Nazi Crimes and the Law

This book examines the use of national and international law to prosecute Nazi crimes, the centerpiece of twentieth-century state-sponsored genocide and mass murder. In its various essays, the contributors reconstruct the historical setting of the crimes committed under the aegis of the Nazi regime and examine why postwar adjudication took place only within limits, within the national and international judicial forums responsible for prosecuting perpetrators. The topics discussed include the impact of the Nazi justice system on postwar justice, postwar legal proceedings against those who committed war crimes and genocide, the work of the Nuremberg tribunal and Allied trials, and judicial investigations and prosecutions in East Germany, West Germany, and Austria. They span the postwar period up to contemporary U.S. legal efforts to deport Nazi criminals within its borders and libel suits brought by Holocaust deniers in British and Canadian courts, and they reveal new perspectives on the present and future implications of these trials.

Nathan Stoltzfus is currently Associate Professor of Modern European History at Florida State University. He has authored, coauthored, or edited four books: *Resistance of the Heart: Intermarriage and the Rosenstrasse Protest in Nazi Germany* (1996), *Social Outsiders in Nazi Germany* (2001), *Shades of Green: Environmental Activism around the Globe* (2006), and *Courageous Resistance: The Power of Ordinary People* (2007). His articles have appeared in publications including *Geschichte und Gesellschaft*, *Central European History*, *The Atlantic Monthly*, and *Die Zeit*. Stoltzfus was named a Harry Frank Guggenheim Foundation Research Scholar and has received research grants from the Fulbright Commission, IREX, the Friedrich Ebert Stiftung, the German Academic Exchange Commission (DAAD), and the Albert Einstein Institution.

Henry Friedlander is a retired professor of Judaic Studies at Brooklyn College, City University of New York. He is the author of *The German Revolution of 1918* (1968/1992) and *The Origins of Nazi Genocide: From Euthanasia to the Final Solution* (1995), which received the Bruno Brand Tolerance Book Award and the DAAD Book Prize. He is also a coeditor of *Archives of the Holocaust* (26 volumes, 1990–95, with Sybil Milton), and he has received numerous research grants, most recently the Deutscher Akademischer Austausch Dienst, the U.S. Holocaust Memorial Museum Ruth Meltzer Senior Fellowship, and The Harry Frank Guggenheim Foundation Fellowship.

PUBLICATIONS OF THE GERMAN HISTORICAL INSTITUTE

Washington, D.C.

Edited by Hartmut Berghoff and Christof Mauch
with the assistance of David Lazar

The German Historical Institute is a center for advanced study and research whose purpose is to provide a permanent basis for scholarly cooperation among historians from the Federal Republic of Germany and the United States. The Institute conducts, promotes, and supports research into both American and German political, social, economic, and cultural history; into transatlantic migration, especially in the nineteenth and twentieth centuries; and into the history of international relations, with special emphasis on the roles played by the United States and Germany.

Recent books in the series:

Roger Chickering, Stig Förster, and Bernd Greiner, editors, *A World at Total War: Global Conflict and the Politics of Destruction, 1937–1945*

Kiran Klaus Patel, *Soldiers of Labor: Labor Service in Nazi Germany and New Deal America, 1933–1945*

Michelle Mouton, *From Nurturing the Nation to Purifying the Volk: Weimar and Nazi Family Policy, 1918–1945*

Peter Becker and Richard F. Wetzell, editors, *Criminals and Their Scientists: The History of Criminology in International Perspective*

Jonathan R. Zatlin, *The Currency of Socialism: Money and Political Culture in East Germany*

Andreas W. Daum, *Kennedy in Berlin*

Joachim Radkau, *Nature and Power: A Global History of the Environment*

Carole Fink and Bernd Schaefer, editors, *Ostpolitik, 1969–1974: European and Global Responses*

Manfred Berg and Bernd Schaefer, editors, *Historical Justice in International Perspective: How Societies Are Trying to Right the Wrongs of the Past*

Nazi Crimes and the Law

Edited by

NATHAN STOLTZFUS
Florida State University

HENRY FRIEDLANDER
Brooklyn College, City University of New York

GERMAN HISTORICAL INSTITUTE
Washington D.C.
and
CAMBRIDGE
UNIVERSITY PRESS

CAMBRIDGE UNIVERSITY PRESS
Cambridge, New York, Melbourne, Madrid, Cape Town, Singapore, São Paulo, Delhi

Cambridge University Press
32 Avenue of the Americas, New York, NY 10013-2473, USA

www.cambridge.org
Information on this title: www.cambridge.org/9780521899741

First published 2008

Printed in the United States of America

A catalog record for this publication is available from the British Library.

Library of Congress Cataloging in Publication Data

Stoltzfus, Nathan.
Nazi crimes and the law / Nathan Stoltzfus, Henry Friedlander.
p. cm. – (Publications of the German Historical Institute)
Includes bibliographical references and index.
ISBN 978-0-521-89974-1 (hardback)
1. War crime trials – Germany. 2. Holocaust, Jewish (1939–1945). 3. World War, 1939–1945 – Law and legislation. I. Friedlander, Henry, 1930– II. Title. III. Series.
KZ1176.5.S76 2008
341.6′90268–dc22 2008006752

ISBN 978-0-521-89974-1 hardback

Contents

Contributors

Christopher R. Browning, Department of History, University of North Carolina at Chapel Hill

Michael S. Bryant, Department of History and Social Science, Bryant College, Smithfield, Rhode Island

Henry Friedlander, Department of Judaic Studies, Brooklyn College, City University of New York (Emeritus)

Winfried R. Garscha, Documentation Center of Austrian Resistance, Vienna

Patricia Heberer, Center for Advanced Holocaust Studies, United States Holocaust Memorial Museum, Washington, D.C.

Dick de Mildt, Institute of Criminal Law, University of Amsterdam

Joachim Perels, Institute for Political Science, Leibniz University Hannover

Nathan Stoltzfus, Department of History, Florida State University

Gerhard L. Weinberg, Department of History, University of North Carolina at Chapel Hill (Emeritus)

Annette Weinke, Independent Historians' Commission for the History of the German Foreign Office during the Nazi Dictatorship and under the Federal Republic

Elizabeth B. White, Office of Special Investigations, U.S. Department of Justice, Washington, D.C.

Nazi Crimes and the Law

Introduction

Nazi Crimes and the Law

NATHAN STOLTZFUS AND HENRY FRIEDLANDER

Although there are substantial differences between the Nuremberg trials and more recent international efforts to bring wartime criminals to justice, there has been a growing literature presenting the Nuremberg trials as a model for prosecuting state-sponsored mass murder.[1] For that reason, the German Historical Institute sponsored a conference in Amsterdam in August 2003 to examine the way the Allied nations and the Germans themselves used the law to prosecute those who had carried out the German state's genocidal crimes during the Nazi period. This volume grew out of papers delivered at that conference. We know a great deal about the crimes of the Nazi regime through the publication of official documents and scholarly works since World War II.[2] The intention of this volume is to discuss and analyze how international as well as national law was used to prosecute Nazi criminals.

Due to its war of aggression and its mass murder of European Jews, Germany must figure centrally in any account of state-sponsored crimes and trials for crimes against humanity. It was clear at the end of the war that the question of what to do about Germany would be crucial to Europe's reconstruction and stability. The victorious Allies intended for their judicial

1 See, for example, Gerhard Werle, *Principles of International Criminal Law* (The Hague, 2005); William A. Schabas, *An Introduction to the International Criminal Court* (Cambridge, 2001); Geoffrey Robertson, *Crimes Against Humanity: The Struggle for Global Justice* (London, 1999).

2 On the history of Nazi genocide and the Holocaust, see Raul Hilberg, *The Destruction of the European Jews* (Chicago, 1961; rev. ed., 3 vols., New Haven, 2003); Gerald Reitlinger, *The Final Solution: The Attempt to Exterminate the Jews of Europe, 1939–1945* (New York, 1953); Gerhard L. Weinberg, *A World at Arms: A Global History of World War II* (Cambridge, 1994); Henry Friedlander, *The Origins of Nazi Genocide: From Euthanasia to the Final Solution* (Chapel Hill, 1995); Saul Friedlander, *Nazi Germany and the Jews: The Years of Persecution, 1933–1939* (New York, 1997) and *Nazi Germany and the Jews 1939–1945: The Years of Extermination* (New York, 2007); Christopher R. Browning, *The Origins of the Final Solution: The Evolution of Nazi Jewish Policy, September 1939–March 1942* (Lincoln, NE, and Jerusalem, 2004).

and political decisions, including the creation of the United Nations, to serve as the basis for a new world order. Proposals for the summary execution of suspected German war criminals were rejected, as was U.S. Secretary of the Treasury Henry Morgenthau's plan to cripple Germany's industrial capacity. Instead, an American-led plan to hold the German leaders accountable before an international court subject to public scrutiny prevailed, "thus pointing the way to an evolution of international law" and the hope of "historical-political enlightenment."[3]

How the international trial of the Nazi leaders fit into the new world order was explained succinctly by the chief U.S. prosecutor at Nuremberg, Supreme Court Associate Justice Robert Jackson, in his opening statement on November 20, 1945: "That four great nations, flushed with victory and stung with injury, would stay the hand of vengeance and voluntarily submit their captive enemies to the judgment of the law is one of the most significant tributes that power has ever paid to reason."[4] Jackson saw it as his task to "establish incredible events by credible evidence," prove that the defendants were responsible for these incredible crimes, and see that they were found guilty.[5] The responsibility of Germans generally in the immediate postwar era was to accept the Nuremberg verdicts and to punish independently those Nazi criminals not tried by the Allies. In time, the West Germans' pursuit of Nazi criminals came to be seen as an indicator of their country's progress toward democracy. Furthermore, as Annette Weinke argues in her contribution to this volume, the pursuit of war criminals itself became a medium for West Germany's democratization.[6]

In the years following VE day, within a Europe Winston Churchill called "a rubble-heap, a charnel house, a breeding ground of pestilence and hate," Germany was ruled by several different authorities that simultaneously pursued justice for the victims of the Nazi regime.[7] In the weeks and months immediately following the German surrender, the U.S. military tried Nazi criminals through newly established military commissions. Patricia Heberer argues in this volume that the chances of justice being done were greatest

3 Norbert Frei, *Adenauer's Germany and the Nazi Past: The Politics of Amnesty and Integration* (New York, 2002), 97. For an overview of the origins of the Nuremberg Trial's charge of "crimes against peace," see Jonathan Bush, "'The Supreme Crime' and Its Origins: The Lost Legislative History of the Crime of Aggressive War," *Columbia Law Review* 102/8 (2002): 2324–424.

4 Cited in Telford Taylor, *The Anatomy of the Nuremberg Trials* (New York, 1992), 167.

5 Robert H. Jackson, *The Nürnberg Case* (New York, 1947), 10.

6 Annette Weinke, "The German-German Rivalry and the Prosecution of Nazi War Criminals During the Cold War, 1958–1965."

7 Churchill's speech in London, May 14, 1947, in *Winston S. Churchill: His Complete Speeches, 1897–1963*, ed. Robert Rhodes James (New York, 1974), 7484.

during the immediate postwar period. Later, even with the great advantage of new tools and precedents, West German jurists failed to convict or even investigate other war criminals. Thus, perpetrators who could lie low initially, living on false papers or enjoying the protection of German professional communities, might escape prosecution altogether; those who had painstakingly organized and implemented Nazi crimes, yet could be linked to those crimes only through time-consuming investigation and tenacious prosecution, could evade prosecution and get away with murder.[8]

In December 1945, in the month following the opening of the trial of "major" Nazis at Nuremberg, the quadripartite Allied Control Council promulgated Law Number 10 authorizing military authorities in the four occupation zones to level charges of crimes against peace, war crimes, membership in an illegal organization, or crimes against humanity for wartime offenses committed in their respective jurisdictions. The four powers occupying Germany – the United States, Great Britain, the Soviet Union, and the French Republic – began to prosecute Nazi criminals in their zones even as they also prosecuted the major war criminals at Nuremberg before what is known as the IMT, the International Military Tribunal.[9] The IMT was able to draw on a series of international agreements that, taken together, had established the core elements of the laws of war.

The turn of the twentieth century saw major advances in the effort to regulate warfare by law. The Hague Convention of 1899 represented a breakthrough by codifying the international effort to establish rules on the conduct of war. The treatment of prisoners of war and the rights of civilian noncombatants were the focus of the Hague Convention of 1907, which was signed by even more states than its predecessor. It also prohibited attacks on enemy soldiers who had already surrendered. The Hague Conventions specified no means of enforcement or penalties for violations, but "the major powers and many other nations" incorporated the substance of many Hague provisions into their military laws. By 1914, the Hague Conventions, as well as previous efforts with similar goals, "had internationalized the whole subject of limits on warfare and laid the basis for an extraordinary expansion of public and political concern with 'war crimes.'"[10]

Like their victorious successors at Nuremberg following the Second World War, the three major victorious powers of the First World War saw the 1919 Paris Peace Conference as an opportunity to salvage meaning from

8 Patricia Heberer, "The American Military Commission Trials of 1945."

9 See also Henry Friedlander, "The Judiciary and Nazi Crimes in Postwar Germany," *Simon Wiesenthal Center Annual* 1 (1984): 27–44.

10 Taylor, *Anatomy*, 10–11.

the war's horrendous toll. President Woodrow Wilson, the most idealistic of the leaders at the conference, had voiced his hope that the Great War would be "the war to end all wars" and would ultimately serve to "make the world safe for democracy." The punishment of war crimes was the first topic on the agenda at Paris, but the "Big Three" – Wilson, David Lloyd George, and Georges Clemenceau – could not agree on what should be done. The provisions of the Versailles Treaty concerning Germany held the Germans collectively responsible for war damages by demanding reparations from Germany, and Kaiser Wilhelm II was held personally responsible. The treaty stipulated that he be arraigned before an international tribunal of judges on charges not of war crimes but of "a supreme offence against international morality and the sanctity of treaties."[11]

Postwar politics soon interfered. World powers, including those whose statesmen had signed the Treaty of Versailles, soon came to believe it had been unfair to hold only Germany responsible for the war, creating a cornerstone of appeasement policy by the Western powers. Early initiatives to put non-Germans on trial for war crimes quickly failed, and little was done about the most egregious violation of human rights, the Turkish genocide of the Armenians; by provision of the Hague Conventions, a state was not criminally liable for actions taken against its own subjects. Brutality against Belgian civilians during the first months of the war topped a list of Germany's offenses. Although Germany would pay reparations until 1932, the Kaiser never faced extradition to stand trial due to the "sovereign immunity" of heads of state. The victors ultimately resolved their disagreement on how Germans should be tried by leaving the matter to Germany. By February 1920, the Allies had instructed German leaders to press for the prosecution of some 854 military and political officials, including such prominent figures as Alfred von Tirpitz and Generals Paul von Hindenberg and Erich Ludendorff. In the face of official German protests, diplomats reached a new agreement for the arraignment of forty-five Germans before the German Supreme Court (Reichsgericht) in Leipzig. The court accepted the superior-orders defense in the case of a German submarine commander who had sunk a British hospital ship; it acquitted him. To the outrage of the French and Belgians in particular, the German court tried just twelve of the forty-five accused and convicted only six, two of whom escaped, apparently with the help of prison guards.[12]

In his opening statement before the Nuremberg tribunal a quarter of a century later, Justice Jackson pointed to the Leipzig trials as an illustration of

11 Ibid., 16.
12 Peter H. Maguire, *Law and War: An American Story* (New York, 2001), 80–2.

the "futility" of allowing a vanquished nation to adjudicate the war crimes of its own nationals.[13] At that point, six months after the end of World War II, the scope of generally accepted laws of warfare did not differ much from that of the Hague Conventions, although public as well as official attitudes had changed, reflected by the agreement of many more nations to be bound by those laws. The Geneva Convention of 1925 had prohibited the use of poisonous gas, and the subsequent Geneva Convention of 1929 specified conditions of care for prisoners of war and those wounded in war. By the mid-1920s, Germany, no longer the pariah of World War I, was an accepted partner in international relations and law. In 1928, it joined other major powers in signing the Kellogg-Briand Pact renouncing war as an instrument of national policy. The following year, Germany agreed to the Geneva Conventions, and in 1930 it became a signatory of the London Treaty regulating submarine warfare. However, by the time of Germany's disregard of the Munich Agreement of October 1938, the notion that wars might be regulated by such international accords had fallen into disrepute: "The summary acquittals at Leipzig, the disengagement of the United States from Versailles and the League of Nations, the complete breakdown of the regulatory regimes for submarines and aerial bombing and the mockery of Kellogg-Briand all suggested that the so-called law of war was bad policy, law, and politics."[14]

Within the first year of the German attack on Poland in September 1939 that started World War II, four governments had officially protested German crimes during the occupation of their countries. Shortly before the United States entered the war, President Franklin D. Roosevelt and Prime Minister Winston Churchill issued statements condemning Germany's execution of "scores of innocent hostages." In November 1941 and again in January 1942, the Soviet Union followed by accusing the German government of "criminal, systematic, and deliberate violation of international law" in its treatment of POWs as well as against innocent civilians and property. The St. James Declaration issued in the name of nine European countries in January 1942 "was the first step toward the formulation of a systematic program" for dealing with war criminals, according to the Nuremberg prosecutor Telford Taylor; it "pointed out that international solidarity is necessary in order to avoid the repression of these acts of violence simply by acts of vengeance on the part of the general public, and in order to satisfy the sense of justice of the

13 Paul Betts, "Germany, International Justice and the Twentieth Century," *History & Memory* 17 (2005): 45–86, 59. Etiene Mantou, *The Carthaginian Peace, or the Economic Consequences of Mr. Keynes* (New York, 1952), shows that in effect Germany never paid any reparations. On the Armenian genocide, see, for example, Sybil Milton, "Armin T. Wegner: Polemicist for Armenian and Jewish Rights," *Armenian Review* 42, no. 4/168 (Winter 1989): 17–40.

14 Bush, "'The Supreme Crime' and Its Origins," 2336.

civilized world."[15] The second major step in developing an international war crimes program came with the simultaneous announcements on October 7, 1942, by President Roosevelt and British Lord Chancellor John Simon that their countries would join with other nations to establish a "United Nations Committee for the Investigation of War Crimes." In all, seventeen nations participated in the committee.[16] The third major step and the only major agreement on the punishment of German war criminals the three major Allies reached during the war was the Moscow Declaration of November 1, 1943. It condemned the Germans responsible for violations of the laws of war and promised that the Allied powers would "pursue them to the uttermost ends of the earth and will deliver them to their accusers in order that justice may be done." While suspected criminals were to be sent to stand trial to the countries where they had committed crimes, "major criminals" were to "be punished by the joint decision of the Governments of the Allies."[17]

The scale of the trials of suspected war criminals after 1945 was unprecedented.[18] The first prosecutions of the Nazi criminals were undertaken by the signatories of the United Nations Declaration of 1942. It is not surprising then that justice under the initial Nuremberg trial in some ways reflected but also departed in several important respects from the pursuit of justice following World War I. The context in Germany, too, was significantly different. During World War I, not a shot had been fired on German soil, making it easy for militarist nationalists to claim the German army had not lost on the battlefield but had been stabbed in the back. In 1945, Germany lay in ruins and, having surrendered unconditionally, was completely subject to Allied will. There was no question about Germany's responsibility for the war, and the Nazi regime itself had left behind comprehensive documentation of many of its atrocities. The nature and extent of German war crimes prompted not only prosecutions on an unprecedented scale, but also significant adjustments to the letter of the law.

First, the court introduced a category of actionable cause called "crimes against humanity," which undermined traditional defenses. The court rejected the superior-orders defense that had prevailed at Leipzig, claiming that a person who had acted according to official orders was necessarily

15 Telford Taylor, *Final Report to the Secretary of the Army on the Nuremberg War Crimes Trials* (Buffalo, 1997 [orig. 1949]), 126–7.

16 Ibid., 26.

17 Arieh Kochavi, *Prelude to Nuremberg: Allied War Crimes Policy and the Question of Punishment* (Chapel Hill, 1998), 57.

18 Michael R. Marrus, *The Nuremberg War Crimes Trial, 1945–1946: A Documentary History* (New York, 1997), 242.

innocent. Acting according to the laws in the circumstances within which persons found themselves was not sufficient cause for acquittal. Following Jackson's criticism of the Leipzig trials, the Germans were not immediately put in charge of judging Germany's suspected wartime criminals. In addition, the court recognized "crimes against peace" as violations of international law, thus repudiating the notion that "reasons of the state" and state sovereignty were inviolable. Also, rejecting the premise of American objections to trying the Kaiser, the Nuremberg court maintained that international law applied to any and all persons, including heads of sovereign states.[19]

The IMT's judgments reflected the premise of the London Charter that individuals were accountable under international law regardless of national law: "crimes against international law are committed by men, not abstract entities . . . individuals have international duties which transcend the national obligations of obedience imposed by the individual state." Collective guilt was no longer an operative concept. Thus, the IMT accepted Robert Jackson's view in his opening statement: "Of course, the idea that a state, any more than a corporation, commits crimes, is a fiction. Crimes always are committed only by persons."[20]

The IMT judges aimed to set a precedent illustrating a fair international judicial response to crimes of aggression and mass murder that would serve to prevent future crimes against humanity. The victorious Allies hoped to build on precedents established in prosecuting Nazi crimes for economic reconstruction and establishment of a new political order. Politics quickly impeded the realization of these aspirations, however: "What had begun in the name of a better future, one illuminated by an imposition of international law, ended on the low ground of political opportunity."[21]

While rebuilding the new economic and political order went hand in hand with a new resolve in the West to contain communism, prosecution of Nazi criminals did not. Rebuilding, in fact, led quickly to reintegration rather than prosecution of Nazi functionaries and other criminals. Germans' views on the Nuremberg trial and on their own responsibility for prosecuting German nationals accused of Nazi-era crimes varied. Especially among nationalists and conservatives, there was little enthusiasm for putting former officials and military personnel on trial. This is not surprising, since Hitler had been generally very popular among the Germans. Furthermore, the

19 Betts, "Germany, International Justice and the Twentieth Century," 58–9.

20 Jackson, *The Nürnberg Case*, 88. See also Cherif M. Bassiouni, *Crimes Against Humanity in International Criminal Law* (The Hague, 1999), 527–8.

21 Frei, *Adenauer's Germany*, 230.

postwar Federal Republic judiciary tended to accept court rulings issued during the Nazi period as valid. Convictions under laws peculiar to the Nazi period (e.g., those dealing with "asocials") were deemed legal in postwar Germany, and those imprisoned under Nazism remained in prison after the war to serve out their terms.[22] The influence of Nazi-era court decisions on the postwar prosecution of Nazi crimes is examined in this volume by Dick de Mildt, who uses the 1943 conviction of an SS officer by an SS court for breaching military discipline in taking the initiative in murdering Ukrainian Jews as a case study. De Mildt's findings confirm Jon Elster's observation that, "In Germany, judges harnessed their undeniable competence to the task of minimizing the guilt of all members of the Nazi regime, beginning with themselves."[23]

The West German judicial system charged with prosecuting Nazi perpetrators was embedded within a society whose members had, by and large, consented to the Nazi dictatorship. Ninety percent of all German judicial officials had belonged to the Nazi Party and had welcomed the self-proclaimed law-and-order state following the disaster of Weimar. Nazi legal guidelines had called for laws to be written in clear, easily understandable language that reflected the "national feeling for justice and morality," as Henry Friedlander writes in this volume. The judicial system played a decisive role in the Nazi regime's efforts to provide the majority with a sense of *Rechtssicherheit*, of stability and legal predictability. Adhering to the formal appearance of the rule of law, the regime anchored the disenfranchisement and dispossession of the German Jews in German law and thereby turned the law into a means of persecution. The German judicial system was one reason the Holocaust resembled machine-like mass murder rather than a Czarist pogrom.[24]

In treating Nazi-era judicial decisions as consistent with the rule of law, West German judges had public opinion solidly behind them, at least during the early years of the Federal Republic's existence. Opinion polls conducted in the 1950s found, for example, that the majority of West Germans thought National Socialism had been more good than bad and that Hitler's would-be assassins had been traitors. In postwar West Germany,

22 Nikolaus Wachsmann, "From Indefinite Confinement to Extermination: Habitual Criminals in the Third Reich," in *Social Outsiders in Nazi Germany*, ed. Robert Gellately and Nathan Stoltzfus (Princeton, 2001), 165–91, 183. See generally Nikolaus Wachsmann, *Hitler's Prisons: Legal Terror in Nazi Germany* (New Haven, 2004).

23 Jon Elster, "Introduction," *Retribution and Reparation in the Transition to Democracy*, ed. Jon Elster (Cambridge; 2006), 1–14, 10. See generally Ingo Muller, *Hitler's Justice*, trans. Deborah Lucas Schneider (Cambridge, MA, 1991).

24 Henry Friedlander, "German Law and Nazi Crimes."

convicted war criminals were not generally ostracized by the population at large; in fact, "the fewer the number of war criminals sitting in Allied prisons, the more uncompromising the solidarity being expressed for them; public pronunciations in the opposite direction were hard to find."[25]

West German public opinion was strongly reinforced by Chancellor Konrad Adenauer's position on former Nazis and war criminals. Like many other Germans, Adenauer was inclined to exonerate professionals who had been part of the bureaucratic apparatus that carried out the "Final Solution" and to shift blame to rougher-hewn members of the working class. Examining the Dachau trials, Michael Bryant shows in his contribution to this volume that traditional social images had considerable impact on West German prosecution of suspected Nazi perpetrators. With the rapid escalation of the Cold War, the Adenauer government increasingly traded German cooperation in the Western alliance for the release of war criminals, and prisons were emptied of convicts during the first half of the 1950s.[26]

Generally, "over time transitional justice in Germany after 1945 became increasingly endogenous and as a result increasingly lenient."[27] Only a small percentage of the West Germans who stood trial for Nazi-era crimes were convicted. In the German Democratic Republic, trials became increasingly awkward not just due to the new political alliances but also because its leaders claimed "the imperialist and Nazi past 'was mastered and overcome long ago.'"[28] Trials and purges were in fact more extensive in East Germany than in the West, even though the Eastern authorities avoided prosecuting certain groups, such as members of the Wehrmacht, and trials tended to target anti-communists as well as Nazis.[29]

West Germany's so-called cold amnesty returned to public service many functionaries, bureaucrats, members of the judiciary, and others whom denazification had removed.[30] By the mid-1950s, many former Nazis were integrated within the public and private sectors in West Germany. When the Adenauer government established an army for the Federal Republic, the Bundeswehr, it relied heavily on Wehrmacht veterans. Of course, the United States, Canada, East Germany, and other countries also drew on the services of many thousands of former Nazis, and continuities of personnel marked the Italian army in the postwar republic as well. Hans Globke, a former interior ministry official who had helped draft amendments to the

25 Frei, *Adenauer's Germany*, 207.

26 David Cohen, "Transitional Justice in Divided Germany after 1945," in Elster, *Retribution and Reparation*, 59–88, 66, 87.

27 Elster, "Introduction," 4.

28 Jeffrey Herf, *Divided Memory: The Nazi Past in the Two Germanys* (Cambridge, MA, 1997), 195.

29 Elster, "Introduction," 4, 7.

30 Cohen, "Transitional Justice," 87.

infamous Nuremberg Laws, famously became Adenauer's national security advisor. It is now known that the CIA helped shield Globke from incriminating statements made by Adolf Eichmann. Moreover, the United States refused to pursue Eichmann even though American officials knew where to find him as early as 1958.[31]

West Germany was in step with its main alliance partner in integrating rather than prosecuting Nazi perpetrators. Thus, by the mid-1950s, as Norbert Frei notes, "little was now left of the moral sweep implicit in a decision to expiate crimes of the 'Third Reich' according to principles of elementary law." The sudden arrival of the Cold War and the division of Germany and Europe played an important role. In addition to these international factors, the transfer of jurisdiction to West Germany resulted in more lenient prosecution and punishment of Nazi crimes. Ultimately, "the most important factor of all was the determined German resistance to the legal efforts nigh from the beginning."[32]

Ironically, during the late 1950s and 1960s, competition between the two Germanys as they jockeyed for legitimacy while casting aspersions on one another, spurred West Germany on to renewed efforts to deal with the Nazi past, as Annette Weinke argues in these pages. Wehrmacht crimes remained an exception, particularly in West Germany, where the myth of the unblemished Wehrmacht held sway for decades. Also, the German judiciary serving during the Nazi period survived virtually intact and was skeptical about, even hostile toward, using the new "crimes against humanity" code to nullify traditional legal arguments that there could be no punishment without preexisting law. Contrary to the impression created by much of the literature on the subject, the pressures of the Cold War were not the sole or most decisive factor behind West Germany's failure to bring Wehrmacht war criminals to justice, as Nathan Stoltzfus illustrates in this volume with a review of the decisions in 1968 and again in 2006 not to prosecute former Wehrmacht members responsible for the massacre of thousands of Italian troops on the Greek island of Cephalonia in September 1943. Persistent German resistance to trials of Nazi-era criminals was the primary reason why no Wehrmacht veteran served prison time in West Germany for war crimes. In fact, while the judiciary had quietly discontinued the case in 1968, the 2006 decision, widely publicized to international protest, accepts the perspective of ex-Wehrmacht officers and in effect shores up the flagging Wehrmacht myth. Since 2002, however, activists have been

31 Scott Shane, "C.I.A. Knew Where Eichmann Was Hiding, Documents Show," *New York Times*, June 7, 2006.

32 Frei, *Adenauer's Germany*, 230.

drawing public attention to Wehrmacht culpability on Cephalonia and may well play a crucial role in shaping public memory of it.[33] Using the 1943 Wehrmacht massacre of the Greek village of Kalavyrta as an illustration, Joachim Perels shows in his chapter in this volume that, in contrast to U.S. courts, West German courts accepted the reasoning that reprisal killings were a lawful response to partisan attacks. This was part of a broader pattern of decisions by the judiciary that ultimately categorized Nazi perpetrators as mere accomplices, making genocide legal, Perels concludes. Rather than acknowledging the collapse of the rule of law under Nazism, West German judges "normalized" the Nazi administration of justice, thus justifying their continued work.[34]

More appalling to civilians throughout the Balkans who had struggled to resist German aggression was the court's conclusion that their resistance outside of nationally mobilized militaries had violated the law of war, and that reprisals during war helped enforce compliance with those laws. Most national military codes allowed reprisals against partisans, including the taking of hostages under limited conditions, and the IMT trial, *United States v. Wilhelm List et al.* (1947–48) charging senior military officials with killing of civilian hostages, also found that there were acceptable levels of hostage murders, and some Wehrmacht reprisals against innocent civilians were deemed lawful. In response, the Geneva Protocols of August 1949 prohibited pillage, wanton destruction, and all collective punishments and reprisals, whether against POWs or civilians.[35]

As for Austria, the third successor state of Nazi Germany, the Moscow Declaration stated that it had been "the first free country to fall victim to Hitlerite aggression." In the Moscow Declaration, the Allies also stated, however, that Austria "has a responsibility for participation in the war on the side of Hitlerite Germany and that in the final settlement, account will inevitably be taken of her contribution to her liberation."[36] Austria's declaration of independence from the Third Reich (April 27, 1945) highlighted the passage identifying it as "Hitler's first victim," while burying the second in an addendum (*Nachsatz*). By the time of the Austrian State Treaty restoring Austria's full sovereignty in 1955, Austrian leaders had convinced the four Allies to strike the notion that "Austria has a certain responsibility"

33 Nathan Stoltzfus, "'A Great Achievement of German Troops in Mountain Warfare': Cold War Pressures and the German Prosecution of Wehrmacht War Crimes in the Case of Cephalonia, 1943."

34 Joachim Perels, "Perceptions and Suppression of Nazi Crimes by the Postwar German Judiciary."

35 Karen Hulme, *War Torn Environment: Interpreting the Legal Threshold* (Leiden, 2004), 128.

36 Moscow Declaration, November 1, 1943: text in *Trials of War Criminals before the Nuremberg Military Tribunals under Control Council Law No. 10*, 14 vols. (Washington, DC, 1950–52), 1: viii.

for participating in World War II.[37] In this volume, Winfried Garscha juxtaposes the energetic prosecution practice of early Austrian Peoples' Courts (*Volksgerichte*) with those after 1955 to conclude about Austria, as Heberer did about Germany, that trials of suspected Nazi perpetrators were more likely to result in conviction during the immediate postwar period than was later the case. The *Volksgerichte* investigated 137,000 individuals before the regular Austrian courts took charge in 1955 and showed very little interest at all in prosecuting war criminals.[38]

The defeat of the Third Reich and prosecution of Nazi criminals has not served as an absolute deterrent to state-sponsored crimes in the years since 1945, as the examples of Cambodia, Yugoslavia, Rwanda, and Darfur make all too clear. This has prompted scholars and practitioners to look back to the successful prosecution of the Nazis at Nuremberg and, indeed, as Gerhard Weinberg reminds us in his essay in this volume, the Nuremberg trial materials still hold unexhausted research potential. The tribunals set up to try those responsible for genocide and/or war crimes in the Balkans and Rwanda have not, however, been as successful as those in Nuremberg in bringing perpetrators to justice. The circumstances in which the Nuremberg trials took place, for one, facilitated prosecution. The two situations are not easily compared. The German state in whose name the crimes of the Nazis had been committed no longer existed at the time of the Nuremberg trials. The leaders of the German state had signed the unconditional surrender that Roosevelt and Churchill had demanded at Casablanca in January 1943. The Allies therefore governed and controlled Germany and Austria and were, under the positive law practiced in Europe, the lawgivers of Germany. This gave them the power legally as well as morally to impose their will. Similarly, the speed with which Nuremberg tried, convicted, and sentenced leading Nazis also stands in marked contrast to the lengthy proceedings in The Hague against Balkan leaders.

The national trials of war criminals in the successor states to the Third Reich might provide a more readily applicable model than Nuremberg. Such an example seems to be needed, considering the fiasco that ensued during the trial of Saddam Hussein by the government of Iraq. The German and Austrian prosecutors and judges trying German and Austrian criminals had a greater understanding of the setting in which these individuals committed crimes, and unlike trials before other courts, convicted defendants could not claim that they had been "victims" of "victors' justice." The

37 David Art, *The Politics of the Nazi Past in Germany and Austria* (Cambridge, 2006), 105.
38 Winfried Garscha, "The Trials of Nazi War Criminals in Austria."

other side of the coin, however, was the refusal of the population at large to support the trials; thus, politics played a role in the consequent limited prosecution and light sentences. Nevertheless, the postwar trials did produce a documentary record that exceeded even that of Nuremberg. Furthermore, a conviction for murder, rape, or larceny in a national court had greater impact than one for crimes against humanity handed down by an occupying power.

This volume thus examines the entire spectrum of postwar legal proceedings in the successor states of Nazi Germany against those who committed, aided, or abetted the genocidal Nazi crimes. In addition, Elizabeth White's essay examines the legal efforts that began decades later to denaturalize and deport Nazi criminals who had illegally entered the United States. The shadow of Nazi criminality has reached even further into our time, as represented in these pages by Christopher Browning's reflections on his experiences as expert witness in trials of Holocaust deniers in the twenty-first century.[39] Considering the connections between historiography and the law and Nazi crimes, his essay reminds us of how vital it is to preserve the integrity of the historical record of the Holocaust.

39 Elizabeth B. White, "History in the Courthouse: The Presentation of World War II Crimes in U.S. Courts Sixty Years Later"; Christopher R. Browning, "Law, History, and Holocaust Denial in the Courtroom: The Zündel and Irving Cases."

1

Nazi Crimes and the German Law

HENRY FRIEDLANDER

In the Moscow "Declaration on German Atrocities" of November 1943, the three Allied powers – the United Kingdom, the United States, and the Soviet Union – warned the "Hitlerite Huns" that they would "pursue them to the utmost ends of the earth" and would "deliver them to their accusers in order that justice may be done."[1] The Allied plan involved the trial of major Nazi war criminals by international Allied courts, while all other criminals would be extradited to countries formerly occupied by Germany to stand trial where they had committed their deeds. And that is what happened after Germany's defeat: the International Military Tribunal tried the major criminals at Nuremberg; the Allied occupying powers held additional trials in Germany, Austria, and Italy; and extradited Nazi war criminals faced their judges in every country formerly occupied by Germany.[2] Before we

An earlier version of this essay appeared in the collection, *The Holocaust's Ghost: Writings on Art, Politics, Law and Education,* edited by F. C. DeCoste and Bernard Schwartz and published by the University of Alberta Press in 2000. The author wishes to thank the University of Alberta Press for permission to make use of the essay here.

1 Moscow Declaration, November 1, 1943. The relevant section of the Declaration reads as follows: "At the time of the granting of any armistice to any government which may be set up in Germany, those German officers and men and members of the Nazi party who have been responsible for, or have taken a consenting part in the above atrocities, massacres, and executions, will be sent back to the countries in which their abominable deeds were done in order that they may be judged and punished according to the laws of these liberated countries and of the free governments which will be created therein. Lists will be compiled in all possible detail from all those countries having regard especially to the invaded parts of the Soviet Union, to Poland and Czechoslovakia, to Yugoslavia and Greece, including Crete and other islands, to Norway, Denmark, the Netherlands, Belgium, Luxembourg, France and Italy." Text in *Trials of War Criminals before the Nuremberg Military Tribunals under Control Council Law No. 10*, 14 vols. (Washington, DC, 1950–52), 1: viii [hereafter *TWC*].

2 For text of the London Agreement, August 8, 1945, and attached IMT Charter, see *TWC* 1: ix–x, xi–xv; also *Trial of the Major War Criminals before the International Military Tribunal*, 42 vols. (Nuremberg, 1947–49), 1: 8–9, 10–16 [hereafter *TMWC*], and Office of United States Chief of Counsel for Prosecution of Axis Criminality, *Nazi Conspiracy and Aggression*, 8 vols. and 2 suppl. (Washington, DC, 1946–48), 1: 1–3, 4–11 [hereafter *NCA*].

proceed, however, let us discuss the nature of the Nazi regime and of the crimes it committed.

The widespread belief that Germany almost immediately became a totally arbitrary state upon the assumption of power by the Nazis on January 30, 1933, is simply not true. The Germans had always prided themselves, and continued to do so during the Nazi period, that theirs was a *Rechtsstaat*, a state ruled by law. They saw such a state as a desirable substitute for the political structure of the parliamentary democracies of the West. This was one of the reasons large numbers of Germans rejected the parliamentary system of the Weimar Republic and welcomed the authoritarian Third Reich. And for this reason the Nazi leaders did everything to assure Germans of *Rechtssicherheit*, that is, assurance for the masses of their own followers that the law would protect their security. Permit me to explain this. *Rechtssicherheit* required that exclusionary, that is, discriminatory, edicts of the state would be clearly defined – both legally and scientifically – so that everyone would know whether he did or did not belong to the excluded group.[3]

Of course, the Hitler regime was a dictatorship, but it imposed its rule to a large degree through properly issued laws and administrative decrees. The earliest were promulgated under the Emergency Decree of the Reich President for the Protection of Volk and State, issued by Hindenburg on February 28, 1933.[4] This was not unprecedented; such emergency decrees had been used during the Weimar Republic. The "emergency" was later regularized by the so-called Enabling Act, passed by a manipulated parliament, the Reichstag, with the required two-thirds majority, and this remained the legal foundation throughout the Nazi period. Under it, the regime imposed its "synchronization" (*Gleichschaltung*) of society; it also used this act to centralize government administration while retaining the form of the federal structure.[5] The regime did also use violence early on in

For the text of Control Council Law No. 10, December 20, 1945, on which all subsequent Allied trials in Germany were based, see *TWC* 1: xvi–xix. For trials of Germans in Allied courts, see German Federal Republic, Der Bunderminister der Justiz, *Bericht über die Verfolgung nationalisozialistischer Straftaten*, Deutscher Bundestag, 4. Wahlperiode, Drucksache IV/3124.

Concerning extradition, see London Agreement, Article 4: "Nothing in this Agreement shall prejudice the provisions established by the Moscow Declaration concerning the return of war criminals to the countries where they committed their crimes." Article 6: "Nothing in this Agreement shall prejudice the jurisdiction or the powers of any national or occupation court established or to be established in any Allied territory or in Germany for the trial of war criminals."

3 See Benno Müller-Hill, "Selektion: Die Wissenschaft von der biologischen Auslese des Menschen durch Menschen," in *Medizin und Gesundheitspolitik in der NS-Zei,* ed. Norbert Frei (Munich, 1991), 146–7.

4 "Notverordnung zum Schutz von Volk und Staat," *Reichsgesetzblatt* 1: 83 (1933).

5 See Karl Dietrich Bracher, Wolfgang Sauer, and Gerhard Schulz, *Die nationalsozialistische Machtergreifung* (Cologne and Opladen, 1962).

the form of storm troopers on the streets, but it realized that public support required "law and order" and moved to limit such popular interference. After the elimination of the SA leadership in the summer of 1934 – the only time force was used within the party – violence in the streets decreased and only reappeared in 1938 in Austria after the Anschluß and throughout the Reich during Kristallnacht; such organized popular violence did not, however, continue, in part because the public did not fully approve.

We may well ask how laws were properly promulgated during the Nazi period. One method was passage by the Reichstag, which had become a rubber stamp, but this method was rarely used, and then mostly for ceremonial purposes. At Nuremberg, Hans-Heinrich Lammers, who served as state secretary in the Reich Chancellery, testified about the proper procedure for enacting a law. A draft law was proposed by a Reich Ministry and had to be circulated to all other interested ministries. The ministries had to negotiate the final draft; Hitler then decided whether there were irreconcilable differences. The final text had to be signed by all concerned ministers and was then presented via Lammers to the Führer, who had to sign it (until 1937, laws were still discussed in cabinet meetings). After Hitler had signed it, the law had to be published in the *Reichsgesetzblatt*, the official legal gazette; otherwise it was not considered a proper law. Obviously, this did not apply to administrative decrees, including implementation decrees for existing laws, which could be issued by individual ministries. But they also required publication – usually in the ministry's gazette – although especially sensitive decrees could be circulated without publication.[6]

Let us look at examples of such laws. In November 1933, the government changed the penal code by enacting the Law Against Habitual Criminals and Measures of Security and Reform (*Gesetz gegen Berufsverbrecher und Maßregeln der Sicherung und Besserung*), which provided inter alia for castration, preventive arrest (*Sicherungsverwahrung*), and prohibition of the exercise of a profession.[7] In December 1934, the government promulgated the Law Concerning Perfidious (*heimtückisch*) Attacks Against the State and the Party, which made it a crime to malign in word or deed the institutions and representatives of the Nazi regime. This law included provisions that also made it a crime to denigrate party uniforms and insignia; this strengthened the May 1933 Law for the Protection of National Symbols.[8] Another decree,

6 U.S. Military Tribunal, Official Transcript of the Proceedings in Case 1, *United States v. Karl Brandt et al.*, 2682–4 (testimony Hans-Heinrich Lammers).

7 *The Statutory Criminal Law of Germany*, edited by Eldon R. James; prepared by Vladimir Gsovski (Washington, DC, 1947), 27–32. See also Gerhard Werle, *Justiz-Strafrecht und polizeiliche Verbrechensbekämpfung im Dritten Reich* (Berlin and New York, 1989).

8 *Statutory Criminal Law of Germany,* 209–10 (Control Council Law No. 1 on repeal of Nazi laws).

issued on the day World War II started and published in the Reich gazette, made it a crime to listen to foreign radio broadcasts.[9]

The racial legislation passed during the 1930s was directed against the three groups targeted for exclusion from the German national community: the disabled, designated as "life unworthy of life"; and Jews and Gypsies, the so-called racial enemies.[10] Although this legislation was overlapping, sometimes written by the same people, let us look at it one group at a time. The government promulgated two important laws against the disabled. On July 14, 1933, the cabinet issued the "sterilization law," named the Law for the Prevention of Offspring with Hereditary Diseases (*Gesetz zur Verhütung erbkranken Nachwuchses*), which provided for the compulsory sterilization of the disabled, and under which approximately 300,000 German nationals were sterilized. It set up an elaborate judicial procedure: cases were judged by newly established hereditary health courts, each staffed by two physicians and one lawyer. This law was modeled after sterilization laws passed in various American states; however, unlike the American laws, the German law did not permit appeals to the regular courts.[11] On October 18, 1935, the government promulgated the Marriage Health Law (*Ehegesundheitsgesetz*), which prohibited marriages where one of the partners was disabled and which required for every marriage a Marriage Fitness Certificate to be issued by the local public health office.[12]

Against the Gypsies, the regime relied on earlier discriminatory anti-Gypsy legislation enacted during the Empire and the Weimar Republic.[13] Thereafter the regime relied on administrative decrees issued by the Reich Ministry of Interior or by the police.[14] However, the major anti-Jewish legislation was also applied against Gypsies.

The first major legislation directed in part against Jews was the Law for the Restoration of the Professional Civil Service (*Gesetz zur Wiederherstellung*

9 *Reichsgesetzblatt* 1: 1683 (1939).

10 See Henry Friedlander, *The Origins of Nazi Genocide: From Euthanasia to the Final Solution* (Chapel Hill, 1995), chap. 1.

11 *Reichsgesetzblatt* 1: 529 (1933), English transl. in Control Commission for Germany (British Element), Legal Division, British Special Legal Research Unit, "Translations of Nazi Health Laws Concerned with Hereditary Diseases, Matrimonial Health, Sterilization, and Castration," November 8, 1945 (mimeograph), 1–5.

12 *Reichsgesetzblatt* 1: 1246 (1935), English transl. in Control Commission for Germany (British Element), "Nazi Health Laws," 33–4.

13 See, for example, Staatsanwaltschaft (StA) Hamburg, Verfahren Ruth Kellermann, 2200 Js 2/84: Preußisches Ministerium des Innern (sig. Bethmann-Hollweg), Verfügung, "Anweisungen zur Bekämpfung des Zigeunerwesens," February 17, 1906; ibid.: Preußisches Ministerium des Innern, "Fingerabdruckverfahren bei Zigeunern," November 3, 1927.

14 See, for example, ibid.: Reich Leader SS circular, "Bekämpfung der Zigeunerplage," December 8, 1938.

des Berufsbeamtentums) enacted in April 1933. Breaching civil service law to permit the regime to fire political opponents from the civil service, the law also included provisions for the removal of so-called non-Aryan civil servants, mostly Jews (but also Gypsies).[15]

The so-called Nuremberg racial laws were enacted in September 1935 as the Reich Citizenship Law and the Law for the Protection of German Blood and German Honor (*Gesetz zum Schutze des deutschen Blutes und der deutschen Ehre*).[16] The drafters of these laws rejected the use of the terms "Aryan" and "non-Aryan," probably because they were imprecise; instead, the laws defined Aryans as persons with "German or related blood."[17] The Blood Protection Law (*Blutschutzgesetz*) excluded Jews from the German national family by prohibiting marriages, and also sexual relations outside marriage, between Jews and citizens with German or related blood. This prohibition applied even outside the borders of the German Reich. However, the law was not retroactive. It also prohibited Jews from employing as domestics females with German or related blood unless they were over forty-five years old.

The Reich Citizenship Law was an afterthought ordered by Hitler and drafted by the bureaucracy in a few hours. This law has been widely misinterpreted and is thus misrepresented in all popular accounts. It is usually argued that this law denationalized Jews, who thereafter were no longer German citizens. In fact, the law did not alter the status of Jews as citizens (*Staatsangehörige*), conceding citizenship (*Staatsangehörigkeit*) to all German nationals, including Jews, and thus retaining for Jews, as we shall see, the rights and protection traditional citizenship conferred. Instead, the law stigmatized Jews as citizens of lesser worth by creating the elevated position of Reich citizen (*Reichsbürger*), which only those with German or related blood could hold. Reich citizens were to be the sole bearers of political rights, but those rights were not defined and, considering the centralization of dictatorial political power, were basically meaningless. In fact, Reich citizenship warrants were never issued.[18]

15 *Reichsgesetzblatt* 1: 175 (1933). See also Joseph Walk, *Das Sonderrecht für die Juden im NS-Staat: Eine Sammlung der gesetzlichen Massnahmen und Richtlinien – Inhalt und Bedeutung* (Heidelberg, 1981), 12, no. 46.

16 *Reichsgesetzblatt* 1: 1146 (1935). See also Walk, *Sonderrecht für die Juden*, 127, nos. 636–7.

17 Arthur Gütt, Herbert Linden, and Franz Maßfeller, *Blutschutz- und Ehegesundheitsgesetz: Gesetz zum Schutze des deutschen Blutes und der deutschen Ehre und Gesetz zum Schutze der Erbgesundheit des deutschen Volkes nebst Durchführungsverordnungen sowie einschlägigen Bestimmungen, dargestellt, medizinisch und juristisch erläutert* (Munich, 1936), 21, 259ff.

18 See Uwe Dietrich Adam, *Judenpolitik im Dritten Reich* (Düsseldorf, 1979), 125–31; Karl Schleunes, *The Twisted Road to Auschwitz* (Urbana, 1970), 121–5.

Although the Nuremberg racial laws were directed primarily against Jews as the minority considered most dangerous to German society and the German gene pool, the provisions of the laws were also applied to other minorities. The Reich minister of interior, Wilhelm Frick, who administered the laws, defined "alien blood" as follows:

> No Jew can become a Reich citizen, because German blood [*Deutschblütigkeit*] is a prerequisite in the Reich citizenship code. But the same also applies to members of other races whose blood is not related to German blood, as, for example, Gypsies and Negroes.[19]

The Blood Protection Law mentioned only Jews, but Article 6 of the law's first implementation decree made it possible to add other groups.[20] It prohibited marriage if offspring from such a union would endanger the purity of German blood. The official commentators saw Article 6 as the means of excluding "other racially alien blood," particularly that of "Negroes and Gypsies."[21]

An exact definition of who belonged to the excluded groups was therefore essential for the administration of the racial laws if *Rechtssicherheit* was to be maintained. But the racial laws did not include a precise definition, leaving such matters to the implementation decrees and regulations. The meaning of the term "Jew," including the various levels of German-Jewish hybrids (*Mischlinge*), was thus not defined until the promulgation of the First Decree to the Reich Citizenship Law. [22]

In addition, a vast number of laws, decrees, and regulations were issued on both the national and local levels to drive Jews from all positions in government, education, the media, and the arts. After 1937, legislation also began to curb the economic activities of Jews, to limit their participation in the social and cultural life of the nation, and to restrict their freedom of movement.[23] Three of these symbolized the system of exclusion. One decree, issued on August 17, 1939, compelled all Jews to add a second name – "Israel" for males and "Sara" for females – and use it at all times.[24] Another decree, issued on October 5, 1938, mandated that all passports and identity cards of Jews be identified with a large "J."[25] Finally, in September

19 Cited in Gütt, Linden, and Maßfeller, *Blutschutz- und Ehegesundheitsgesetz* (1st ed.), 21. The German words used to define the status of blood were *artverwandt* for "related" and *artfremd* for "alien."

20 *Reichsgesetzblatt* 1: 1334 (1935). See also Gütt, Linden, and Maßfeller, *Blutschutz- und Ehegesundheitsgesetz*, 225ff.

21 Gütt, Linden, and Maßfeller, *Blutschutz- und Ehegesundheitsgesetz*, 16.

22 *Reichsgesetzblatt* 1: 1333 (1935).

23 The various decrees and regulations are listed chronologically in Walk, *Sonderrecht für die Juden*.

24 *Reichsgesetzblatt* 1: 1044 (1938). See also Walk, *Sonderrecht für die Juden*, 237, no. 524.

25 *Reichsgesetzblatt* 1: 1342 (1938). See also Walk, *Sonderrecht für die Juden*, 244, no. 556.

1941, months after the killings had already started in the East, a decree prohibited all German and Austrian Jews above the age of six to appear in public without wearing the so-called Jewish star; at the same time, they were forbidden to wear any decorations.[26]

Of course, not all repressive measures were publicly legislated during the 1930s. There were also extralegal measures of intimidation, harassment, and terror, but even these were usually based on legislation. The concentration camps are a good example. The imposition of the so-called *Schutzhaft*, that is, protective custody, was an administrative procedure and not a judicial one. In the beginning, in the period of the "wild" camps, the judicial authorities still concerned themselves with the random violence practiced in these camps. In some, judicial investigations led to trials; in March 1934, for example, the Reich Minister of Justice, commenting on a murder at the Hohnstein camp in Saxony, argued that "The nature of the assault, especially the use of water torture, reveals a brutality and cruelty on the part of the perpetrator that is alien to German sensibilities and feelings. These cruelties, reminiscent of oriental sadism, can neither be explained nor excused by even the most extreme form of hatred in battle."[27] In Dachau, the commandant, Hilmar Wäckerle, had attempted to regularize murder by issuing draconian camp regulations that included as punishment the "execution" of inmates. Thereafter, several prisoners were found dead;[28] they had supposedly committed suicide or had been shot trying to escape. As the law required a medical examination whenever the cause of death was not natural, the state attorney in Munich ordered an autopsy. The medical examiner found that neither suicide nor escape had been a cause of death; the state attorney indicted the commandant and two members of his staff and issued arrest warrants.[29] Such interference did not continue, however; soon laws were issued to legalize the camps as state institutions and to regulate the arrest of prisoners. But these laws granted total control over the camps to the executive and prohibited any appeals to the regular courts.[30]

26 *Reichsgesetzblatt* 1: 542 (1941). See also Walk, *Sonderrecht für die Juden*, 347, no. 229.

27 *TMWC*, 42 vols. (Nuremberg, 1947–49), vol. 26, Nuremberg Doc. PS-783. See also ibid., Nuremberg Docs. PS-784, PS-785, PS-786, PS-787, PS-788.

28 For the camp regulations, see *TMWC*, vol. 35, Nuremberg Doc. D-922.

29 *TMWC*, vol. 26, Nuremberg Docs. PS-641, PS-642; vol. 35, Nuremberg Docs. D-923, D-926.

30 See Martin Broszat, "Nationalsozialistische Konzentrationslager, 1933–1945," in *Anatomie des SS-Staates*, Hans Buchheim et al. (Munich, 1967), 2: 11–133; Henry Friedlander, "The Nazi Concentration Camps," in *Human Responses to the Holocaust*, ed. Michael Ryan (New York, 1981), 33–69; Friedlander, "Die Entwicklung des NS-Konzentrationslagersystems," *Revue d'Allemagne* 27 (1995): 151–64.

Adhering to legal procedures did not preclude the use of the legal system in a barbarous and criminal way. There are a vast number of examples of how the regular courts as well as the special courts (*Sondergerichte*) abused their authority to hand down draconian sentences – applying, for example, the death sentence in race defilement cases – and this increased exponentially during the war, especially in cases before the Peoples' Court (*Volksgerichtshof*). However, the normal legal system did continue to function as long as a larger issue did not intervene, as the following case demonstrates. During the 1930s, the city of Alzey near Mainz embarked on a project of urban renewal, and for this purpose it bought real estate in the inner city. The project involved Kloster Street, designated for new sewers and wider pavements. Kloster Street No. 8 was the property of a Jewish woman, the late Johanna Koch née Strauss. In the 1930s, the property belonged to her three heirs: Albert Koch, who had emigrated to Toledo, Ohio; Luise Koch, an invalid who had died in 1937 owing the city of Alzey RM 10,000 for institutional care; and Bertha Franken née Koch, a resident of Berlin. In March 1941, the city of Alzey – fearful that a private company might preempt the city by purchasing No. 8 and nearby properties – expropriated this real estate. The Alzey Magistrate Court issued the order, and the urban renewal commission set compensation at RM 4,500. Bertha "Sara" Franken received her one-third share of RM 1,500. She contested the financial award, demanding an additional RM 4,800 for a total compensation of RM 9,300. Although Germany was at war and the plaintiff was Jewish, the Magistrate Court granted her appeal and ordered the city to pay the additional money to the three heirs.[31]

Until the war, the regime could thus impose its will while retaining the structure, if not the content, of the *Rechtsstaat*, and assure the *Rechtssicherheit* of the German population. But with the implementation of mass murder, this became more difficult. After all, throughout the Nazi period the German Penal Code, the *Strafgesetzbuch* (StGB), remained in force, including its prohibition of intentional killings.

To carry out mass murder operations, obtain the cooperation of those charged with carrying them out, and retain the appearance of *Rechtssicherheit*, the regime could not make such killings public. At no time was it "legal" to kill Jews or Gypsies; no law legalizing such killings was ever promulgated. The first killing operation of the war – the so-called euthanasia program named Operation T4 – was the systematic mass murder of institutionalized

31 See Henry Friedlander, "The Deportation of the German Jews: Postwar German Trials of Nazi Criminals," *Leo Baeck Institute Yearbook* 29 (1984): 204–5.

disabled German nationals. To accomplish this, the T4 organization established killing centers at Brandenburg, Grafeneck, Hartheim, Bernburg, Sonnenstein, and Hadamar. Operation T4 was a secret enterprise, and Hitler resisted all pressures to legalize it through the promulgation of a law. T4 operated under an order of the Führer, and Hitler signed a totally unofficial authorization; this assured cooperation from those charged with implementing T4. Although this authorization did not have the force of law, it did assure that there would be no prosecutions; this satisfied the physicians and administrators involved. But the killings did not remain secret, and the population, no longer assured of *Rechtssicherheit*, became restless. The regime had to alter the killing operation. The use of killing centers was discontinued, and the murders were thereafter carried out with even greater secrecy in various institutions, many at the borders of the German Reich.[32]

The same did not apply to the murder of Jews and Gypsies. These ethnic groups had already been isolated from the German population, and the *Rechtssicherheit* of Germans was not threatened by their murder. But this did not apply, for example, when Germans and Jews were still associated, which explains the continued concern of the German bureaucracy with the status and fate of Jews in mixed marriages and of Jewish hybrids. Still, Jews and Gypsies were not murdered on German soil; the perpetrators established the killing centers in the occupied east. For the same reason, no law was passed denationalizing all Jews or confiscating their property. When the systematic deportation of German and Austrian Jews commenced in October 1941, their citizenship with all its rights – including property and pension rights – had to be revoked one by one through the application of two 1933 laws: the "Law Concerning the Confiscation of Communist Property" and the "Law Concerning the Confiscation of Subversive Property."[33] Eventually the bureaucracy replaced this cumbersome method with the Eleventh Decree to the Reich Citizenship Law of November 25, 1941, which provided for automatic loss of citizenship and confiscation of property if a German Jew took up residence outside the borders of the German Reich; involuntary deportation to the eastern territories occupied by the Wehrmacht counted as such a change of residence.[34] To underline this fact, on December 3, 1941, the Directive for the Implementation of the Eleventh Decree specifically

32 See Friedlander, *Origins of Nazi Genocide*, chapters 6 and 8.

33 "Gesetz über die Einziehung kommunistischen Vermögens," May 26, 1933 (*Reichsgesetzblatt* 1: 293) and "Gesetz über die Einziehung volks- und staatsfeindlichen Vermögens," July 14, 1933 (*Reichsgesetzblatt* 1: 479).

34 Walk, *Sonderrecht für die Juden*, 357, no. 272, and 358, no. 279.

included the Ostland and the Government General in those foreign areas falling under the provisions of the decree.[35]

After Germany's unconditional surrender, Allied military courts tried German nationals for crimes committed against members of the United Nations, but these courts had no jurisdiction for crimes committed against other German nationals and stateless persons, including German Jews. These were left to the German judicial system, which no longer existed. Germany's unconditional surrender had placed all governmental powers into the hands of the Allies, who became Germany's de facto lawgiver. All German courts had ceased to function and were not permitted to reopen until late 1945.[36] But even then it was not business as usual. The Allies repealed the most important discriminatory laws and decrees "upon which the Nazi regime rested."[37] They also demanded the exclusion of jurists implicated in the crimes of the Nazi regime. Because more than 90 percent of all judicial officials had belonged to the Nazi Party,[38] there were not enough unimplicated judges, prosecutors, and court clerks available to staff the ordinary courts. In the Soviet zone, Nazi jurists were absolutely excluded, and there the occupation authorities appointed lay judges who were legally unqualified but were politically reliable.[39] In the western zones, only qualified professional jurists were eligible for judicial office; the one concession allowed was the appointment as prosecutors or judges of non–civil service lawyers. In the U.S. zone, strict screening meant few appointments; the courts were understaffed and slow to commence functioning. In the British zone, the absence of jurists who were not implicated led to pragmatic compromise: the British introduced a 50:50 rule known as the "piggyback system" by which every unimplicated jurist could bring along one Nazi colleague.[40]

35 Ibid., 357, 358. See also Adam, *Judenpolitik*, 292ff.

36 See *Festschrift für Wilhelm Kiesselbach* (Hamburg, 1947), 39; Friedrich Scholz, *Berlin und seine Justiz: Die Geschichte des Kammergerichtsbezirks 1945 bis 1980* (Berlin and New York, 1982), 3.

37 Control Council Law No. 1 (September 20, 1945), in Library of Congress, *The Statutory Criminal Law of Germany with Comments*, ed. Eldon R. James (Washington, DC, 1947), 209–11. Also Law No. 3, ibid., 211–12; Law No. 11, ibid., 213–15; Law No. 55, in *Justiz und NS-Verbrechen: Sammlung deutscher Strafurteile wegen nationalsozialistischer Tötungsverbrechen*, 22 vols., ed. Adelheid L. Rüter-Ehlermann and C. F. Rüter (Amsterdam, 1968–81), Registerheft, 77–8 [hereafter *JuNSV*]. See also Karl Loewenstein, "Law and Legislative Process in Occupied Germany," *Yale Law Journal* 57 (1948): 730; Eli E. Nobleman, "The Administration of Justice in the United States Zone of Germany," *Federal Bar Journal* 8 (1946): 91.

38 Joachim Reinhold Wenzlau, *Der Wiederaufbau der Justiz in Nordwestdeutschland 1945 bis 1949* (Koenigstein/Ts, 1979), 103–4.

39 Martin Broszat, "Siegerjustiz oder strafrechtliche Selbstreinigung," *Vierteljahrshefte für Zeitgeschichte* 29 (1981): 487.

40 Ibid., 103–4, 113, 130ff. See also Elmer Plischke, "Denazification Law and Procedure," *American Journal of International Law* 41 (1947): 814.

The trials of Nazi war criminals in German courts commenced late in 1945 and continued into the twenty-first century.[41] We are all well aware of their failings: too few perpetrators were actually indicted; far too few were convicted; and far too many received lenient sentences. Justice was not served. Nevertheless, the importance of the German trials cannot be overestimated. First, they have proven invaluable for historians, because they have generated a vast number of interrogations, collected previously undiscovered documents, and compiled accounts in investigative reports, indictments, and decisions.[42] Second, they judged Nazi criminals on their home turf. The criminals were examined by police officers and prosecutors of their own nationality, who undoubtedly understood them better than had Allied interrogators; they were tried in their own courts under their own law, one that had been in effect at the time they committed their crimes. They could no longer claim to be victims of retroactive "victors' justice." Nazi criminals thus faced their judges as ordinary criminals who had violated the regular provisions of the penal code; although they and their public might claim political victimization, they appeared in court as killers and thieves. Third, it applied national law, showing both the benefit and the liability of applying such law to judge state-sponsored international crimes.[43]

Let us be clear about the differences between the German continental civil law and the Anglo-American common law. The German system is based on positive statutory law; in criminal cases, the penal code serves as the basis for all proceedings. Although courts of appeal can and do alter interpretations on how the law should be applied, the lawgiver rules supreme. Equally important are the differences in procedure. German judges – like prosecutors – are civil servants. German judges cannot be compared to independent Anglo-American judges; for example, they do not possess the power of "contempt" and therefore cannot discipline misbehaving lawyers.[44]

During the late 1940s, the period of military government, the German courts exhibited a welcome severity toward the Nazi criminals they tried.

41 See Adalbert Rückerl, *NS-Verbrechen vor Gericht: Versuch einer Vergangenheitsbewältigung* (Heidelberg, 1982); Henry Friedlander, "The Judiciary and Nazi Crimes in Postwar Germany," *Simon Wiesenthal Center Annual* 1 (1984): 27–44.

42 For court decisions in capital cases, see *JuNSV*; for interrogations and documents generated by German proceedings, see, for example, Henry Friedlander and Sybil Milton, eds., *Zentrale Stelle der Landesjustizverwaltungen, Ludwigsburg*, Archives of the Holocaust, vol. 22 (New York, 1993).

43 Nazi war criminals were tried under the German Code of Criminal Procedures (*Strafprozessordnung*, or StPO), in force since 1877, by German courts, who applied the German Penal Code (*Strafgesetzbuch*, or StGB) of 1871.

44 See, for example, Hans Julius Wolff, "Criminal Justice in Germany," *Michigan Law Review* 42 (1944): 1067, and 43 (1944): 155.

They rejected the vestiges of racial law, classifying, for example, the confiscation of Jewish property as invalid.[45] They struck down secret Hitler decrees, refusing, for example, to accept as a defense the legality of his euthanasia authorization.[46] They imposed death sentences on defendants found guilty of mass murder; after the death penalty was abolished, they handed down life sentences.

But in less obvious criminal cases, the courts often refused to acknowledge that German law had been corrupted under the Nazi regime. Just one example: a deserter from the Wehrmacht had been sentenced to death by a military court in wartime Germany. He escaped and eventually reached Switzerland. However, he was able to escape only by attacking and wounding a police officer. Upon his return to Germany in 1946, the Lübeck District Court convicted him, and the Circuit Court in Kiel upheld the sentence under Article 224 (Causing Serious Bodily Injury) and Article 113 (Resisting Lawful Arrest) of the Penal Code.[47]

The language used by the courts at times also showed a lack of sensitivity to Nazi criminality, as is evident in the following two examples:

> The Federal Supreme Court condemned the activities of a German civil servant who aided Jews in contravention of Nazi laws as a "violation of official duties."[48]
>
> In sentencing a concentration camp administrator for killings committed in the Sachsenhausen concentration camp, the District Court in Nuremberg-Fürth concluded: "The Court did not find sufficient reason to revoke the defendant's civil rights, because it could not be proven that, as an SS officer, he lacked honorable character."[49]

Equally bizarre were reasons sometimes advanced to explain the unusual leniency shown Nazi criminals. For example, in one case a court ruled as follows: "In passing sentence, the Court considered as mitigating circumstances that the defendant suffered protracted psychological stress because, fearful of unjust punishment and extradition to foreign powers, he concealed himself for years in his apartment."[50]

During the 1940s, German courts had great flexibility in their pursuit of Nazi criminals, because alongside German law they were able to use Control

45 Amtsgericht (AG) Wiesbaden, in *Süddeutsche Juristenzeitung* 1 (1946): 36.

46 See, for example, Landgericht (LG) Berlin, March 25, 1946, 11 Ks 8/46, in *JuNSV* 1: 33; Kammergericht, in *Juristische Rundschau* 2 (1948): 139.

47 Oberlandesgericht (OLG) Kiel, in *Süddeutsche Juristenzeitung* 2 (1947): 323, and comment by Adolf Arndt, ibid., 330. A similar case in the Soviet zone led to a "not guilty" verdict (ibid., 1 [1947]: 107).

48 Bundesgerichtshof (BGH), in *Neue Juristische Wochenschrift* 15 (1962): 431, note 3.

49 *JuNSV* 17: 150.

50 *JuNSV* 12: 599.

Council Law No. 10, including its provision of "crimes against humanity."[51] But the application of Law No. 10 where no German law had been violated disregarded the legal principle *nullum crimen sine lege* (without a law there is no crime); judges objected that it forced them to act contrary to their convictions.[52] In the Tillessen case, for example, the French occupation authorities had to intervene before the District Court in Konstanz would convict Matthias Erzberger's killer by applying Law No. 10 to the political murder committed in 1921.[53] Although the courts eventually accepted this retroactive law as binding, judges objected that it forced them to act contrary to their principles; they demanded the reestablishment of the legal positivism that had characterized the German *Rechtsstaat*. The British Legal Division observed that "German jurists have wasted much time and energy in academic debates concerning the problems of Law No. 10."[54] In the end, the argument prevailed that, because the Allies were the lawgivers in post-surrender Germany, Law No. 10 had to be applied. Not satisfied with such a pragmatic solution, the courts sought other justifications. The District Court in Siegen, for example, found that retroactive law could be applied as long as it covered crimes "whose severity absolutely demanded punishment in the interest of substantive law, and whose mighty injustice thus also appears to justify for ethical reasons the abrogation of the precept *nulla poene sine lege*, although this rule is retained in principle."[55] Finally, in 1951, the Allies yielded to massive German pressure and prohibited the use of Law No. 10 in German courts. Thereafter, unlike the German Democratic Republic and even Austria, the legislature and the courts of the Federal Republic of Germany refused with Teutonic thoroughness to apply new, and therefore retroactive, law to Nazi crimes of genocide, and conviction of Nazi criminals could thus be obtained only on the basis of the German penal code.

51 Control Council Law No. 10, Article 2, Section 1c, in *TWC* 1: xvii. The text of Crimes Against Humanity read as follows: "Atrocities and offenses, including but not limited to murder, extermination, enslavement, deportation, imprisonment, torture, rape, or other inhumane acts committed against any civilian population, or persecution on political, racial, or religious grounds whether or not in violation of the domestic laws of the country where perpetrated."

52 For a leading attack on Law No. 10, see Hodo Frhr. von Hodenberg, "Zur Anwendung des KRG Nr. 10 durch deutsche Gerichte," *Süddeutsche Juristenzeitung* 2 (1947): 113. For opinions more or less supporting Law No. 10, see August Wimmer, ibid., 123; Gustav Radbruch, ibid., 2 (1947): 131; Richard Lange, ibid., 3 (1948): 655; R. H. Graveson, in *Monatsschrift für Deutsches Recht* 1 (1947): 278; Wilhelm Kiesselbach, ibid., 2 (1947): 2.

53 LG Konstanz, in *Süddeutsche Juristenzeitung* 2 (1947): 337, with comments by Gustav Radbruch, ibid., 343.

54 Cited in Wenzlau, *Wiederaufbau der Justiz*, 249–50.

55 Landgericht Siegen, 4 KLs 23/47, 9 September 1947, in *JuNSV* 1 (1968): 668 (citing OLG Hamm).

During the 1950s, the number of trials in Germany dropped precariously for a number of reasons: the desire to be finished with war crimes trials, the belief that the Allies had tried all criminals, and local prosecutors' lack of jurisdiction over crimes committed in the East. In the late 1950s, the Ulm Einsatzgruppen trial – soon followed by the Eichmann trial – made Germans aware that many crimes had never been adjudicated. The Zentrale Stelle Ludwigsburg, the Central Office for the Investigation of Nazi Crimes in Ludwigsburg, was created to aid local prosecutors, and trials concerning major crimes and involving many defendants started with the first Auschwitz trial in 1963, and continued throughout the 1960s and 1970s and, to a lesser extent, in the 1980s.[56]

By that time, the statute of limitations had expired on all crimes except homicide; it expired on manslaughter in 1960, leaving only the crime of murder for future prosecutions. Until 1941, an intentional killing was classified as murder if it was premeditated, and was considered manslaughter if it was not. On September 4, 1941, the homicide provisions of the German Penal Code were changed to conform to those of several other European countries. The revised murder and manslaughter provisions of the German penal code read as follows:[57]

> Art. 211. The murderer shall be punished by death [changed in 1949 to life in prison]. A murderer is someone who kills a human being out of bloodthirst, for the satisfaction of sexual desires, for greed or any other base motives, in a cunning or cruel manner or by means causing common danger, or to make possible or conceal another felony.
>
> Art. 212. Whoever without being a murderer intentionally kills a human being shall be guilty of manslaughter and shall be punished by confinement in a penitentiary for not less than five years.

The new Article 211 thus defined murder as a killing that is "particularly reprehensible." At the same time, the article listed various attributes that classified an intentional killing as reprehensible; only one such attribute had to apply. Some of them, for example, cruelty, defined the nature of the deed; others, for example, greed, defined the perpetrator's motives. With regard to Nazi crimes, however, usually only three attributes applied:

56 See Richard Henkys, *Die nationalsozialistischen Gewaltverbrechen* (Stuttgart, 1964); Adalbert Rückerl, ed., *NS-Prozesse* (Karlsruhe, 1971); Rückerl, *Die Strafverfolgung von NS-Verbrechen, 1945–1978* (Heidelberg and Karlsruhe, 1979); Ulrich-Dieter Oppitz, *Strafverfahren und Strafvollstreckung bei NS-Gewaltverbrechen* (Ulm, 1979); Bundesminister der Justiz, "Bericht."

57 My translation. See also *Statutory Criminal Law of Germany*, 128.

cruelty, cunning, and base motives.[58] The courts judged killings for racial reasons as base motives, the killings by mass executions or gas chambers as cruel, and the use of subterfuge to lure people to their death as cunning. In general, the courts defined these attributes in the following way:

Cruelty (*Grausamkeit*). A killing is cruel if the victim suffers particularly serious physical or mental pain or torture, due to the reprehensible attitude of the perpetrator as reflected by the execution of the deed.[59]

Cunning (*Heimtücke*). A killing is cunning if the perpetrator exploits the innocence and helplessness of the victim to accomplish the deed. This applies especially if he abused a special relationship of trust.[60]

Base Motives (*niedrige Beweggründe*). This vague concept includes those motives for an intentional killing that are utterly unacceptable in standard ethical judgment. They are contemptuous, even abominable, motives because they are governed by uninhibited and animalistic selfishness.[61]

One might assume that Nazi killings were always judged to be murder, but this was not true. A crass example can serve as an illustration. Early in 1945, two members of the Gestapo were assigned to collect an American pilot at a village where he had been captured after parachuting from his damaged plane. During the trip to city headquarters, they killed the U.S. officer, shooting him with a machine pistol while he walked before them. One of the Gestapo men was convicted and executed by an Allied court. In the 1962 trial of the second Gestapo man, the District Court in Koblenz did not find any of the attributes defined in Article 211; it did not judge the killing of the U.S. officer as "particularly reprehensible." The killing was not cruel; the officer died immediately and thus did not suffer special tortures. The killing was not cunning; the pilot had no reason to trust his captors. The killing did not reflect base motives; the Gestapo men shared the understandable popular antagonism toward Allied pilots. For these reasons the court convicted for manslaughter.[62]

Since under the law conviction for murder required a mandatory sentence of life in prison, we might assume that henceforth all convicted Nazi criminals received life. Nothing could be further from the truth, and

58 At times bloodthirst could apply in cases of the so-called *Exzesstäter*, and greed in cases where officials stole without government authorization; concealment of a felony was applied only in cases involving Commando No. 1005, the enterprise of exhuming and burning the corpses from mass graves, where the workers were shot after the job had been completed.

59 See *Entscheidungen des Reichsgerichts in Strafsachen* (*RGSt.*) 77 (1943): 45, and *Entscheidungen des Bundesgerichtshofs in Strafsachen* (*BGHSt.*) 3 (1952): 180, 264.

60 See *RGSt.* 77 (1943): 44, and *BGHSt.* 2 (1951): 60.

61 See *BGHSt.* 3 (1952): 133.

62 *JuNSV* 18: 538.

we must ask why lighter sentences were handed down. Defense claims of duress, often advanced as an explanation, do not usually apply. The defense of duress under orders, which was granted even to senior Nazi functionaries in the early days, has been discounted since it became clear that no one who refused to kill ever suffered harm to life or limb.[63] Although the courts granted the defense of putative duress from time to time, it did not play a major role.[64] And the defense that under the law superior orders required subordinates to carry out the killings was never admissible, because Article 47 of the Military Code of Justice (*Militärstrafgesetzbuch*), in force during World War II, stated that a subordinate carrying out an order must be punished as a fellow perpetrator "if he knew that the order of his superior involved the commission of a crime."

The reason light sentences could be handed down for murder can be found in the changing legal interpretation of the role of the "accomplice" and the nature of "aiding and abetting." The crucial decision, known as the Bathtub Case, was issued by the German Supreme Court in February 1940:

> The female defendant had drowned her sister Maria's newly born illegitimate infant in a bathtub. The lower court had convicted for murder. The Supreme Court reversed. Both women had killed the infant together. One would be perpetrator, the other accomplice. The fact that the defendant had personally drowned the baby, and had thus actually committed the killing, is not relevant in determining the degree of participation. That is based on the motivation of the perpetrator – his or her personal interest in the success of the undertaking. Maria, the mother of the baby, had this interest; she would have suffered the stigma if the infant had lived. The defendant, her sister, did not have a personal interest in the outcome; she only acted to support the deed of another. She is therefore only an accomplice.[65]

This so-called subjective interpretation enabled the courts to convict as an accomplice someone who had personally killed another human being. The courts concluded "that someone who personally wants the crime to succeed is a fellow perpetrator; one who supports the crime of another is an accomplice." In the immediate postwar years, some courts still rejected this interpretation. They refused to classify Nazi killers as accomplices; they saw the "degree of personal interest" as only one criterion of how

63 Herbert Jäger, *Verbrechen untcr totalitärer Herrschaft: Studien zur nationatsozialistischen Gewaltkriminalität* (Frankfurt, 1982), 81–138. For an egregious example in which duress was granted to a senior Nazi functionary, see Henry Friedlander, "The Deportation of the German Jews: Postwar German Trials of Nazi Criminals," *Leo Baeck Institute Yearbook* 29 (1984): 219–21.

64 But see, for example, *JuNSV* 17: 519.

65 *RGSt.* 74: 84.

to judge participation.[66] In the Federal Republic, however, the subjective interpretation assumed the putative status of law.

Almost all court decisions followed a pattern. First, the courts correctly classified the crimes as murder. In the first Auschwitz trial, for example, the court classified the killing of hundreds of thousands of Jews in the Birkenau gas chambers as a crime characterized by cruelty, cunning, and base motives. Second, the courts listed the chief perpetrators, who were almost always dead. In the Auschwitz trial they were Adolf Hitler, Heinrich Himmler, Hermann Göring, and Reinhard Heydrich. In the Treblinka trial against Kurt Franz and others, they were listed as Hitler, Göring, Himmler, Heydrich, Odilo Globocnik, and Christian Wirth.[67]

The defendants were convicted as accomplices. In the Auschwitz trial, the chief defendant Robert Mulka, adjutant to the camp commandant, was classified as an accomplice, because he was only "a small cog in the machine of destruction." The fate of the Jewish victims arriving by RSHA (Reich Security Main Office) transport had already been sealed. The participating Auschwitz SS members "could not control events" and "had little leeway for independent action." The court thus "assumed that the participating subordinates wanted only to aid and abet the deeds ordered by the state." Mulka received fourteen years, one year less than the maximum sentence permissible under German law.[68]

Fourteen years is a reasonable sentence, if fifteen years is the longest term German law permits. But the law also provides for life sentences, and these are mandatory in a conviction for murder. Why then does an accomplice to murder not receive a life sentence? Prior to 1939, Articles 49 and 44 of the penal code required that the accomplice receive a lighter sentence than the perpetrator. In September 1939, Paragraph 4 of the Decree Against Violent Criminals permitted the courts to impose on the accomplice the same sentence as on the perpetrator. In 1943, Articles 49 and 44 were altered to reflect this change; lighter sentences were no longer required but only permitted.

The courts were therefore not required to lower the sentence of the accomplice; they could impose a life sentence. But as we have seen, this did not happen in the case of Robert Mulka. Similarly, in the Chelmno (Kulmhof) trial of 1963, the defendant Gustav Laabs received a fifteen-year sentence as an accomplice. He had operated the gas van at Chelmno; the

66 See, for example, OLG Frankfurt in *JuNSV* 1 (1948): 268, 269.

67 Landgericht (LG) Düsseldorf, Urteil Kurt Franz u.A, 8 I Ks 2/64, September 3, 1965.

68 *JuNSV* 21: 595 (LG Frankfurt, Urteil Robert Mulka u.A., 4 Ks 2/63, August 19–20, 1965).

court found mitigating circumstances in the fact that Laab had behaved correctly during the trial and had once requested to be relieved of his gas-van duty.[69] In the Treblinka trial, two accomplices – the T4 operatives Otto Stadie and Franz Suchomel – received, respectively, seven and six years in prison. Both men had used guns and whips to drive Jews from arriving transports toward the gas chamber. But the court found mitigating circumstances because otherwise their behavior toward Jewish camp workers had been relatively proper. Another defendant convicted as an accomplice to the murder of at least 300,000 human beings, the T4 mason Erwin Lambert, who had built the gas chambers in Treblinka but otherwise had not mistreated prisoners, received a sentence of four years.[70] In the trial of Einsatzkommando 8 in 1964, the defendant Werner Schönemann, a member of the Cologne Gestapo who commanded a subcommando, received a sentence of six years as an accomplice in the murders of Einsatzgruppe B; the court found mitigating circumstances since he had been just twenty-nine years old, had not joined the police for ideological reasons, had not requested but only accepted induction into the SS, had been forced to join the Einsatzgruppe, and had believed a Führer order had the force of law. The court also counted in his favor that he always behaved correctly during the trial, concluding that he would have lived a good bourgeois life if circumstances had not placed him into an Einsatzgruppe.[71]

In 1968, a change of the German penal code made obtaining conviction and stiff sentences for accomplices even more difficult. That year the legislature enacted a change in Article 50 of the penal code (Article 28 after the renumbering of 1975). The changes mandated a reduction in sentence if the accomplice did not also share the perpetrators' personal motives. In Nazi war crimes cases, this involved "base motives." Prior to 1968, it had been sufficient for the accomplice to be aware of the perpetrators' base motives; after 1968 he had to share them. Absence of base motives changed a charge from abetting murder to abetting manslaughter; as the statute of limitation on manslaughter had expired by that time, most bureaucratic killers could not be convicted. Although it is usually assumed that this change was an unintended consequence of judicial reform, some have speculated that the bureaucrats who proposed this change had intended to aid Nazi criminals.

The change of Article 50 did not, however, alter the status of the accomplice if cruelty or cunning were involved, but without base motives even such accomplices usually received lesser sentences. A good example is the

69 *JuNSV* 21: 594 (LG Bonn, Urteil Gustav Laabs u.A., 8 Ks 3/62, March 30, 1963).
70 LG Düsseldorf, Urteil Kurt Franz, 8 I Ks 2/64, September 3, 1965.
71 *JuNSV* 20: 573 (LG Köln, 24 Ks 1/63, May 12, 1964).

decision of the Düsseldorf court in the Maidanek trial, which commenced in 1975 and ended in 1981.[72] Due to Article 50 and all the preceding interpretations of the law, the reasoning behind the court's decision appeared truly Byzantine.

Two of the defendants, Hermine Braunsteiner (who had been extradited from the United States) and Hildegard Lächert, were feared female guards; Lächert was known to the prisoners as "bloody Brigitta." Together they participated in the same killing operations – the murder of Jewish children and the selection of their mothers for the gas chamber. The court found that neither Braunsteiner nor Lächert had shared the racial ideology of the Nazi leaders. But in the case of Braunsteiner the court concluded nevertheless that base motives applied because "driven by selfish ambition, she had acted in brutal disregard of human and moral precepts to advance her career." In the case of Lächert, however, the court concluded that her intellectual and emotional instability did not indicate that she shared the base motives of the perpetrators. Braunsteiner received a life sentence; Lächert received twelve years' imprisonment.

I have tried to sketch the salient features of the trials of Nazi criminals under German national law. These national trials, different from the international and Allied trials at Nuremberg and elsewhere, point toward an alternate legal approach to the crimes of genocide and mass murder.

72 LG Düsseldorf, Urteil Hermann Hackmann u.A., 8 Ks 1/75, June 30, 1981.

2

The Setting and the Significance of the Nuremberg Trials

A Historian's Perspective

GERHARD L. WEINBERG

The formal opening of what is today referred to as the "Nuremberg trials" actually took place in Berlin, primarily at Soviet insistence. There was a double symbolic significance in this: the proceedings were opened in what had been the capital of the Third Reich, and this was a capital that the Red Army had taken in the final stages of the war. The actual conduct of the international trial – the only one because the Allies eventually decided not to hold another with the same format[1] – took place at Nuremberg, as did the subsequent twelve trials conducted by the United States under Control Council Law No. 10. Nuremberg had been selected for both practical and symbolic reasons. The practical factor was simply the availability of a number of courtrooms with an adjacent facility for holding prisoners – all still standing in the Germany of 1945, not an easy thing to find in the rubble of the Reich. The symbolic factor in this choice was the association of the city of Nuremberg with the annual rallies of the Nazi Party, rallies shown throughout the world of the 1930s in pictures and movies, newsreels and other media. Furthermore, in this city the German parliament, the Reichstag, had met in its one session outside Berlin during the Third Reich and had enthusiastically approved a series of measures against the less than 1 percent of the country's population which was Jewish, measures that had generally come to be known as the "Nuremberg Laws."

But such issues of symbol and memory were less important – even if today more widely remembered – than quite another concern at the time

1 See the section devoted to this question in Telford Taylor's *Final Report to the Secretary of the Army on the Nuernberg War Crimes Trials under Control Council Law No. 10* (Washington, DC, 1949), 22–7.

the key decisions were made: the memory of the failed war crimes trials after World War I. The victorious powers at that time had eventually, and reluctantly, allowed the Germans to run their own trials. A small number of these had been held in Leipzig, and although many of the technical legal issues discussed at Nuremberg and in the subsequent literature on them had already come up at Leipzig, the trials had been a farce and were seen to have been just that.[2] In this instance as in so many others, what were believed to be the lessons of the prior conflict greatly influenced thinking during World War II. On this occasion, the Allies would avoid what in retrospect had been a mistake; they would establish the tribunal and conduct the trial or trials themselves. Years would pass before German courts were entrusted with the responsibility of conducting trials of war criminals.

For the historian, surely one of the most dramatic aspects of both the first trial and the "Subsequent Proceedings," as the twelve American trials at Nuremberg under Control Council Law No. 10 were called, was that they provided for the almost immediate accessibility of a vast quantity of documentation on dramatic events of the most recent past. Not only were masses of documents made available, but key actors in a past of most recent memory as well as witnesses in considerable numbers were heard about events still alive in the minds of scholars as well as other onlookers.

It is essential to stress a generally neglected aspect of this early opening of documents. What was opened up to those interested was not only the trial record itself, including the documents actually introduced into evidence. The vast majority of the documents collected for the prosecution all over Europe, and especially those culled from the German archives captured in the final stages of World War II, were *not* introduced as evidence by either prosecution or defense, but still became accessible in the document series into which they had been organized when these were deposited in the U.S. National Archives and in many libraries and other institutions. I myself recall most vividly my own experience of opening the crates of Nuremberg materials in the basement of the Law Library of the University of Chicago in 1950–51 and helping the librarians there set up the system under which these materials were held until transferred to the Midwest Interlibrary Loan

2 There are summaries in *Foreign Relations of the United States: The Paris Peace Conference 1919*, vol. 13 (Washington, DC, 1947), 371–80; Johann W. Brügel, "Das Schicksal der Strafbestimmungen des Versailler Vertrags," *Vierteljahrshefte für Zeitgeschichte* 6 (1958): 263–70. Detailed studies are Gordon Wallace Bailey, "Dry Run for the Hangman: The Versailles-Leipzig Fiasco, 1919–1921, Feeble Foreshadow of Nuremberg," Ph.D. diss., University of Maryland, 1971; James F. Willis, *Prologue to Nuremberg: The Politics and Diplomacy of Punishing War Criminals of the First World War* (Westport, 1982). A rather more favorable view of the German handling of the cases may be found in Claud Mullins, *The Leipzig Trials* (London, 1921).

Center, now the Center for Research Libraries. There was something quite extraordinary about holding in my hand a photocopy of a volume of the war diary of the German navy of a few years earlier.[3]

In this context it is important to note the extent to which the revelations of the trials and the availability of enormous quantities of information about recent events both challenged and assisted the scholarly community. The challenge was threefold. First, in this as in all other cases, the historian had to be exceedingly careful in the utilization of testimony and documentary evidence presented at a trial or gathered for use in the courtroom. Second, the sheer mass of material – transcripts running into tens of thousands of pages, document series containing thousands of items of which many are themselves whole files, interrogations, and affidavits without number – forced all scholars who wanted to make systematic use of these vast treasures to possess what the Germans appropriately call *Sitzfleisch*, the ability and willingness to plow through huge masses of material. Third, scholars had to be very careful always to remember that the documentary evidence had been collected to incriminate or exculpate; perhaps other relevant but contrary evidence might turn up later. And the historian then and now had always to keep in mind the fact that much had been destroyed and that many surviving documents might well have been deliberately slanted to serve a variety of purposes when originally written.

On the other hand, historians were provided an essentially unprecedented look at materials of the most recent past and were thereby enabled to take a new look at the 1930s and the war years much sooner than would otherwise have been the case. Both the published record of the international trial and the availability of huge collections of documents gathered in various series, primarily by the prosecution, opened up opportunities which greatly influenced the writing of accounts of major aspects of the 1933–45 era during the 1950s and 1960s. Such books as Alexander Dallin's study of *German Rule in Russia* (1957), Raul Hilberg's *Destruction of the European Jews* (1961), and my own *Germany and the Soviet Union* (1954) necessarily relied very heavily on materials which the trials had made accessible.[4] It is worth noting that each of these three works was subsequently reissued in a new

3 The diary has now been published: *Kriegstagebuch der Seekriegsleitung, 1939–1945*, ed. Werner Rahn and Gerhrd Schreiber with the assistance of Hansjoseph Maierhöfer (Osnabrück, 1988–97). There is an early but still useful discussion of the Nuremberg materials as a whole in Robert M. W. Kempner, "The Nuremberg Trials as Sources of Recent German Political and Historical Materials," *American Political Science Review* 44 (1950): 447–59.

4 Alexander Dallin, *German Rule in Russia* (London and New York, 1957); Raul Hilberg, *The Destruction of the European Jews* (Chicago, 1961); Gerhard L. Weinberg, *Germany and the Soviet Union, 1939–1941* (Leyden, 1954).

edition; each with some added details, but each able to retain its original basic structure.

One significant aspect of the trials that affected the work of historians has not generally received the attention it deserves. During the international trial, documents were challenged in court or subsequently impugned by some apologists for the Third Reich.[5] It must now be noted that one by one, the key items subjected to such attacks have turned out on subsequent scholarly investigation to have been authentic and accurate. Three examples of highly important documents once attacked as unreliable or even forged will illustrate the point.

First, the famous "memorandum" by Friedrich Hoßbach on Hitler's extensive November 5, 1937, discussion of his plans for war, endlessly discussed and challenged, has now been fully authenticated.[6] Second, what is now recognized as the best, most reliable, and most complete account of Hitler's August 22, 1939, address to the generals was the one most disputed at the trial and afterward.[7] Third, there is the case of the letter of General Werner von Fritsch of December 11, 1938 – written after the November 1938 pogrom, and after a filthy intrigue had led to the general's dismissal as commander-in-chief of the German army – showing Firtsch's sympathy for Hitler and especially for the Nazi war against Jews, Catholics, and workers. This letter was disregarded by the tribunal because the prosecution could not produce the original; it has turned up in the papers of Sir John Wheeler-Bennett. Surely worthy of note in this connection is that the news of this discovery and a photographic reproduction of the original appeared in the *Vierteljahrshefte für Zeitgeschichte*, a periodical published by the Institute for Contemporary History in Munich.[8]

The materials made available by the trials at Nuremberg have not, however, been exhausted as a source for scholarly research. Let us consider three areas where these materials point in directions that may serve to exemplify the possibilities still open. Considerable attention was justifiably paid to the meetings in Poznan-Posen in the fall of 1943 at which Heinrich Himmler described the murder of the Jews in considerable detail to several

5 See, for example, Hans-Günther Seraphim, "Nachkriegsprozesse und zeitgeschichtliche Forschung," in *Mensch und Staat in Recht und Geschichte: Festschrift für Herbert Kraus* (Kitzingen/M, 1954), 436–55.

6 Bradley F. Smith, "Die Überlieferung der Hoßbach-Niederschrift im Lichte neuer Quellen," *Vierteljahrshefte für Zeitgeschichte* 38 (1990): 329–36.

7 See Winfried Baumgart, "Zur Ansprache Hitlers vor den Führern der Wehrmacht am 22. August 1939. Eine quellenkritische Untersuchung," *Vierteljahrshefte für Zeitgeschichte* 16 (1968): 120–48, and the subsequent exchange between Baumgart and Hermann Boehm, *Vierteljahrshefte für Zeitgeschichte* 19 (1971): 294–304.

8 Nicholas Reynolds, "Der Fritsch-Brief vom 11. Dezember 1938," *Vierteljahrshefte für Zeitgeschichte* 28 (1980): 358–71.

large audiences of German military, administrative, and Nazi party leaders.[9] The audience that attended these presentations warrants further study. How many were there? Who were they? What reactions, if any, were there? Some of those present later swore under oath that they had only heard about these mass killings after World War II.

The second topic concerns oaths. After the Third Reich had been defeated and in the decades since, a great deal has been said and written about the oath to Hitler. One might have thought that this was the only oath most high German officials and officers had sworn in their lives. That, on a moment's reflection, can be seen as nonsense. They had for the most part sworn an oath to uphold the constitution and laws of the Weimar Republic. Nothing suggests that most of them took that oath particularly seriously. On the contrary. The Treaty of Versailles was one of the laws passed by the Reichstag and duly published in the *Reichsgesetzblatt*, the German equivalent of the Statutes at Large. Far from honoring their oath, German officers were proud of breaking it as frequently as possible, and several documents among those revealed at Nuremberg show them boasting about their actions. For example, Admiral Erich Raeder told the officers of the German navy in June 1940 how proud he was of all that the navy had done illegally in the Weimar years after having a special seventy-nine-page booklet on these illegalities issued as a secret 1937 *Marine Dienstvorschrift*, a service regulation for the German navy.[10] It is of interest to note that, in a service regulation, illegality was thus held up as a model for members of a branch of the armed forces.

As early as 1955, Karl Dietrich Bracher reviewed the pre-1933 discussion of these illegalities as contrary to the oath taken by officers and officials during the Weimar Republic.[11] In Bracher's work and elsewhere, one can read about Gerd von Rundstedt's implementation of the July 20, 1932, coup against the Prussian government, but not a word about his oath to the constitution, which that famous general broke with evident enthusiasm.

It is in this general context that the Nuremberg trials may shed light on a significant but hitherto unexplored aspect of the Third Reich. How did those who swore to tell the truth as defendants or witnesses at Nuremberg

9 Some preliminary work on these speeches may be found in Bradley F. Smith and Agnes Peterson, eds., *Heinrich Himmler: Geheimreden 1933 bis 1945* (Frankfurt, 1974), 162–83, 300–3; Richard Breitman, *The Architect of Genocide: Himmler and the Final Solution* (New York, 1991), 242–3, 308.

10 For Raeder's statement, see *Trial of the Major War Criminals before the International Military Tribunal (Blue Series)*, 42 vols. (Nuremberg, 1949) 34: 529; for the *Dienstvorschrift*, see ibid., 530–607.

11 *Die Auflösung der der Weimarer Republik,* 5th ed. (Villingen, 1971), 210–11 and Anhang 4. The issue is also reviewed in Karl Dietrich Bracher, Wolfgang Sauer, and Gerhard Schulz, *Die Nationalsozialistische Machtergreifung* (Cologne and Opladen, 1962), 778–9.

see their oaths on *this* occasion? What light does their attitude then shed on the protestations of some that they felt bound by the oath of loyalty to Hitler, which they had taken after their oath to the constitution of the Weimar Republic and prior to their postwar oaths at Nuremberg? If they felt bound by only one of the many oaths they had sworn during their lifetime, how did they come to select that one?

A third area for further exploration involves von Rundstedt as well as a considerable number of other higher commanders of the German army. In October 1941, an explanation of the mass killing of Jews was distributed to all German armies on the eastern front with the demand that German soldiers accept these terrible events as "just punishment" (*gerechte Sühne*) for the Jews. Although von Rundstedt swore as a witness at Nuremberg that he knew nothing about this extraordinary justification of mass murder, at the time he actually declared himself in writing to be in full agreement with it and ordered its distribution within the army group he then commanded.[12]

This notorious directive was discussed at some length during the international trial and several subsequent proceedings. The question of why these orders were thought necessary or appropriate in the first place needs to be investigated. German field marshals and generals were not ordinarily in the habit of explaining themselves to the troops. I have put forth in my history of World War II the theory that these orders were most likely issued in response to questions and objections from within the German military to what they saw going on around them and many times involving them directly.[13] Now that we have available to us the war diaries of the army and army group headquarters where these orders were issued, we can see that they represent almost the only instance when commanders thought that something had to be explained. Why was such instruction of the troops thought necessary, unless it was needed to quiet the rumblings aroused by such events as the Babi Yar massacre of over thirty thousand Jews, which took place in the area of Rundstedt's army group at the end of the preceding month? It is too late to ask any of the field marshals and generals to explain why they believed that shooting can be a just punishment for a two- or three- or four-year-old child, but it is certainly not too late to raise the question, why did they have to offer an explanation?

12 For Rundstedt's false testimony, see *Trial of the Major War Criminals* 21: 45–6; for the true story, see Helmut Krausnick and Hans-Heinrich Wilhelm, *Die Truppe des Weltanschauungskrieges: Die Einsatzgruppen der Sicherheitspolizei und des SD, 1938–1942* (Stuttgart, 1981), 259–61.

13 Gerhard L. Weinberg, *A World at Arms: A Global History of World War II*, 2nd ed. (Cambridge, 2005), 302.

These three matters are, of course, not the only issues that await examination, but they are mentioned here to remind everyone that the research potential of the trial materials is by no means exhausted. And new approaches to history will no doubt make still more new questions worth pursuing in the great storehouse of records left behind by the Nuremberg trials.

It may be appropriate to conclude by drawing attention to an entirely different aspect of the trials, which seems to this historian to be of current and continuing relevance. There is a perspective on the trials which is, in a way, the reverse of that which led to the way the trials were held in the first place. As we have seen, the experience after World War I was very much in the minds of those who during World War II consciously wanted to handle differently the problem of what to do about war criminals. In the process of implementing the decision to conduct trials themselves, they were forced to develop a whole host of rules and procedures. They had to combine Roman Law and Common Law legal concepts, arrange ways of making a trial function effectively and efficiently, make sure that the interests of defendants were properly protected, and they had to institute for the first time a system of simultaneous translation.

Those who conducted the international trial and the subsequent proceedings at Nuremberg may not have done everything perfectly – human justice should never be confused with divine justice – but they did make a new beginning. In November 1995, Dr. Jutta Limbach, the then chief justice of the German Constitutional Court, described the international trial as both fair and necessary during the commemoration in Nuremberg of the trial's fiftieth anniversary.[14] This suggests that there is no need today or in the future to reinvent the wheel. Different situations, legal systems, and other details, as well as the prior experience itself, will no doubt indicate modifications to be necessary if and when any further trials of war criminals are conducted. But there is now a precedent that deserves attention, as a positive rather than a negative model. If the will is there, a useful precedent is indeed available.

14 As the U.S. participant in the commemorative session in the original courtroom in Nuremberg, I heard Dr. Limbach make these comments; they were subsequently reported in newspapers.

3

The American Military Commission Trials of 1945

PATRICIA HEBERER

On December 20, 1945, a month after formal proceedings in the trial of "major" Nazi criminals began before the International Military Tribunal at Nuremberg, the quadripartite Allied Control Council promulgated its Law Number 10. A chief feature of this legislation was Article 2, which allowed military authorities in the four zones of occupied Germany to level charges of crimes against peace, war crimes, membership in an illegal organization, or crimes against humanity for wartime offenses committed in their respective jurisdictions.[1] Before this time, Allied officials were limited to adjudication of crimes under the confining strictures of international law. This essay seeks to explore the military commission trials occurring in the U.S. zone during these earliest months of occupation. It will discuss policies and procedures governing such proceedings in the American sector and, through two case studies, examine how U.S. military authorities wielded international law both to adjudge traditional war crimes and in a more challenging vein, to confront Nazi policies of mass murder before Control Council Law No. 10 lent prosecutors and jurists greater flexibility in administering postwar justice.

American efforts to adjudicate Axis crimes found focus through the United States War Crimes Branch (USWCB), established in 1944 by the Judge Advocate General of the U.S. Army to aid in Allied collection of evidence and in the apprehension of alleged war criminals. Its history was intrinsically linked with that of the United Nations War Crimes Commission (UNWCC) and thus with the Allied decision, in the face of mounting Nazi atrocities against prisoners of war and civilian populations, to prosecute perpetrators of war crimes at war's end. Movement toward such a decision

1 *Trials before the Nürnberg Military Tribunals under Control Council Law No. 10* (Green Series), vol. 1 (Nürnberg, 1949), xvi–xix.

began on October 25, 1941, when the American President Franklin Delano Roosevelt, referring specifically to Nazi executions of hostages in France, warned that such acts of violence would "only sow the seeds of hatred which will one day bring fruitful retribution."[2] On the same day, British Prime Minister Winston Churchill, having conferred with his government, announced that "punishment of these crimes should . . . be counted among the major goals of the war."[3] These statements were followed on January 13, 1942, by the St. James Declaration in which the governments-in-exile of nine Allied nations affirmed their resolve to punish Nazi war criminals found guilty of violence against civilian populations through a judicial process.[4] In the fall of 1942, the United States and Great Britain issued simultaneous declarations that a United Nations War Crimes Commission should be created to bring to justice those guilty of war crimes and to collect and evaluate evidence for this purpose. The Allied governments-in-exile and the French National Committee approved and adopted this convention. Of the Allied nations, only the Soviet Union refused to join the UNWCC, instead establishing on November 2, 1942, its own agency, the Soviet Extraordinary State Commission to Investigate War Crimes.

In the winter of 1942, a significant event steeled Allied determination to punish Nazi offenders. On December 17 of that year, in possession of incontrovertible evidence, the Allied powers, including the Soviet Union, issued the first joint declaration officially noting the mass extermination of Jewry in Europe and reasserting their resolution to prosecute those responsible for these atrocities.[5] The UNWCC was officially established in London in October 1943 and was immediately empowered to compile lists of possible war criminals and to collect data submitted by national commissions in participating countries. In the same month, at the Moscow Conference, the foreign ministers of the United States, Great Britain, and the Soviet Union resolved that at the time of an armistice, those persons deemed responsible for war crimes would be sent back to the countries in which their crimes had been committed, and prosecuted according to the laws of the nation concerned. Excepted from this rule were persons whose crimes could not be assigned a specific geographical location, particularly those who had made broad-reaching policy decisions. These "major" war

2 Franklin Delano Roosevelt, quoted in Whitney Harris, *Tyranny on Trial: The Evidence at Nuremberg*. 2nd ed. (Dallas, 1982), 3. Of course at this time the United States was not yet a belligerent in World War II.

3 Winston Churchill, quoted in Harris, *Tyranny on Trial*, 3.

4 Ann Tusa and John Tusa, *The Nuremberg Trial* (New York, 1984), 21.

5 Telford Taylor, *The Anatomy of the Nuremberg Trials* (New York, 1992), 26.

criminals, it was determined, would be punished by joint decision of the Allied governments.[6]

The dilemma of how to deal with Nazi perpetrators of atrocities and war crimes absorbed certain members of the American administration. On September 6, 1944, Secretary of the Treasury Henry Morgenthau presented his famous "pastoralization" plan for a defeated Germany to President Roosevelt in which he suggested that the occupying powers strip the *Ruhrgebiet* and other strategic areas of their industries, thus preventing the return of German economic might. In the same memorandum, Morgenthau called for the preparation of a list of German war criminals, proposing that those persons whose guilt was generally recognized should be shot upon capture.[7] In the Roosevelt cabinet, the so-called Morgenthau Plan met stiff opposition from Secretary of War Henry Stimson. Stimson argued that the "pastoralization" plan outlined in Morgenthau's memorandum was utterly impracticable; more important for our purposes, he contended that the punishment of German war crimes should follow a defined legal procedure, which should include such hallmarks of the American judicial system as notification of the accused, the right to be heard, and the right to call witnesses in one's own defense. Leading members of the Nazi government whose policies had led to aggressive war or war crimes should be called before "an international tribunal constituted to try them."[8]

In the end, Stimson and other American supporters of judicial action won the day, and the secretary of war's call for Allied adjudication of major Nazi officials came to fruition in the International Military Tribunal (IMT) and in twelve subsequent Nuremberg proceedings, which, under the aegis of the American military authorities, tried leading branches of the German civil, economic, and judicial administrations, the army, police, and free professions implicated in major crimes. Yet American officials, like their British, French, and Soviet counterparts, had to prepare for the eventuality of organizing proceedings for offenses committed in their respective zones of occupation. On September 25, 1944, Stimson, with the approval of the Departments of State and the Navy, designated the U.S. Army's Office of the Judge Advocate General (JAG) within his War Department as the central agency for the prosecution of violations of international law, particularly those perpetrated against American military and civilian personnel. One of the Judge Advocate General's first tasks was to create a War Crimes Office

6 The Moscow Declaration, quoted by Taylor, ibid., 27.

7 Taylor, *Anatomy of the Nuremberg Trials*, 34; Harris, *Tyranny on Trial*, 7.

8 Bradley F. Smith, *Reaching Judgment at Nuremberg: The Untold Story of How Nazi War Criminals Were Judged* (New York, 1977), 25.

under Brigadier General John M. Weir, to collect evidence, arrange for the capture of alleged war criminals, and to ensure an expeditious trial of those persons for whom a prima facie case could be made.[9] Both European and Asian theaters of operation were to establish War Crimes Branches for the investigation of evidence, including information relating to crimes against nationals of other countries, which was to be relayed to the governments concerned. After the liberation of France, the U.S. War Crimes Branch in the European theater established its headquarters in Paris. In early July 1945, the Branch then moved to American occupation headquarters in Wiesbaden. At the same time, the Combined Chiefs of Staff authorized the Supreme Headquarters of the Allied Expeditionary Forces (SHAEF) to adjudicate war crimes in accordance with international law under the auspices of the commanding general of the European theater.[10] Colonel Claude B. Mickelwait, a regular army man and able lawyer, became the first Deputy Theater Judge Advocate General, succeeded in May 1946 by Colonel Clio E. Straight.[11] Under Mickelwait, the JAG established a Trial Section within the War Crimes Branch, tasked with creating military commissions capable of trying alleged war criminals in the American zone of occupation. The American government had engaged in thirteen major occupations by 1950: twice in Mexico, in Florida, the Confederate States of America, Cuba, Puerto Rico, the Philippines, the demilitarized Rhineland after World War I, Japan, Austria, Italy, Germany, and Korea. In each case, the U.S. occupying force protected its nationals and punished offenders against military and international law by means of its military courts. Although such tribunals were not new to American military or legal history, the extraordinary nature of Axis crimes and Allied commitment to punish these offenses signaled a complete departure in the courts' traditional function and purpose.

Trials conducted by military commissions under the auspices of the USWCB began in earnest shortly after Allied victory in Europe.[12] Among the first significant proceedings in the U.S. zone was the so-called Rüsselsheim Death March Trial, held in Darmstadt in July 1945. The case involved the murder of six American servicemen after their capture by German authorities. While in many instances Wehrmacht soldiers or other members of the German armed forces proved responsible for the killing of

9 Harris, *Tyranny on Trial*, 8.

10 On July 16, 1945, SHAEF was dissolved, and U.S. Forces, European Theater (USFET) (formerly European Theater of Operations, U.S. Army, or ETOUSA) took over as theater headquarters for all U.S. military commands in Europe.

11 Judge Advocate Association, *The Judge Advocate Journal* 4 (January 1950): 5.

12 An exception was the trial of Curt Bruns (Case No. 6–56), tried and sentenced to death by a military commission of the U.S. First Army for shooting Jewish POWs, on April 7, 1945.

Allied POWs, here the accused perpetrators were civilians angered by a string of deadly Allied bombings in the region. The small city of Rüsselsheim on the Main had been the focus of repeated aerial bombardment, the most intense attack coming on the night of August 25, 1944. The raids targeted the town's strategic Opel-Werke, but bombs also fell in residential neighborhoods, causing extensive damage and loss of life.[13] Citizens emerging from air raid shelters and bunkers on the morning of August 26 found their attention drawn to the sight of a small German guard unit marching captured American fliers John Sekul, William Dumont, Thomas Williams, Elmore Austin, and four unidentified comrades through the center of town.[14] Ironically, the men had been shot down near Hannover and were being transported to a prisoner-of-war camp near Frankfurt for interrogation and so had taken no part in the nighttime bombing itself.[15] In the Frankfurterstrasse, the small ensemble encountered an angry mob. At the edge of the crowd, shop owners Margarete Witzler and Käthe Reinhardt incited the throng to violence, shouting, "Beat them to pieces; beat them to death," themselves heaving bricks and roof tiles in the direction of the airmen. At this juncture, many of their neighbors joined in the assault, utilizing any implements they had at hand. Local deputy Ortsgruppenleiter Josef Hartgen struck several of the Americans with a hoe, encouraging others in the assembly to join him and reportedly threatening an onlooker who protested. Townsmen Johannes Seipel, Georg Daum, and Heinrich Barthel were seen to strike or kick the prisoners, or to pelt them with stones. Friedrich Wust assaulted at least two of the fliers with a hammer. Johann Opper, observed by several witnesses as standing at the front of the crowd, beat the unarmed men with a broomstick. Philipp Gutlich, echoing the women's cry, "Beat them to pieces," wielded a wooden beam, possibly a two-by-four.[16]

When the frenzy was over, the eight airmen lay dying or unconscious in the street. After townspeople loaded the broken bodies onto a borrowed

13 National Archives and Record Administration II at College Park, Maryland (hereafter NARA), Record Group 549 (Records of the United States Army, Europe (USAREUR)), War Crimes Cases Files – Cases Tried, Case 12–1497, *United States v. Josef Hartgen et al.*, Boxes 167–170 (hereafter *U.S. v. Hartgen et al.*), Review of the Staff Judge Advocate, *U.S. v. Hartgen et al.*, Headquarters of the U.S. Seventh Army, August 23, 1945; Clemency Petition of Frieda Hartgen to the Commander of the Seventh Army in Heidelberg, August 12, 1945.

14 *U.S. v. Hartgen et al.*, Review of the Staff Judge Advocate, 2–4; Deputy Theater Judge Advocate General's Office, War Crimes Branch, USFET, Reviews and Recommendations of the Deputy Theater Judge Advocate re *U.S. v. Hartgen et al.*, September 29, 1945.

15 Leon Jaworski, *After Fifteen Years* (Houston, 1961), 68.

16 *U.S. v. Hartgen et al.*, Reviews and Recommendations of the Deputy Theater Judge Advocate re *U.S. v. Hartgen et al.*, September 29, 1945.

pushcart, local Nazi leader Hartgen appeared with his service revolver to apply the "coup de grâce" to the defenseless men, firing shots into the heads of at least four of them. The handcart was trundled off to the local cemetery, but its handlers abandoned it as the town's air raid siren sounded. Toward nightfall, two of the soldiers, miraculously still alive, regained consciousness and under the cover of darkness made their escape.[17] The corpses of the remaining fliers were interred the next day in a remote part of the cemetery, with Hartgen, clad in full SA attire, in attendance.[18] On a tip from Polish and French forced laborers who had witnessed the events, American forces discovered the servicemen's remains in a mass grave on June 28, 1945. The men were still clothed in their U.S. Air Corps uniforms; four of them still wore dog tags.[19] American army pathologist reports indicated that two of the deceased died from skull fractures, one from bullet wounds, and three as a combined result.[20]

The Rüsselsheim Death March is emblematic of the majority of military commission cases tried in the first months of American occupation. The murder of six American fliers represented a classical contravention of international law, a traditional war crime in violation of both Hague (1907) and Geneva Conventions. When it became clear to lead USWCB investigator Luke P. Rogers that the Rüsselsheim case would warrant a legal proceeding, American Deputy Theater Judge Advocate Mickelwait began looking for a suitable jurist to serve as Trial Judge Advocate, the term applied to the chief prosecutor in American military courts. Several options presented themselves, but in the end Mickelwait chose a formerly obscure corporate lawyer from Houston, Texas named Leon Jaworski. Destined to gain national fame during the Nixon administration as Watergate Special Prosecutor, then Colonel Jaworski headed the USWCB Trial Section's Investigation and Examinations Divisions, and had in this capacity proved instrumental in preparing prosecution evidence against the Rüsselsheim defendants.[21] On July 11, 1945, Jaworski and his prosecution team succeeded in indicting eleven German civilians – Josef Hartgen, Friedrich

17 Jaworski, *After Fifteen Years*, 84–5. The two men fled the town that night and roamed for several days; they were ultimately captured by a German patrol and spent the rest of the war in a POW camp. Following their release, the pair pledged never to reveal their gruesome experience in Rüsselsheim, hoping to spare their comrades' family members the details of their grisly deaths. When press coverage of the trial revealed the dead fliers' names and fates, the two came forward with their story to General Davidson, head of the military commission.

18 *U.S. v. Hartgen et al.*, Review of the Staff Judge Advocate, August 23, 1945.

19 Ibid., August 23,1945; Jaworski, *After Fifteen Years*, 67.

20 *U.S. v. Hartgen et al.*, USFET Stayback Abstract, Record of Trial in Case of Hartgen, et al. [Case] 12–1497, sign. Brig. Gen. Ed C. Betts, October 9, 1945.

21 Jaworski, *After Fifteen Years*, 66–8.

Wust, Margarete Witzler, Käthe Reinhardt, August Wolf, Johannes Seipel, Heinrich Barthel, Georg Daum, Johann Opper, Philipp Gutlich, and Karl Fugmann – on the charge of "violation of the laws of war" in the beating deaths of the six American servicemen.[22] Because in a last act of brutality he had shot the wounded men, Hartgen figured as chief defendant in the ensuing proceedings.

The trial of the *United States v. Josef Hartgen et al.* began on July 25, 1945, in Darmstadt before a six-member military commission led by Brigadier General Garrison Davidson, commanding general of the U.S. Seventh Army. Davidson and the other officers had been advised by JAG authorities that they were to respect the recognized rules of procedure and evidence governing U.S. courts-martial. In accordance with Military Government policy, however, the commission might make such rules which they deemed necessary in order to assure a fair and impartial trial. In particular, they were instructed to "admit any evidence having probative value to the reasonable man."[23] In practice, this regulation effectively allowed the admission of hearsay, inadmissible in standard American jurisprudence, while permitting the commission to dismiss any evidence which it might find irrelevant. Balanced against these seemingly arbitrary powers were the fundamental rights guaranteed by Ordinance No. 2 of the Military Government Gazette, German U.S. Zone, to all persons brought before American military tribunals. These rights, printed on the reverse of every charge sheet and court summons, included the right to see a copy of the indictment in advance of trial, to be present at said trial, to give evidence in one's own defense, and to cross-examine all witnesses giving opposing testimony. Each defendant was permitted to introduce his or her own material witnesses, or have them summoned, and to conduct his or her own trial or be represented by a lawyer of his or her own choosing.[24] If the alleged crime warranted the death penalty, U.S. authorities also provided an Allied officer as legal counsel. For Hartgen and his codefendants, Lieutenant Colonel Roger E. Titus of Massachusetts served as military defense counsel, assisted by several German attorneys, including Heinrich von Brentano, who was to serve as West German foreign minister in the latter years of the Adenauer government.[25]

22 *U.S. v. Hartgen et al.*, Charge Sheet, sign. Capt. Luke Rogers and Lt. Col. Henry Mize, JAG, with German translation for counsel, July 11, 1945.

23 *U.S. v. Hartgen et al.*, Review and Recommendations of the Theater Judge Advocate, September 29, 1945.

24 Eli Nobleman, "American Military Government Courts in Germany," *The Annals of the American Academy of Political and Social Sciences* 267 (January 1950): 89.

25 Ibid., 89; Jaworski, *After Fifteen Years*, 76.

In addition to these fundamental rights, a number of procedures had been introduced to war crimes proceedings in the American zone to ensure the accused a fair trial. Naturally, all trial proceedings conducted in American-occupied Germany were to be translated into German for the benefit of defendants, counsels, and witnesses. All trials were to be open to the public unless circumstances (e.g., the protection of witnesses) made such a practice impossible.[26] Although the military commission reserved the right to call a defendant to the stand for questioning at the conclusion of the trial, the new rules of procedure specified that the accused, upon taking the stand either to answer the commission's questions or to speak in his or her own defense, could choose to make an unsworn statement and thus avoid cross-examination by the prosecution.[27] Once both the prosecution and defense had rested, a two-thirds majority vote was required for conviction and sentencing. In the event of conviction, the entire trial transcript was to be examined by the Staff Judge Advocate of the U.S. War Crimes Branch as reviewing authority. If the proceedings were found to be procedurally correct and the sentences fitting, the trial documents were passed on to the superior officer who had appointed the commission – in this case, the commanding general of the Seventh Army, in whose power it was to approve or reduce the sentences or to overturn the convictions.[28] If the sentence of the court were death, the entire proceedings were turned over to the Theater Army Commander for his approval before executions could be carried out. Precautions against the appearance of "victors' justice" fit in with early American democratization efforts and despite occasional deviation from Continental and Anglo-American legal practice, acknowledged by the trial's reviewing authority,[29] the zone's first major effort at war crimes adjudication scored high marks in terms of fairness, even among German defense counsel.[30]

The Rüsselsheim Death March Trial lasted one week, with the verdict read on July 31, 1945. With the exception of the defendant Karl Fugmann, against whom the prosecution itself was forced to admit it had insufficient evidence, Trial Judge Advocate Jaworski won convictions of the remaining ten accused. Pointing to a ruling of the U.S. Judge Advocate General which

26 Jaworski, *After Fifteen Years*, 58.

27 NARA, National Archives Microfilm Publication M1078, *United States of America v. Alfons Klein et al.* (hereafter *U.S. v. Alfons Klein et al.*), Case Files 12–449 and 000-12-31, 3 rolls, HQ statement, August 25, 1945, p. 1, Reel 2.

28 Jaworski, *After Fifteen Years*, 58.

29 *U.S. v. Hartgen et al.*, Review and Recommendations of the Theater Judge Advocate, September 29, 1945.

30 Jaworski, *After Fifteen Years*, 83.

struck down distinctions between principal perpetrators and their aiders and abettors, Jaworski seized upon the principle of common design, a strategy which he would also turn to his advantage in subsequent trials, as we shall presently see. "All who join in a common design to commit an unlawful act," quoted Jaworski, "the natural and probable consequences of which involve the contingency of taking human life, are responsible for a homicide . . . although not specifically contemplated by the parties."[31] Because Josef Hartgen had beyond doubt shot several of the airmen as they lay unconscious, the chief defendant received the death penalty, as did Friedrich Wust, Johann Opper, Johannes Seipel, and Philipp Gutlich, who had been witnessed striking the victims with deadly force. In accordance with protocol, the sentences of these men were reviewed and confirmed by Theater Commander Dwight D. Eisenhower on October 23 and the executions carried out the following month.[32] The court also sentenced to death Margerete Witzler and Käthe Reinhardt, the sisters who had initially incited the converging mob to violence. Reluctant to confirm death by hanging for the two women, however, the Reviewing Authority of the Seventh Army commuted these sentences to a thirty-year prison term in each case.[33] Georg Daum was initially sentenced to twenty-five years, and Heinrich Barthel and August Wolf to fifteen years, respectively. Barthel and Wolf, along with Witzler and Reinhardt, were paroled in 1953.[34]

The Darmstadt case of July 1945 commenced a stream of proceedings under War Crimes Branch auspices. By the end of January 1946, thirty-three trials had been held throughout the U.S. zone, involving 110 accused and resulting in 97 convictions.[35] As with the Rüsselsheim affair, the majority of these proceedings focused solely upon classical violations of international law, principally upon the murder of captured Allied service personnel. Yet by late summer 1945, occupation authorities began to prepare their first effort to confront Nazi policies of mass murder with the so-called Hadamar Murder Factory Trial. The Landesheilanstalt Hadamar (Hadamar

31 *U.S. v. Hartgen et al.*, JAG 29 Juris Corpus, Section 46, quoted by Leon Jaworski, Trial Protocol, Closing Arguments of the Prosecution, July 31, 1945.

32 *U.S. v. Hartgen et al.*, Review of *U.S. v. Hartgen et al.* by European Theater Commander, sign. Dwight D. Eisenhower, October 23, 1945.

33 Jaworski, *After Fifteen Years*, 101; *U.S. v. Hartgen et al.*, Review of case of Margarete Witzler, War Crimes Modification Board, sign. Brig, Gen. Mark McClure, August 17, 1951; Order of Parole, USAREUR Office of the CIC, Case 12–1497, *U.S. v. Kathe [sic] Reinhardt*, October 15, 1953. Both sentences were reassessed and reduced to twenty-five years in the early 1950s.

34 *U.S. v. Hartgen et al.*, Order of Parole, USAREUR Office of the CIC, Case 12–1497, *U.S. v. Heinrich Barthel*, undated, c. October 15, 1953; Order of Parole, USAREUR Office of the CIC, Case 12–1497, *U.S. v. August Wolf*, undated, c. October 15, 1953.

35 Jaworski, *After Fifteen Years*, 61.

State Sanatorium) near Limburg on the Lahn, in the state of Hessen-Nassau, had during the war years been a major site of the infamous "euthanasia," or "T4," program that targeted institutionalized patients throughout Germany and Austria. From January until August 1941, Hadamar had served as a killing center where 10,072 mentally and physically disabled individuals were gassed before a halt in the "euthanasia" action brought an interruption of murder operations.[36] Thanks to the efforts of Hessen-Nassau's administrator for state hospital and care facilities, Fritz Bernotat, "euthanasia" killings began again at the institution in August 1942, this time by means of lethal overdose of medication.[37] In this second murder phase – often, and inappropriately, labeled "wild euthanasia" – the killing process at Hadamar expanded beyond severely disabled adults, the program's chief focus, to include a new and ever-widening circle of victims. From 1942 on, mentally retarded and physically deformed children and juveniles were murdered at Hadamar, not in the "special pediatric wards" (*Kinderfachabteilungen*) that belonged to the child "euthanasia" effort, but as an extension of adult T4 procedures at the facility.[38] In addition, Jewish *Mischling*[39] children were killed at Hadamar. These victims were for the most part perfectly healthy children who had become wards of the state after both parents had been arrested, or where the Jewish parent had been imprisoned or deported, leaving the gentile partner unable to supervise or provide for their offspring.[40] Official records also show that a small number of Waffen-SS and Wehrmacht soldiers were killed at Hadamar. Although T4 guidelines had specifically excluded German soldiers from both World Wars from the gassing phase, a handful of Wehrmacht soldiers whose "incurable" psychiatric disorders had prompted their release from military service fell victim to the killing machine at Hadamar after 1943.[41] In 1944, foreign members of the

36 "Die Zahl der Vergasten, verteilt auf die einzelnen Anstalten, für die Monate der Jahre 1940/1941" (Hartheim Statistics), reprinted in Ernst Klee, *Dokumente zur "Euthanasie"* (Frankfurt/Main, 1985), 233.

37 For a detailed examination of the Hadamar facility, see Patricia Heberer, "'Exitus heute in Hadamar': The Hadamar Facility and 'Euthanasia' in Nazi Germany," Ph.D. diss., University of Maryland, 2001.

38 There is no available documentation to indicate that Hadamar had a *Kinderfachabteilung;* children were killed in both murder phases at the facility, but all evidence suggests that children were transported, housed, and murdered in the same manner as Hadamar's adult victims. See Susanne Scholz and Reinhard Singer, "Die Kinder in Hadamar," in *Psychiatrie im Faschismus: Die Anstalt Hadamar, 1933–1945*, ed. Dorothee Roer and Dieter Henkel (Bonn, 1986), 214–36.

39 Literally, "mixed breed"; in Nazi terminology, a person with both Jewish and German gentile ancestry. The term was classified in legislation surrounding the Nuremberg Laws of September 1935, which described a *Mischling* of the second degree as someone having one Jewish grandparent; a *Mischling* of the first degree had two Jewish grandparents.

40 Scholz and Singer, "Die Kinder in Hadamar," 230–2.

41 Gerhard Baader, Johannes Cramer, and Bettina Winter, "*Verlegt nach Hadamar": Die Geschichte einer NS-"Euthanasie"-Anstalt. Historische Schriftenreihe des Landeswohlfahrtsverbandes Hessen*, catalogue vol. 2 (Kassel, 1991), 149.

Waffen-SS deemed incurable after two months' confinement at the Neurological and Psychiatric Observation Station for Mentally Ill Waffen-SS Members in nearby Giessen were transferred to Hadamar for "special treatment."[42] At least 100 victims of Allied bombing also perished at Hadamar. Disoriented or suffering from shock, many such persons were temporarily housed in custodial or welfare institutions for observation or until relatives could collect them. Unable to locate friends or family members who might take them in, municipal authorities often admitted these individuals – almost invariably female and elderly – to local asylums, whence they were deported to their deaths at "euthanasia" sites.[43]

Finally, transports of physically and mentally ill forced laborers, principally *Ostarbeiter* (Eastern workers), were murdered at Hadamar in the last years of the war.[44] Before mid-1943, foreign laborers incapacitated by illness or exhaustion for more than three weeks were simply sent back to their countries of origin.[45] But as the military situation on the eastern front began to deteriorate, the Plenipotentiary for Labor Allocation (*Generalbevollmächtiger für den Arbeitseinsatz*), Fritz Sauckel, began to rethink this strategy. It is most likely that a stop order for repatriation of "Eastern workers" came in June 1943, coinciding with a decree from Sauckel ordering "mentally ill" Soviet and Polish forced laborers who were unable to work be placed in German asylums.[46] Hadamar was one of eleven "collection institutions" (*Sammelstellen*) that existed for mentally ill *Ostarbeiter* by September 1944.[47] It is believed that from mid-1944 through March 1945, some 100 mentally ill "Eastern workers" were murdered at the facility.[48] Nevertheless, most Soviet and Polish workers killed at Hadamar did not suffer from mental disorders but rather from tuberculosis, contracted in the crowded and unsanitary forced labor camps of Hessen-Nassau. There is strong evidence to indicate that Hadamar was the only institution at which tubercular "Eastern workers" were murdered within the context of "euthanasia" operations.

42 Ibid., 150. With their transfer, these individuals were automatically stripped of SS membership.

43 See Götz Aly, "Die 'Aktion Brandt': Bombenkrieg, Bettenbedarf und 'Euthanasie,'" in *Aktion T4, 1939–1945: Die "Euthanasie"-Zentrale in der Tiergartenstrasse 4*, ed. Götz Aly (Berlin, 1989), 168–78.

44 For a comprehensive account of the murder of Eastern European forced laborers in German mental health facilities, see Matthias Hamann, "Die Morde an polnischen und sowjetischen Zwangsarbeitern in deutschen Anstalten," in *Aussonderung und Tod: Die klinische Hinrichtung der Unbrauchbaren*, ed. Götz Aly et al. (Berlin, 1985), 121–87; Holker Kaufmann and Klaus Schulmeyer, "Die polnischen und sowjetischen Zwangsarbeiter in Hadamar," in *Psychiatrie im Faschismus: Die Anstalt Hadamar, 1933–1945*, ed. Dorothee Roer and Dieter Henkel (Bonn, 1986), 256–82.

45 Hamann, "Die Morde an polnischen und sowjetischen Zwangsarbeitern," 122. Before October 1941, the period of debilitation allowed before "repatriation" was two weeks.

46 Kaufmann and Schulmeyer, "Die polnischen und sowjetischen Zwangsarbeiter in Hadamar," 260.

47 Bundesarchiv Berlin-Lichterfelde (hereafter BABL), R 1501 (Reichsministerium des Innern), Akte 3763, Runderlass des Reichsministers des Innern, betr. geisteskranke Ostarbeiter und Polen, September 6, 1944.

48 Hamann, "Die Morde an polnischen und sowjetischen Zwangsarbeitern," 148.

In this case, the 468 tubercular forced laborers killed at Hadamar came to the "euthanasia" center upon the initiative of the Hessian labor offices (*Arbeitsämter*), and it is clear that the impetus for their murders issued not from a central directive from Berlin but from a local public health imperative.

"Euthanasia" killing at Hadamar continued until the arrival of Allied forces in the spring of 1945. In all, the institution had claimed nearly 15,000 lives. On March 26, 1945, troops of the U.S. First Army's Second Infantry Division entered the town of Hadamar. When Captain Alton H. Jung received disturbing reports from villagers that thousands of persons had been murdered in the sanatorium above the town, he decided to investigate. American officials conducted their first visit to the Hadamar facility on March 29. Although a visit to the basement morgue yielded only five bodies, further investigation uncovered 481 mass graves in the institution's cemetery; a death register containing the names of Hadamar victims was discovered in the wine cellar.[49] Convinced that the team's findings confirmed the worst fears of local residents, Captain Jung alerted the United States War Crimes Branch (USWCB), then still headquartered in Paris.

The case of the "Hadamar Murder Factory," as the facility became known in the American press, represented the first mass atrocity trial conducted in the American zone of occupation.[50] Given the high-profile nature of the endeavor and his own recent success in the Darmstadt Trial, Leon Jaworski was once again assigned to prepare the prosecution of the Hadamar proceeding, or United Nations War Crimes Commission Case No. 4, as it was also known. Originally, American authorities had been eager to try Hadamar staff personnel for the murders of the 15,000 mentally ill and disabled patients killed at the institution. Here, though, the prosecution team encountered a setback when on July 28 they were advised that it would be impossible to prosecute the Hadamar defendants for the murders of the German patients. As these crimes had been carried out by German citizens against their fellow nationals, they could not be considered a violation of international law; and as the Hadamar trial preceded the December 1945 promulgation of Control Council Law No. 10, which allowed the more elastic charge of "crimes against humanity," an American military tribunal would have no jurisdiction to try such a case.[51] Only one option remained

49 John Thompson, "Twenty Thousand Slain in Nazi House of Shudders," *New York Times Herald*, April 10, 1945.

50 For a closer examination of the American 1945 Hadamar Trial, see Patricia Heberer, "Early Post-War Justice in the American Zone: The 'Hadamar Murder Factory' Trial, in *Atrocities on Trial: The Politics of Prosecuting War Crimes in Historical Perspective*, ed. Patricia Heberer and Juergen Matthaeus (Lincoln, NE, 2008).

51 *U.S. v. Alfons Klein et al.*, Robert W. Mapes, War Crimes Branch, to Lt. Col. Mize, War Crimes Branch, July 28, 1945, Reel 1.

for American prosecutors. An American military court *was* empowered to investigate and adjudicate crimes against Allied servicemen or civilians, and among the Hadamar dead there had been 476 Soviet and Polish forced laborers. These, then, were the victims upon which Jaworski and his team would build their case.

A shift in focus in the nature of the crimes at Hadamar signaled a redefinition of the circle of perpetrators whom the prosecution could indict for the killings. Limiting the trial to the murders of the "Eastern workers" meant that some suspects who were heavily implicated in the killing of German patients would have to be released as suspects,[52] while other Hadamar personnel not originally listed among the accused, such as chief nurse Irmgard Huber, would have to be taken into custody. Prosecutors were certain from the outset that the elderly chief physician Adolf Wahlmann, who had overseen the deaths of the *Ostarbeiter*, would figure as one of the accused. Hadamar's administrative head, Alfons Klein, who had transmitted the fatal order to murder the forced laborers from local administrator of state hospitals, Fritz Bernotat, and from the *Gauleiter* of Hessen-Nassau, Jakob Sprenger, to his staff, became the lead defendant. Also included on the charge sheet were male nurses (*Pfleger*) Heinrich Ruoff and Karl Willig, who admitted to the actual killings of the "Eastern workers," and head female nurse Irmgard Huber, responsible for dispensing the deadly quantities of morphine and scopolamine from the pharmacy under her control. Finally, the prosecution added to the roster Hadamar clerk Adolf Merkle, who had falsified the death records of the tubercular Soviets and Poles, and handyman Philipp Blum, who had supervised the interment of Hadamar victims, including the dead workers.[53] The indictment, served on September 25, 1945, charged these Hadamar personnel with violation of international law in that they

> Acting jointly and in pursuance of common intent, and acting for and on behalf of the then German Reich, did, from on or about 1 July 1944 to on or about 1 April 1945, at Hadamar, Germany, willfully, deliberately, and wrongfully aid, abet, and participate in the killings of human beings of Polish and Russian nationality, their exact name and number being unknown but aggregating in excess of 400, and who were then and there confined by the then German Reich as an exercise of belligerent control.[54]

52 Ibid., July 28, 1945.

53 Blum figured on the investigative unit's original suspect list, as witnesses had implicated him in administering lethal overdoses of medication to "Eastern workers" on at least one occasion, but this was never proven.

54 Willard B. Cowles, "Trials of War Criminals (Non-Nuremberg)," *American Journal of International Law* 42 (April 1948), 311. Two names were missing from the indictment. Fritz Bernotat, administrator of hospitals and care facilities in Hessen-Nassau, and Jakob Sprenger, the region's *Gauleiter*, had arranged the transfer of workers to the Hadamar facility, and both were originally to have been chief

On the morning of October 8, 1945, U.S. military commission members Colonel John Dicks, Colonel Trevor Swett, Colonel David Waystaff, Jr., Colonel Daniel Stevenson, Colonel Daniel A. Richards, and Lieutenant Colonel James C. Dobbins assembled at the former district court building in Wiesbaden to hear the case of the *U.S. v. Alfons Klein et al.* Trial Judge Advocate Leon Jaworski had specifically requested that he might prosecute the case before a military commission rather than before a newly defined U.S. Military Government court; the proceedings would have been the first effort for the latter body, a fact that Jaworski was convinced would entail considerable confusion and delay.[55] The trial lasted seven days. With the preponderance of evidence on his side, Jaworski's prosecution strategies were relatively straightforward and reworked themes that he had used so successfully in the Rüsselsheim case. His arguments emphasized the assembly-line nature of the killings at the Hadamar "murder factory," and stressed that each of the defendants had played an integral role in the killing process. Citing as an example Title 18, Section 550 of the U.S. Penal Code, which several years earlier had eliminated distinctions between accomplices and accessories before and after the fact in American federal law, Jaworski argued that each of the Hadamar defendants had been a principle in "a production line of death":[56]

> Not a single one of these accused could do all of the things that were necessary in order to have the entire scheme of things in operation.... For instance, the accused Klein, the administrative head, couldn't make the arrangements and receive those people and very well attend to undressing them and make arrangement for their death chamber and at the same time go up there and use the needle that did the dirty work, and then also turn around and haul the bodies out and bury [them] and falsify... the death certificates. No, when you do the business on a wholesale production basis... it means that you have to have several people doing different things... in order to produce the results and you cannot draw a distinction between the man that may have initially conceived the idea of killing them and those who participated in the commission of those offenses.[57]

Parallel to his "assembly-line" argumentation, Jaworski had two other considerations. The first was to show that the Soviet and Polish workers discussed in the indictment had not suffered from mental illness. In doing

defendants in the proceedings. Sprenger and his wife had committed suicide near Kitzbühl, Austria, and their bodies were discovered shortly before the trial. Bernotat evaded arrest until his death in 1951.

55 *U.S. v. Alfons Klein et al.*, Col. Leon Jaworski, Trial Judge Advocate, to Col. Claude Mickelwait, Theatre Judge Advocate General, September 13, 1945, Reel 1.

56 *U.S. v. Alfons Klein et al.*, Leon Jaworski, Closing arguments of the Prosecution, October 15, 1945, Trial transcript, p. 372, Reel 2.

57 Ibid., 372, Reel 2.

so, he hoped to avoid discussion of the murder of German patients and a 1939 Hitler authorization for the "euthanasia" killings – which might be construed as a state directive – and to waylay defense attempts to apply the authorization to the deported "Eastern workers."[58] Likewise, he hoped to show that the Soviets and Poles did not exhibit advanced or incurable stages of tuberculosis upon their arrival at Hadamar and that no effort had been made there to examine or treat them for their illness. For this, Jaworski relied heavily upon the testimony of USWCB pathologist Major Hermann Bolker, who had conducted autopsies on the bodies of selected "Eastern workers" buried in the Hadamar institution's cemetery. Summarizing from the autopsies of six remains, Bolker was able to show that none of the individuals he examined had suffered from advanced stages of tuberculosis, nor had they died from the illness from which they had suffered.[59] Bolker further testified that he had discovered no equipment on the premises employed to treat tubercular patients (e.g., an X-ray or pneumothorax machine), and that the only two drugs uncovered in the Hadamar pharmacy had been morphine and scopolamine, hardly treatments that the psychiatrist Wahlmann would have prescribed to persons with tuberculosis, particularly as morphine "depresses [the] centers for breathing and heart action in the brain," and thus is never prescribed to patients suffering from lung ailments.[60] Bolker's testimony represented, for all practical purposes, the close of Jaworski's case, and in its entirety proved the most damning evidence against the Hadamar defendants.

Perhaps the most significant aspect of the 1945 Hadamar trial was the degree to which it tested Allied military tribunals' efforts to prosecute civilians of foreign governments under international law. In common practice, an occupying power was authorized to try alleged war criminals for offenses against its own military or civilian personnel, if those offenses occurred at the time in which the occupying country maintained de facto control over the area in question.[61] As American prosecutors began to prepare the Hadamar case, a controversy ensued among occupation officials as to whether the United States held jurisdiction in the proceedings, since none of the victims of the Hadamar institution had been American nationals and since American forces had not occupied Hadamar or its environs at the time when the crimes had taken place.[62] Likewise, legal scholars pondered how the U.S.

58 *U.S. v. Alfons Klein et al.*, Mapes to Mize, Reel 1.

59 *U.S. v. Alfons Klein et al.*, Testimony of Hermann Bolker, October 9, 1945, Trial transcript, 116–17, Reel 2.

60 Ibid., 118–19.

61 Cowles, "Trials of War Criminals (Non-Nuremberg)," 312.

62 Ibid.

Judge Advocate General's Office might pursue arraignment of the seven Hadamar defendants on the charge of war crimes, when neither the victims nor the perpetrators had belonged to the armed forces and when the offenses occurred hundreds of miles from front-line activity. Appointed American chief defense counsel Lieutenant Colonel Juan Sedillo used these arguments as a major line of defense, disputing American jurisdiction in the case. All charges should be dropped, Sedillo argued, on the grounds that "there is no rule of law existing under International Law such as the specification alleges the accused of violating."[63] Sedillo mustered traditional American military policy and War Department memoranda in defense of the Hadamar accused. Citing a confidential dispatch to Headquarters, European Theater of Operations, "Establishment of War Crimes Branches," dated February 24, 1945, he showed that USWCB policy itself dictated that "action by members of the United States forces in cases involving ... nationals of other United Nations will normally be limited to cooperation with the appropriate [national] agencies investigating such matters."[64] Thanks to the early efforts of USWCB legal experts, Jaworski could parry Sedillo's arguments with a comprehensive memorandum on the issue of American jurisdiction, penned by Captain Charles H. Taylor of the Prosecution Subsection. It had already been suggested that the military commission was within its rights to note "that hundreds of thousands of Soviet and Polish citizens from occupied territories had been compulsorily deported to Germany for work," that the German government had viewed deportation and application of foreign forced laborers as measures necessary to the war effort, and that as such the murder of those deported aliens represented a war crime.[65] In his "Has the Commission Jurisdiction to Hear and Determine the Hadamar Case?" Taylor supported this interpretation and bolstered the commission's claims of competence with articles of the 1907 Hague Convention on the Rules of Land Warfare. Taylor further cited the Judge Advocate General of the U.S. Army, who in 1943 wrote: "An offense against the laws of war is a violation of the laws of nations, and is a matter of general interest and concern. Whether committed by their forces or those of the enemy, all civilized belligerents have an interest in the punishment of offenses against

63 *U.S. v. Alfons Klein et al.*, Juan Sedillo, Defense Pleas for Abandonment of the Proceedings, n.d., Reel 1.

64 *U.S. v. Alfons Klein et al.*, War Department Memorandum to Headquarters, European Theater of Operations, "Establishment of War Crimes Branches," February 24, 1945, cited by Juan Sedillo, Defense Pleas for Abandonment, Reel 1.

65 Cowles, "Trials of War Criminals (Non-Nuremberg)," 312.

the laws of war."[66] Pursuant to this statement, Taylor suggested that in the case of Hadamar, "custody of the accused is sufficient basis for jurisdiction, at least where, as here, the victims were nationals of our war allies."[67]

In the end, the commission held with the prosecution, upholding its charges based on the

> general doctrine recently expounded and called "universality of jurisdiction over war crimes," which has the support of the United Nations War Crimes Commission and according to which every independent state, has, under International Law, jurisdiction to punish not only pirates, but also war criminals in its custody, regardless of the nationality of the victim or of the place where the offense was committed, particularly where for some reason the criminal would otherwise go unpunished."[68]

In the late evening of October 15, 1945, the six-man tribunal convicted all seven Hadamar accused of violation of international law in the murders of the 476 Soviets and Poles. At 9:45 PM, commission president Colonel Dicks pronounced the sentence of death by hanging for chief defendant Alfons Klein and the male nurses Heinrich Ruoff and Karl Willig. Dr. Adolf Wahlmann, because of his advanced age and poor physical health, was spared the death penalty, instead receiving a life sentence at hard labor. For Adolf Merkle and Philipp Blum, the commission decreed prison terms at hard labor for periods of thirty-five and thirty years, respectively. Irmgard Huber received the mildest sentence – that of twenty-five years at hard labor. By March 7, 1946, the sentences had been approved by Commanding General of the U.S. Seventh Army and by the Theater Commander, General Dwight D. Eisenhower. On March 14, Klein, Ruoff, and Willig went to the gallows. American authorities transferred the remaining prisoners – Wahlmann, Merkle, Blum, and Huber – from the district jail in Wiesbaden, where they had remained interned since proceedings began, to Bruchsal Prison, near Karlsruhe, to serve out the remainder of their sentences.

Although the pair had escaped the "supreme penalty," trouble for Dr. Wahlmann and Nurse Huber was just beginning. On October 30, 1945, as a step toward democratization, the Allied occupying powers issued Control Council Law No. 4, whose Article 3 extended the authority of German courts to all punishable acts except those perpetrated by German citizens against Allied nationals or their property. Two months later, the quadripartite

66 *U.S. v. Alfons Klein et al.*, Judge Advocate General of the U.S. Army, quoted by Charles Taylor, "Has the Commission Jurisdiction to Hear and Determine the Hadamar Case?" n.d., Reel 1.

67 Taylor, "Has the Commission?" Reel 1.

68 Hadamar Military Commission, quoted in Cowles, "Trials of War Criminals (Non-Nuremberg)," 313.

Allied Control Council cemented its commitment to involve German justice in the adjudication of war crimes and crimes against humanity. On December 20, 1945, it promulgated Control Council Law No. 10, which stated that "The occupying powers *may* authorize German courts of law to pass sentence on crimes committed by German subjects or German citizens against other German subjects or German nationals, or against stateless persons."[69] Following the example set at the 1945 American Hadamar Trial and by its precedents in international law, occupation forces left "euthanasia" offenses – for the most part a German-on-German crime – to newly reconstructed German tribunals.[70] In February 1946, the Frankfurt public prosecutor's office initiated proceedings against personnel of the Landesheilanstalt Hadamar for the murders of the nearly 15,000 *German* patients killed at the facility between 1941 and 1945. Wahlmann received a death sentence for his role in the deaths of 900 patients, while Nurse Huber, convicted as an accomplice, garnered an additional eight-year prison term.[71]

Like their counterparts in the Rüsselsheim Death March proceedings, none of the four surviving defendants of the original 1945 Hadamar trial served the balance of their sentences. Spared execution when the new Federal Republic of Germany outlawed capital punishment,[72] the aging Dr. Wahlmann was paroled in 1952, as was Nurse Huber. As a result of the personal intervention of Senator Patrick McCarran of the U.S. Senate Judiciary Committee, Hadamar clerk Adolf Merkle obtained release on March 22, 1950, the War Crimes Modification Board concurring with McCarran's conclusion that the time served "was sufficient for the degree of Merkle's participation in the crime."[73] Philipp Blum, a sort of *Sorgenkind* (problem child) for American authorities, was the last to be paroled, in 1954.

69 Allied Control Council Law No. 10, quoted in Adalbert Rückerl, "Nazi War Crimes," *Leo Baeck Institute Yearbook* 29 (1984): 622 (emphasis in original). This authorization was usually granted, although German courts were required to petition occupation authorities to obtain jurisdiction.

70 By 1958, German courts had adjudicated some 16 "euthanasia" trials, with several proceedings against high-ranking T4 perpetrators continuing into the 1960s and 1970s. Other trials involving German-on-German offenses tried in the years before 1950 included the deportation of German Jews and Gypsies (Roma) and the denunciation of German Jews and other political or ideological opponents of the National Socialist regime to Gestapo or police officials.

71 Hessisches Hauptstaatsarchiv Wiesbaden [hereafter HHStAW], 461/32061–7, LG Frankfurt/Main, *Verfahren gegen Adolf Wahlmann et al.*, 4a Kls 7/47 (4a Js 3/46), Protokoll der Öffentlichen Sitzung der 4. Strafkammer des Landgerichtes Frankfurt am Main [hereafter *Verfahren gegen Adolf Wahlmann et al.*], Verdict, 44.

72 HHStAW 461/32061//14, Dr. Kosterlitz, Oberstaatsanwalt bei dem LG Frankfurt/Main, an Dr. Hans Bodo Gorgass, z. Zt. Strafanstalt Ziegenhain; an Herrn Director der Strafanstalt Ziegenhain oder Vertreter im Amt; an Dr. Adolf Wahlmann, z. Zt. Landsberg a. Lech, und an Herrn Amtsgerichtsrat Dr. Landgraf, Landsberg a. Lech, July 20,1949.

73 *U.S. v. Alfons Klein et al.*, Outgoing message to Judge Advocate General, Department of the Army, Review of the Merkle Sentence, March 22, 1950, Reel 3.

Indeed, by 1956, not one of the surviving Hadamar staff from either the 1945 or 1947 trials remained in captivity.[74] Bowing to Cold War pressures, the War Crimes Modification Board began issuing a wave of amnesties in 1950. Parole, even for serious crimes, was the rule, not the exception, for those incarcerated following conviction by early military commissions. The belief that initial sentencing by these tribunals had been too stringent is suggested by parole board recommendations of convicted war criminals like Käthe Reinhard, a principal in the Rüsselsheim atrocities. "This was one of the first war crimes trials held," wrote Board officials. "In subsequent trials for similar offenses, the sentences adjudged were generally not so severe as that adjudged in this case."[75]

In the history of war crimes adjudication, the early American commission proceedings quickly sunk into obscurity beneath the long shadow of Nuremberg. If trials like the Hadamar Murder Factory case are remembered at all, it is usually in the writings of legal scholars who recall it as America's first major effort to punish Nazi criminality or who remark upon the legal maneuvers of its prosecutors, fettered by international law in those brief months before the charge of "crimes against humanity" greased the wheels of postwar adjudication. The swift, certain attempts at justice these tribunals reflected in their sentencing clearly remained an unequaled standard in subsequent years. In the immediate postwar, perpetrators could expect conviction and relatively stiff sentences, even – sometimes unfortunately – for minor collaboration. In light of later proceedings, the record suggests that tough-minded justice for the victims of Nazism was a possibility only in the immediate postwar. Those perpetrators who could lay low, living on false papers or enjoying the protection of German professional communities, might escape prosecution altogether. And those inevitable criminals – whether jurists, bureaucrats, policemen, or physicians – who had carefully organized and implemented Nazi crimes, yet whose links to those crimes required time-consuming investigation and tenacious prosecution, *could* literally get away with murder. The Hadamar case in particular taught this lesson. At the time of preparations for the Hadamar trial in 1945, American military authorities had also attempted to bring proceedings against President Ernst Kretschmann of the *Gau* Labor Office Rhein-Main and against the office's chief physician, Dr. Hans Welcker. These men had been instrumental in transferring the tubercular "Eastern workers" to their deaths at Hadamar when it was clear that the ailing laborers had fulfilled their purpose

74 Baader, Cramer, and Winter, "*Verlegt nach Hadamar*," 180–1.

75 *U.S. v. Josef Hartgen et al.*, Parole Application of Käthe Reinhardt, Case 2–1497, undated, c. October 15, 1953.

and when it was no longer feasible to repatriate them. Establishing definitively that Kretschmann and Welcker knew transport to Hadamar meant a death sentence for the forced laborers proved difficult, and the proceedings foundered.[76] They were never prosecuted. And what of Fritz Bernotat, whose direct orders had occasioned the murder of the "Eastern workers" and whose ruthless energy and ambition had shaped Hadamar into a killing center which claimed 15,000 lives? Bernotat slipped into obscurity, living under an assumed name until his death in 1951. He died in his sleep.

76 Hamann, "Die Morde an polnischen und sowjetischen Zwangsarbeitern in deutschen Anstalten," 176.

4

Punishing the Excess

Sadism, Bureaucratized Atrocity, and the U.S. Army Concentration Camp Trials, 1945–1947

MICHAEL S. BRYANT

> Other sinnes onley speake;
> Murther shreikes out.
> John Webster,
> "The Duchess of Malfi"

In one of his earliest anti-Semitic writings, a 1919 letter to his commander while still an army private in Munich, the thirty-year-old Adolf Hitler cautioned that the "anti-Semitism of pure emotion" would never progress beyond sporadic pogroms. To curb the noxious influence of the Jews, a different kind of anti-Semitism was required – the "anti-Semitism of reason," which alone would form a legal basis for the systematic deprivation of Jewish "privileges" and, ultimately, their total "removal" (*Entfernung*). An uncanny sensation steals over us as we read Hitler's distinction, articulated a full two decades before the outbreak of World War II, between the two varieties of anti-Semitic perpetration: the one excited by passion, vented locally by individuals or small groups, and destined to subside with little impact; the other grounded in a sober "recognition of facts," committed to the step-by-step process of first restricting, then eliminating the Jews through the instrumentalities of a "government of national power." The first, subjective and short-lived, would quickly burn itself out; the second, objective and enduring, promised a racially pure community.[1]

The sense of uncanniness evoked by Hitler's words may reside in their prescient anticipation not only of the Nazis' war on the Jews between 1933

1 Adolf Hitler, "Brief an Adolf Gemlich," September 16, 1919, letter 61 of *Hitler: Sämtliche Aufzeichnungen 1905–1924*, ed. Eberhard Jäckel (Stuttgart, 1980), 88–90. I am indebted to Raul Hilberg for directing my attention to this extraordinary datum from Hitler's early career.

and 1945, but of a fissure that runs through the thousands of postwar trials of the Holocaust's perpetrators – the dichotomy between emotional killers motivated by private impulse and professional killers who merely followed criminal orders. The defense of "superior orders" (*Befehlsnotstand*) hovers over the postwar prosecution of National Socialist crimes, hinting that the courts were trying, convicting, and punishing "good soldiers" who had answered the call of duty and followed orders conscientiously, only to face severe punishment for their efforts. Although the International Military Tribunal (IMT) had ruled that the superior-orders defense was inadmissible in the findings portion of the trial, compliance with military orders could be considered in extenuation/mitigation during sentencing. Some of the fiercest struggles between prosecution and defense counsel in the American trials of German war crimes defendants hinged on what image of the defendant the judges would endorse: the freelancing sadist lording absolute power over his defenseless victims, or the restrained, dispassionate agent of the state, acting strictly within his orders.

This theme recurs in the U.S. Army's prosecution of concentration camp personnel. The first of 225 trials of concentration camp defendants began in November 1945 and continued until December 1947. The U.S. Army's jurisdiction over these defendants was derived from Joint Chiefs of Staff (JCS) Directive 1023/10 (issued on July 8, 1945), which assigned authority for war crimes trials to military theater commanders. Under the terms of JCS 1023/10, responsibility for conducting the trials was reserved to the Office of Military Government for Germany (OMGUS) and the Deputy Judge Advocate for War Crimes, European Command. Dwight Eisenhower, the commander of U.S. Forces–European Theater (USFET), delegated this authority to the commanding generals of the Western Military District (Bavaria, occupied by the U.S. Third Army) and Eastern Military District (Hessen, Baden Württemberg, and Bremen, occupied by the U.S. Seventh Army). The general of the Western Military District was to hold the trials at the site of the former concentration camp at Dachau, chosen both because it was a subject of the Army's prosecution and because its facilities were adequate to accommodate the trial participants. In the Eastern Military District, plans were made to convene a military court in Ludwigsburg, but in October 1946 all Army trials in the American zone of occupation were consolidated at Dachau – a decision actuated by the enormous volume of cases and investigations. Thereafter, all trials by the U.S. Army would take place at Dachau.[2]

2 Pamphlet describing M 1217, NARA, RG 338. See also Joshua M. Greene, *Justice at Dachau: The Trials of an American Prosecutor* (New York, 2003), 29; Frank M. Buscher, "Bestrafen und erziehen: 'Nürnberg' und das Kriegsverbrecherprogramm der USA," in *Transnationale Vergangenheitspolitik:*

The trials prosecuted four separate categories of cases: (1) main (or "parent") concentration camp offenses; (2) subsidiary (or "subcamp") concentration camp offenses; (3) attacks on downed American fliers, typically by German civilians; and (4) a miscellaneous catchall that included the Malmedy massacre and the murders of Eastern European workers at the Hadamar mental hospital. The Dachau trials of concentration camp crimes included the main camps of Dachau, Buchenwald, Flossenburg, Mauthausen, Nordhausen, and Mühldorf, as well as the sprawling network of subsidiary camps attached to each.[3] Juries were not impaneled for these trials; rather, a commission of no fewer than five officers and a "law member," the latter a senior officer with extensive experience in military law, were the fact finders. In all the Dachau trials, only offenses against Allied nationals would be tried, leaving to the German court system the prosecution of crimes committed by Germans on other Germans. (U.S. policymakers considered diversity of citizenship between victims and defendants essential to sustain a prosecution for war crimes.) By the time the military court had permanently adjourned in December 1947, it had tried 1,200 defendants for war crimes in German concentration camps, achieving a conviction rate of approximately 73 percent. For the most part, the defendants were the *hoi polloi* among Nazi perpetrators: lower-ranking camp guards (interspersed with an occasional commander of a main camp or subcamp), inmates and capos, block elders, and sometimes civilian contractors provided with labor drafts of camp inmates. A typical case from the Buchenwald trial complex is illustrative: the defendants, tried in aggregate, were a bank employee, a locksmith, a mechanic, a tailor, and a glasscutter. From time to time, SS doctors were hauled into the dock for giving phenol and gasoline injections or performing lethal experiments on camp inmates, particularly at Dachau, Buchenwald, and Mauthausen. In the main, however, the defendants hailed from working-class or lower-middle-class backgrounds.[4]

Unlike the indictment of the twenty-four major war criminals by the IMT at Nuremberg, which charged them with four substantive offenses

Der Umgang mit deutschen Kriegsverbrechern in Europa nach dem Zweiten Weltkrieg, ed. Norbert Frei (Göttingen, 2006), 114; Holger Lessing, *Der erste Dachauer Prozess (1945/46)* (Baden-Baden, 1993), 62–4.

3 Due to space limitations, I will restrict my discussion to U.S. Army prosecution of the leading camps: Dachau, Buchenwald, and Mauthausen. The basis for this essay is the Reviews & Recommendations [hereafter "R&R"] of the Theater Judge Advocate for War Crimes, which reviewed the findings and sentences of the U.S. Army concentration camp trials for their legal propriety. Each review includes a comprehensive summary of the facts of the case, assessments of the court's findings, and the confirming authority's recommendations as to upholding, commuting, or reducing the sentence given. The R&Rs were intended for the U.S. military governor for the American zone of occupation.

4 R&R of the Deputy Theater Judge Advocate for War Crimes, January 22, 1948, NARA, RG 549, M 1217, Roll 4 (Case of *U.S. v. Anton Stinglwagner et al.*); Greene, *Justice at Dachau*, 42.

(war crimes, crimes against humanity, crimes against peace, and conspiracy to commit each of these acts), the U.S. Army's charges against concentration camp personnel adhered to a single model based on "violation of the Laws and Usages of War." Numerous charges could be alleged against individual defendants under this heading. Whether the case related to a main camp or one of its subcamps, defendants were usually accused of "wrongfully" participating in a "common plan" to commit war crimes through beatings, assaults, killings, tortures, starvations, abuses, cruelties, and mistreatment of camp prisoners. In the parent Dachau case, the indictment refers to the victims as either "civilian nationals of nations then at war with the then German Reich" or as "members of the armed forces of nations then at war with the then German Reich," whose identities were "unknown" but numbered in the "many thousands." This language from the Dachau charge sheet is often reprised in other concentration camp cases, indicating that many of the victims were anonymous and their numbers legion. The enormity of the crimes – in the Dachau parent case, forty defendants were charged with killing, torturing, and beating thousands of inmates – imparts a chilling, surreal touch to the proceedings, a quality that would later prompt Konrad Adenauer in 1952 to identify Nazi criminality with these "true criminals," the "asocials" who filled the ranks of the SA and concentration camp staffs.[5]

It is tempting, of course, to agree with Adenauer that many of the defendants tried by Army courts were sadists who gave free rein to their sociopathy within the brutal, permissive conditions of the concentrationary universe. The hair-raising accounts of their deeds automatically guide us to such a conclusion. However, the special condemnation reserved for the sadistic perpetrator blunts our perception of an important aspect of the Holocaust – namely, that much of the destruction it wrought was done by dispassionate bureaucrats acting under orders, rather than by the "asocials" whose lurid crimes seized headlines across the world.[6] The tendency to impose the harshest punishment on brutal perpetrators may have ancient roots in millennia of cognitive-ethical development; as a paradigm for dealing with modern forms of bureaucratic criminality, however, it may be both anachronistic and counterproductive.[7] Already at the age of thirty, Hitler

5 The Adenauer quotes are from his *Teegespräche, 1950–1954*, cited in Ulrich Herbert, *Best: Biographische Studien über Radikalismus, Weltanschauung, und Vernunft 1903–1989* (Bonn, 1996), 456.

6 Based on his analysis of judicial records in West Germany between August 1958 and August 1963, Herbert Jäger estimated that 60 percent of Nazi defendants had acted in strict accordance with a superior order. H. Jäger, "Strafrecht und nationalsozialistiche Gewaltverbrechen," *Kritische Justiz* 1 (1968): 147.

7 In his 1967 study, *Verbrechen unter Totalitärer Herrschaft*, Herbert Jäger referred to the need to locate a direct act of violence by the defendant before punishment can be imposed as "archetypal" and

had realized that only an authoritarian government could move beyond the violent excesses of the pogrom to permanent exclusion of a persecuted minority. Bureaucratic rationality as expressed in the "anti-Semitism of reason," and not the wild excesses of the "anti-Semitism of feeling," was the indispensable precondition to effectual, long-term exclusion. In the Dachau concentration camp trials and their aftermath, we can discern this understandable yet regrettable inclination to mete out the severest punishment to "deviant" perpetrators while according favored treatment to the cool-headed bureaucratic killer.

THE DACHAU CONCENTRATION CAMP TRIALS

Established near Munich in March 1933 by Heinrich Himmler, at the time the Munich police president, Dachau began as a detention center for "protective custody" prisoners, primarily Communists and Social Democrats, under the command of the Bavarian state police. In April 1933, the SS assumed control of the camp, and in June of that year Theodor Eicke became its commandant. Eicke was responsible for instituting the system of regulations that governed life in the Dachau camp; when he later became inspector general for all concentration camps, he adopted the Dachau system as his model for camp structure and administration. Beginning in 1935, other types of internees entered the ranks of the Dachau camp population: prisoners who had served their prison term after judicial conviction; Jehovah's Witnesses, imprisoned for flouting the draft; Gypsies, in order to segregate them from German society; churchmen, for resisting the Party's encroachment on the churches; homosexuals, due to their "deviant" sexuality; and miscellaneous individuals accused of criticizing the regime. The first Jews who entered the camp in the years after 1935 were well-known critics of the Nazi government. The number of Jewish internees spiked considerably after Kristallnacht in November 1938, when more than ten thousand German Jews were sent to the camp. (Most of these *Kristallnacht* inmates were released after several months.)[8]

The deportation of thousands of Austrian prisoners to Dachau after the Anschluss in 1938 established a grim precedent that would be followed during the war years of transporting to Dachau "undesirables" – partisans,

"atavistic," adjectives suggesting that this urge to focus on overt acts of wrongdoing may have evolved over centuries, if not millennia, of human reflection on crime and punishment. Jäger, *Verbrechen unter Totalitärer Herrschaft: Studien zur nationalsozialistischen Gewaltkriminalität* (Olten, 1967), 297.

8 *Encyclopedia of the Holocaust*, 1st ed., s.v. "Dachau," by Barbara Distel; Johannes Tuchel, "Planung und Realität des Systems der Konzentrationslager 1934–1938," in *Die nationalsozialistischen Konzentrationslager*, Band 1, ed. Ulrich Herbert, Karin Orth, and Christoph Dieckmann (Frankfurt am Main, 2002), 43ff.

Jews, and those unwilling to collaborate – from each country the Nazis invaded. In this fashion, the Dachau camp population soared between 1939 and 1945 as prisoners from thirty or more countries poured into it, rapidly transforming the German inmates into a minority in the camp. By 1944, the camp population included Russians, Jews, Germans, Czechs, Spaniards, Dutch, Belgians, Norwegians, Lithuanians, Austrians, Italians, and French. These prisoners constituted a potential source of labor that was quickly tapped by the camp commandant, who put them to work in stone quarries, draining marshes, and road construction. As the camp population skyrocketed and the need for war production became acute, the SS centralized control of concentration camp labor in the SS Wirtschafts-Verwaltungshauptamt (Economic-Administrative Main Office, or WVHA). The Germans' war economy was voracious, and soon the work of concentration camp inmates had become essential. Additional camps were formed throughout Germany and Central Europe. Dachau grew into a forced labor Leviathan, embracing at least 85 subsidiary and branch camps in which some 65,000 prisoners toiled on German armaments. They worked not only for the WVHA, but for private contractors who paid the WVHA for the use of the inmates' slave labor.[9]

Although Dachau was not a death camp per se, camp conditions were designed to harass, humiliate, intimidate, starve, exhaust, and brutalize the camp inmates. Beyond the daily fear of being beaten or killed at the whim of SS guards, inmates had to contend with the fatal medical experiments of camp physicians. Dr. Klaus Schilling freely took advantage of the limitless supply of human guinea pigs to test his homeopathic theories of malaria prevention by injecting prisoners with the disease. Dr. Sigmund Rascher conducted the notorious high altitude and freezing experiments that resulted in the deaths of between eighty and ninety inmates. Moreover, Dachau became the venue for the mass murder of Soviet POWs (6,000–8,000 of whom were shot just outside the camp in the spring of 1942) and prisoners deemed unable to work in the winter of 1941–42. This latter group fell into the net of the "14f13" program, which sought to relieve overcrowding in the camps by transferring the ill and infirm to "euthanasia" centers for killing. Transports of prisoners were sent from Dachau to the euthanasia center at Hartheim (near Linz), where 3,166 of them were gassed.[10]

9 Ibid.; R&R, March 1946 [date illegible], NARA, RG 549, M 1217, Roll 3 (*U.S. v. Martin Gottfried Weiss et al.*).

10 *Encyclopedia of the Holocaust*, 1st ed., s.v. "Dachau," by Barbara Distel; R&R, March 1946, NARA, RG 549, M 1217 (*U.S. v. Martin Gottfried Weiss et al*).

The Parent Dachau Case (November 15–December 13, 1945)

The first of the U.S. Army trials of Dachau camp defendants began on November 15, 1945. The indictment enumerated the names of forty defendants, including the camp commandant from 1942 to 1943, Martin Gottfried Weiss; Dr. Klaus Schilling, a renowned expert in tropical diseases who operated an independent malaria station in the camp; and sundry camp guards and capos. The accused were charged with participating in a "common design" to commit war crimes ("killings, beatings, tortures, starvation, abuses and indignities") on thousands of foreign civilian nationals and military members of belligerent nations. The relative earliness of the Dachau case, which began six days before the IMT at Nuremberg, meant that the prosecuting authorities had little by way of precedent to follow in drafting their charges. For guidance, they looked to the Bergen Belsen case tried by a British military court (September–November 1945) at Lüneburg, which, as noted in the Review and Recommendation of the Deputy Theater Judge Advocate, "was the first instance of a mass trial for war crimes committed by persons acting in concert." In terms of the defendant numbers (forty-five in the Belsen case, forty in Dachau), the diversity of nationality among the victims, and the nature of the crimes alleged, the two cases were closely analogous. Following the British at Belsen, the Americans used the notion of a "common plan" to tie the Dachau accused to the war crimes perpetrated in the camp. The technique of alleging participation in an overall plan to commit violations of the laws of armed conflict was common to the U.S. prosecutions of Nazi criminality, appearing in most of the concentration camp trials, the trials of the Hadamar staff, the IMT trial of the major war criminals, and the twelve "subsequent" national trials at Nuremberg. Although often used interchangeably with the doctrine of "conspiracy" as a theory of criminal liability, the Review and Recommendation carefully distinguished between the two, noting that "common plan" required a lesser quantum of proof against the defendants: a showing of a "community of intention" between them was sufficient. Thus, to prosecute the Dachau accused successfully, the prosecutor needed only to prove that the defendants were aware that a "definite *practice* of cruelties and abuses, violative as to foreign nationals, military and civilian, of many of the laws and usages of war" had occurred, and that they "took active parts in encouraging" this practice (emphasis in the original). "Such a course of conduct," the R&R concludes, "we believe, constitutes acting in pursuance of a common design to violate" the laws of war.[11]

11 R&R, March 1946, NARA, RG 549, M 1217, Roll 3 (*U.S. v. Martin Gottfried Weiss et al.*).

Proving the "practice of cruelties and abuses" at Dachau was a comparatively simple matter. Before the trial commenced, the Army's lead prosecutor, William Denson, had decided to make oral eyewitness testimony the crux of the prosecution's case against the defendants. (In this regard, the trial differed from the "trial by document" conducted by Robert Jackson at Nuremberg.) Accordingly, the pretrial documentation Denson submitted to Judge Advocate General Headquarters listed 170 witnesses, many of whom offered testimony during the trial of the appalling conditions within the camp. The parade of horrors included starvation rations, extreme overcrowding that fostered typhus epidemics, the mass executions of Soviet POWs, the murders of mentally and physically ill patients by injections of phenol into their hearts, lethal medical experiments, clothing inadequate to protect the prisoners from the cold, "invalid transports" to killing centers, and an omnipresent round of beatings and abuse that included the practice of forcing newcomer prisoners to stand naked for hours in wintry weather.[12]

The Army prosecutors argued that this shocking bill of particulars, coupled with proof of the defendants' participation in the common plan to perpetrate the atrocities, proved their inherent sadism. In his closing argument, Denson referred to the defendants at least three times as "sadistic," and, in his peroration, called the accused "beasts" who "cannot lay claim to being human in any respect." German defense counsel Hans Karl von Posern, by contrast, portrayed the defendants as loyal soldiers acting on superior orders: "*Befehl ist Befehl* – an order is an order. It had to be obeyed, however its quality was." The clash between prosecution and defense centered on how the military court would interpret the interior psychologies of the defendants: that is, whether they would be seen as enterprising sadists acting within the spirit of a vague "common plan," or as normal, law-abiding men who merely carried out their orders in a time of war. The conviction of all the accused along with the death sentences dealt to nearly all of them signal that the prosecutors' conception prevailed.[13]

The Subsidiary Dachau Camp Trials (October 1946–September 1947)

Dachau's theater of cruelty was not restricted to the stage of the main camp, but extended to the myriad subsidiary camps of the Dachau complex. The trials of personnel associated with these camps, as well as those

12 Ibid.; Greene, *Justice at Dachau*, 36.

13 Greene, 101–4; R&R, March 1946, NARA, RG 549, M 1217, Roll 3 (*U.S. v. Martin Gottfried Weiss et al.*).

of other main camp defendants, ensued after the close of the parent case in December 1945. As noted previously, the mounting demands of the German war economy after 1939 occasioned an expansion of main camps like Dachau, Buchenwald, and Mauthausen, so that hundreds of "subcamps" arose around them. Some of these subcamps, like the Kaufering site located 25 miles southwest of Munich, are perhaps best thought of as complex, epicyclical organizations that themselves embraced numerous subsidiary camps. Kaufering, for example, was created pursuant to Albert Speer's *Jägerstab* program between June and October 1944, its fifteen subcamps devoted to exploiting Jewish slave labor in the underground construction of German military aircraft. The first prisoners of Kaufering, a group of Lithuanian Jews, arrived in June 1944. Beginning in October 1944, transports of Hungarian, Czechoslovak, Polish, and Romanian Jews from Auschwitz were sent there. Starvation rations, lack of health care, daily physical abuse, and grinding hard labor were the lot of the Kaufering inmates. Precise figures of the camp population are unavailable; however, a prisoner who worked in the camp record office estimated a figure of 28,000 for the duration of its brief existence. Many of the prisoners who survived the harsh conditions of the camp perished at the hands of SS guards during forced marches in the last phases of the war, shortly before Kaufering was liberated by the U.S. Army in late April 1945.[14]

One of the hallmarks of the Kaufering subcamp trials was the number of hyperviolent direct perpetrators involved. A few cases in point are the trials of Hermann Zisch (January 3–February 3, 1947), Martin Schreyer (February 26–March 6, 1947), Josef Neuner (March 27–28, 1947), Karl Ehrenboeck (July 2–7, 1947), and Franz Millenz (August 14–15, 1947). Zisch, a Waffen-SS sergeant in charge of the supply room at Kaufering XI (Landsberg) from December 1944 to April 1945, was a machinist; Neuner, an SS master sergeant who served at the main Dachau camp prior to service as roll call leader at Allach (an outcamp of Kaufering), was a miner; and Ehrenboeck, a Waffen-SS sergeant at both the main camp and Allach, was a glass painter. (The civilian occupations of Schreyer and Millenz, both SS sergeants and guards at the Kaufering complex, were not identified in the Review and Recommendation.) Evidence against each of them rested on the testimony of eyewitnesses. Zisch was accused of forcing ill prisoners to do vigorous exercises for eight consecutive hours every Sunday; of causing the death by hypothermia of prisoners by removing their coats; of administering constant beatings to the so-called *Muselmänner*, the emaciated, terminal prisoners in

14 *Encyclopedia of the Holocaust*, s.v. "Kaufering," by Barbara Distel.

the camp; of tying the hands of prisoners behind their backs and hoisting them into the air for fifteen minutes; and of senseless atrocities during the prisoner march from Kaufering in April 1945, which included shooting a Czech prisoner for trying to drink from a stream and others for being too exhausted to continue the march. It was alleged that Schreyer routinely beat prisoners, some of them so severely that they later died from their wounds; forced inmates to stand in the cold without shoes for twenty-four hours or longer; reported prisoners for fashioning their blankets into rags for their feet (the prisoners were hanged as punishment); selected ill prisoners for "invalid transports" to locations where they were murdered; confined prisoners in a cellar without food or adequate clothing, thereby causing their deaths; and hanged prisoners from their wrists. Witnesses accused Neuner of hanging Russian escapee POWs, severely kicking prisoners and beating them with a stick, and shooting numerous prisoner evacuees during the forced march of April 1945. Ehrenboeck was accused of setting his dog on prisoners with the apparent object of either punishing them for failing to work fast enough or to train the dogs in attacking human body parts; beating an inmate with a rubber hose and then, when the victim lay helpless on the ground, administering fatal kicks to his groin; beating and whipping prisoners for failure to remove their caps promptly; and participating in the mass executions of Russian POWs (presumably at the main camp). The evidence against Millenz alleged that he had forced all inmates at Kaufering – including those enfeebled with illness – to attend roll calls that could last up to four hours, no matter the weather, during which he often punched, kicked, or beat them with a club, causing the deaths of some of them; that he ordered the extraction by inmate dentists of healthy teeth from prisoners' mouths; that he beat to death a Polish inmate for being unable to work due to a foot injury and two others for complaining of the inadequacy of their clothing to protect them against the cold as they worked; that he pistol-whipped to death Hungarian and Polish prisoners on work details; and that he testified shortly before liberation of the camp that "one should liquidate the entire bunch [of prisoners] before the Americans come." Each of these defendants was sentenced to death, his punishment upheld on review.[15]

15 R&R, July 17, 1947, NARA, RG 549, M 1217, Roll 4 (*U.S. v. Hermann Zisch*); R&R, June 12, 1947, NARA, RG 549, M 1217, Roll 4 (*U.S. v. Willi Fischer et al.*); R&R, June 13, 1947, NARA, RG 549, M 1217, Roll 4 (*U.S. v. Josef Neuner*); R&R, March 2, 1948, NARA, RG 549, M 1217, Roll 4 (*U.S. v. Karl Ehrenboeck*); R&R, November 10, 1947 NARA, RG 549, M 1217, Roll 4 (*U.S. v. Franz Millenz*). Millenz's statement was hardly an idle threat. The SS administration at Dachau in the waning months of the war did, in fact, plan to murder all the prisoners with bombs and poison before the Americans arrived – a plan that was soon overtaken by events.

THE BUCHENWALD CONCENTRATION CAMP TRIALS (APRIL 1947–DECEMBER 1947)

Like Dachau, the Buchenwald concentration camp five miles north of Weimar (Thüringen) was a concentrationary megalopolis with 130 subsidiary camps. The main camp was founded in 1937 as a detention center for political dissidents and criminals; the following year, the population of the camp escalated from 2,500 to 18,000 as "asocials" and Austrian and German Jews were sent there. (Most of the Jewish inmates were released, reducing the prisoner population to 11,000.) The onset of the war in September 1939 brought new prisoner accessions to the camp, including fresh waves of political prisoners and thousands of Poles. Like Dachau, too, Buchenwald became a crucial supplier of forced labor in the German war industry: the needs of armament factories built near Buchenwald drew thousands of inmates into the camp system, swelling the population to over 63,000 by late 1944 and to 86,232 by February 1945. During its eight-year existence, almost 239,000 inmates were imprisoned at Buchenwald or in its subcamps, including prominent political prisoners like Leon Blum (prime minister of France), Peter Zenkl (prime minister of Czechoslovakia), and the sister of Charles de Gaulle. The total number of fatalities associated with Buchenwald is believed to be just over 43,000, yielding a mortality rate of 18 percent.[16]

The Buchenwald Parent Case (April 11–August 14, 1947)

The parent case began on April 11, 1947, charging thirty-one defendants with participating in a common plan to commit war crimes at Buchenwald and its subcamps on "many thousands" of foreign nationals in the form of "killings, beating, tortures, starvation, abuses and indignities." The crimes committed there were of exceptional brutality, even by concentration camp standards. Dr. Ding-Schuler's typhus experiments on guinea pig prisoners in the notorious block 46, the shooting of thousands of Soviet POWs in the Buchenwald "horse stables" under the ruse of administering a medical exam, and the paracriminal fetishism of Ilse Koch, wife of the camp commandant Karl Koch, which allegedly expressed itself in the crafting of lampshades

16 *Encyclopedia of the Holocaust*, s.v. "Buchenwald," by Yehoshua R. Büchler. Generally on Buchenwald, see Eugen Kogon, *Der SS-Staat: Das System der deutschen Konzentrationslager* (Frankfurt am Main, 1946); *The Buchenwald Report*, trans. David A. Hackett (Boulder, 1995); Harry Stein, "Funktionswandel des Konzentrationslagers Buchenwald im Spiegel der Lagerstatistiken," in *Die nationalsozialistischen Konzentrationslager*, 167ff.

from the tattooed skin of murdered prisoners, lends a grotesqueness to the trial proceedings that may actually surpass that of the Dachau parent case.[17]

As in the Dachau main camp trial, the defendants in the Buchenwald case raised a superior-orders defense. According to this argument, the executions of prisoners at Buchenwald (such as the "detail 99" killings) were under the 1942 orders of Gestapo Chief Heinrich Müller and the Reich Security Main Office. According to the defendants, Müller's orders concerned reprisals to be carried out on selected Jewish and Polish inmates. On the strength of these orders, the defense argued that executions like detail 99 were not illegal. Neither the military court nor the subsequent reviewing authorities were moved by the defendants' argument, the latter noting that executions of spies and saboteurs could occur only after a fair trial (which did not occur at Buchenwald) and that reprisals against POWs were in any event illegal. The defendants knew or should have known that the killings were patently unjust and in violation of international law. Accordingly, the court convicted all thirty-one of the Buchenwald accused, sentencing all but eight to death.[18]

Subsequent Buchenwald Main and Subsidiary Camp Trials (September 1947–December 1947)

Following the parent Buchenwald trial, the U.S. Army prosecuted an assortment of main and subsidiary camp cases. Like their Dachau counterparts, most of these trials involved predominantly camp guards from working-class and petit bourgeois backgrounds charged as direct perpetrators with acts of breathtaking ferocity. The trials of Heinrich Buuck, Victor Hantscharenko,

17 The charge against Ilse Koch of participating in the murder of camp inmates in order to process their tattooed skin into lampshades and photo albums became, both within Germany and worldwide, a symbol of National Socialist criminality. When Koch's life sentence, dispensed by the U.S. Army court in 1947, was reduced to a four-year prison term by an Army review board, the international sensation aroused by her release from prison led to her indictment by the *Landgericht* (state court) of Augsburg in 1951, which sentenced her to life in prison. She committed suicide in 1967.

Koch emerged from her two trials as an infamous, even monstrous, figure, the "bitch of Buchenwald" whose alleged crimes both shocked and titillated consumers of the German and international press. Significantly, as Ulrich Herbert notes, Koch lived out the rest of her life in jail while "former Gestapo chiefs, generals of the Waffen-SS, and Einsatzgruppen commanders responsible for shooting tens of thousands of Jews regained their freedom after a handful of years in prison, and often quickly became esteemed and prosperous citizens." Ulrich Herbert et al., *Die nationalsozialistischen Konzentrationslager*, 18–19. See also Alexandra Przyrembel, "Ilse Koch – 'normale' SS-Ehefrau oder 'Kommandeuse von Buchenwald'?" in *Karrieren der Gewalt: Nationalsozialistische Täterbiographien*, ed. Klaus-Michael Mallmann and Gerhard Paul (Darmstadt: Wissenschaftliche Buchgesellschaft, 2004), 127–9.

18 R&R, November 15, 1947, NARA, RG 549, M 1217, Roll 4 (*U.S. v. Josias Prince zu Waldeck et al.*). Several of these sentences were either commuted or reduced on review, including that of Ilse Koch (see note 17).

Ignaz Seitz, Adam Ankenbrand, and a group of SS guards who participated in detail 99 at the main camp illustrate the kind of sensational brutality that increasingly defined the worst excesses of Nazi criminality. Witnesses accused Buuck, a farmer and guard at subcamp Sonnenberg, of shooting numerous prisoners at both the Sonnenberg camp and during the evacuation march in April 1945, allegedly for eating potatoes or being too weak to continue. Hantscharenko, a Russian national, laborer, and SS guard at the main camp, faced accusations that he had shot and killed twelve prisoners during the forced march from the camp in April 1945 for being unable to continue the march or for eating beets along the roadside. Seitz, a farmer and SS guard at both the main camp and the Leau subcamp, confessed to shooting under orders eleven prisoners for being physically incapable of marching during the evacuation of Leau. Ankenbrand, a laborer and SS technical sergeant at the Schlieben subcamp, was charged with several acts of pure sadism: shooting and wounding one prisoner as he lay on the ground, then killing another as the first cried out in pain; sniping at a distance of 40 meters a starving prisoner who had briefly left a transport train to pick grass to eat; and shooting and killing five prisoners during the same prisoner transport for trying to eat grass. Evidence against the detail 99 defendants – all SS guards at the main camp from the lower rungs of the German socioeconomic ladder – indicated that a former horse stable had been remodeled to convey the appearance of a medical exam room. SS personnel led Russian POWs into this bogus facility, ostensibly for the purpose of a medical exam; as they stood with their backs against the wall to have their height measured, the defendants, standing behind the wall in a secret compartment, inserted the barrels of their guns into a hidden aperture and shot the POWs in the back of the head. In this manner, between two thousand and three thousand Russians were murdered (from late 1941 to mid-1942).[19]

In three of the five cases above, the defendants unsuccessfully raised a superior-orders defense. In each instance, the military court and reviewing authorities dismissed the defense arguments. According to the Reviews and Recommendations of the trials, "compliance with superior orders does not constitute a defense to the charge of having committed a war crime." The R&Rs did note, however, that compliance with orders was relevant

19 R&R, December 5, 1947, NARA, RG 549, M 1217, Roll 3 (*U.S. v. Heinrich Buuck*); R&R, January 8, 1948, NARA, RG 549, M 1217, Roll 3 (*U.S. v. Victor Hantscharenko*); R&R, February 27, 1948, NARA, RG 549, M 1217, Roll 3 (*U.S. v. Ignaz Seitz*); R&R, NARA, RG 549, M 549, Roll 3 (*U.S. v. Adam Ankenbrand*); R&R, February 20, 1948, NARA, RG 549, M 1217, Roll 3 (*U.S. v. Werner Alfred Berger*).

in mitigation/extenuation of punishment, but only when the defendant proved:

(a) that he received an order from a superior in fact . . . ,
(b) that he did not know or, as a reasonably prudent person, would not have known that the act which he was directed to perform was illegal or contrary to universally accepted standards of human conduct, and
(c) that he acted, at least to some extent, under immediate compulsion.[20]

In denying any grounds for accepting defense claims of superior orders, the military courts essentially identified the defendants as direct perpetrators freely choosing to commit acts of gratuitous cruelty on helpless camp inmates.

THE MAUTHAUSEN CONCENTRATION CAMP TRIALS (MARCH 1946–NOVEMBER 1947)

The third of the major concentration camp trial complexes focused on Mauthausen and its subsidiaries. Established after the 1938 Anschluss near a stone quarry in Upper Austria, the camp first housed convicted criminals and "asocial elements" transferred to it from Dachau. In the ensuing four years, the camp population grew with infusions of political prisoners (German, Czech, and Spanish) and Dutch Jews. In 1942 alone, 13,000 new prisoners flooded into the camp, among them both civilians and POWs from Czechoslovakia, the Netherlands, the USSR, Yugoslavia, France, Belgium, Greece, and Luxembourg. The following year, the prison population grew by 21,028, spiking again in 1944 as large transports of Jews from Auschwitz arrived in Mauthausen and its subcamps. In March 1945, the population of the main camp and the subcamp of Gusen reached 84,000.[21]

Estimates reckon that of the 199,404 prisoners to pass through Mauthausen during its existence, around 119,000 of them perished. The mortality rate of 60 percent is particularly jarring as compared with Dachau and Buchenwald (15 and 18 percent, respectively). The remarkable lethality of Mauthausen within the concentration camp system may have its origins in an August 19, 1942, decree of Reinhard Heydrich, chief of the Reich

20 R&R (*U.S. v. Heinrich Buuck*). The language quoted is boilerplate that appears verbatim in hundreds of the R&Rs that considered the issue of the superior-orders defense.

21 *Encyclopedia of the Holocaust*, s.v. "Mauthausen," by Benyamin Eckstein. See also Michel Fabréguet, "Entwicklung und Veränderung der Funktionen des Konzentrationslagers Mauthausen 1938–1945," in *Die nationalsozialistischen Konzentrationslager*, Band 1, 193–214; Bertrand Perz, "Der Arbeitseinsatz im KZ Mauthausen," ibid., Band 2, 533–57; Florian Freund, "Häftlingskategorien und Sterblichkeit in einem Außenlager des KZ Mauthausen," ibid., 874–86.

Security Main Office, who introduced a grading scale of I to III for concentration camps based on the harshness of their conditions, with Category I camps rated the mildest and III the harshest. Only Mauthausen and Gusen were classified as Category III camps. Accordingly, "problem" prisoners – recidivists, negativists, and those in "protective custody" – were transferred to Mauthausen after Heydrich's decree. The mortality rates as recorded in the camp *Sterbebuch* (Death Book) confirm this trend: in 1942, between 50 and 150 prisoners died per day; in 1943, between 200 and 300; in 1944, between 350 and 400. At the time of the camp's liberation in April 1945, deaths from starvation alone had risen to 400–500 per day.[22]

The Mauthausen Parent Case (March 29–May 13, 1946)

The subject matter of the Mauthausen parent case resembles an act from the *Théâtre du Grand Guignol*, a resemblance that may explain why, of the sixty-one defendants tried and convicted, sixty were sentenced to death by hanging. The indictment charged the defendants with participating in a "common design" to commit war crimes ("killings, beatings, tortures, starvation," etc.) against foreign nationals and POWs at the Mauthausen concentration camp and its subcamps. Newcomers to Mauthausen were bathed and forced to stand outdoors for hours in bitter winter temperatures. On one occasion in February–March 1945, 300 sick prisoners who arrived in a transport were subjected to hot and cold showers, then exposed to the cold, leading to the deaths of 230 of them. Clothing and food were inadequate as a matter of camp policy. As at Dachau and Buchenwald, Mauthausen prisoners sometimes became human guinea pigs for camp doctors. In July 1942, the chief medical officer at Gusen had his inmate physicians operate on 300 prisoners to instruct them on surgical technique. Of this group of "patients," who were selected for their debilitated condition, only 150 survived. The survivors later disappeared on invalid transports. The violence inflicted on camp inmates was without limit, as the R&R of the Deputy Theater Judge Advocate for War Crimes observed: "Virtually every known form of killing was used at Mauthausen. To list some, inmates were killed by gassing, hanging, clubbing, heart injections, driving inmates into the electric fence, kicking in genitals, being buried alive and by putting a red hot poker down the throat."[23]

22 Ibid.; R&R, February 25, 1947, NARA, RG 549, M 1217, Roll 4 (*U.S. v. Hans Altfudisch et al.*).

23 R&R, February 25, 1947, NARA, RG 549, M 1217, Roll 4 (*U.S. v. Hans Altfudisch et al.*).

This statement was not hyperbole. Prisoners selected for extermination on account of their physical debility were injected with cyanide, gasoline, magnesium sulphate, and Lysol. Lethal injections were supplemented with asphyxiation in the "blue automobile" (a gas van) and in the camp gas chamber, which, as in the death camps and the Reich's euthanasia centers, was disguised as a shower room. The gas used to kill prisoners was the fumigant Zyklon B, employed to the same effect in the gas chambers of Auschwitz. Two crematoria installed in the camp incinerated the bodies. The Mauthausen trial court found that a large but unspecified number of Czech women and children were gassed there in October 1942. As the Third Reich veered toward its final collapse in April 1945, at least 1,400 camp patients were dispatched in the Mauthausen gas chamber.[24]

The military court formulated "special findings" during the trial that would prove fateful to the defendants. As trier of fact, the court would assume the following postulates as proven by the evidence:

(1) that the Mauthausen Concentration Camp was essentially a criminal enterprise;
(2) that it was impossible for anyone to be employed at or present in the camp without acquiring definite knowledge of the criminal practices;
(3) that every employee and official connected with the camp, regardless of his capacity, is guilty of the crime of violating the laws and usages of war.

To rebut their guilt under the presumptions above, defendants could show either that they were not present at Mauthausen, or, if present, were unaware (and should not have been aware) of the camp's criminal operations, or that their participation in such operations did not in any way promote the commission of war crimes. The majority of the defendants, being SS camp guards, were unable to meet this burden.[25]

The Mauthausen Subsidiary Camp Cases (March–November 1947)

After the parent case had concluded, the Army launched an extensive series of trials of Mauthausen subcamp defendants, including those of Gros-Raming, Linz (Kleinmünchen), Wiener-Neudorf, Gusen, Ebensee, Oberilzmühle, Steyr, St. Aegyd, and St. Lambrecht. Defendants were primarily SS guards from lower-class backgrounds, intermingled with occasional capos and subcamp commandants. Hans Bergerhoff, a factory worker and SS block leader at Linz III, was convicted of beating inmates with a rubber cable and blackjack for "trivial reasons." Friedrich Felsch, a baker and

24 Ibid.

25 Ibid.

guard at subcamp Linz III, was charged with pistol-whipping at least one inmate to death and beating others with his rifle butt. Willy Auerswald, a textile worker and SS roll call leader at the Steyr subcamp, beat prisoners with his fists, a club, a riding crop, and an oxtail whip. In addition, witnesses charged that he severely beat a Russian prisoner during a work detail, then, as the prisoner begged on his knees for his life, threw him against the electrical fence that encircled the camp, instantly killing him. When defendants raised the superior-orders defense, as Auerswald did, the military court tersely rejected it, indicating that superior orders was not a defense to a war crimes charge, and that the defendants (like Auerswald) acted under neither ignorance nor compulsion.[26]

CONSTRUCTIONS OF EXCESS IN THE DACHAU TRIALS: TYPOLOGIES OF PERPETRATION

"We were the bottom of the basement, not even pebbles in their shoes," Paul Guth, assistant trial counsel to William Denson at Dachau, groused about the kinds of defendants he and his team prosecuted.[27] His standard of comparison was the trial by the IMT at Nuremberg of the major war criminals, which roughly coincided with the parent Dachau case in November 1945. In contrast with the former leadership corps of the Nazi regime at Nuremberg, the Dachau defendants were farmers, factory workers, glass-cutters, bakers. With the exception of a commandant like Martin Weiss or a medical doctor like Klaus Schilling, the accused filled the lower echelons within the concentration camp apparatus, occupying positions that guaranteed them daily, intimate exposure to their victims and boundless opportunity to harass, torture, beat, degrade, and murder them with their own hands.

Guth's distinction between the IMT defendants and the accused at Dachau hints at a significant criminological dimension of Nazi perpetration: the difference between "direct perpetrators" and "facilitators," distinguished from each other by their relative distance from the crime. In the language of the criminal law, direct perpetrators commit the criminal act (*actus reus*) intentionally (*mens rea*) and without either justification or excuse. Facilitators, on the other hand, do not directly perform the *actus reus* themselves, but knowingly contribute to a chain of actions that lead to it. At their trials, both Rudolf Höss and Adolf Eichmann staked their

26 R&R, February 26, 1948, NARA, RG 549, M 1217, Roll 4 (*U.S. v. Hans Bergerhoff et al.*); R&R, January 23, 1948, NARA, RG 549, M 1217, Roll 4 (*U.S. v. Willi Auerswald et al.*).

27 Quoted in Greene, *Justice at Nuremberg*, 62.

defense on the remoteness of their connection with atrocity, Höss boldly asserting at his trial that he "never abused or killed anyone." The absence of a proximate relationship between the facilitator's actions and the violence of his crime attenuates the impression of culpability. Thus, at the Eichmann trial in 1961, despite the voluminous evidence of Eichmann's central role in the deportation of European Jews to their deaths, the prosecution strove unsuccessfully to prove direct acts of violence committed by Eichmann – a tactical move amounting to a virtual admission that the facilitator was something less than a true murderer. By contrast, proximity between the direct perpetrator's willful acts and the crime alleged confirms the actor as a real criminal deserving of the harshest sanctions the law can impose. Most of the defendants tried at Dachau fall into the latter category.[28]

Herbert Jäger's typology of individual participation in totalitarian criminality enables us to locate the crimes of the Dachau accused on a spectrum of perpetration. Jäger divided it into three types: (1) crimes without orders, or "crimes of excess" (*Exzesstaten*); (2) carrying out orders with relative independence, or "crimes of initiative" (*Initiavtaten*); and (3) carrying out orders in a situation in which the actor exerts little personal influence on the event, or "crimes of command" (*Befehlstaten*).[29] In this framework, the offenses of the Dachau trial defendants largely fall into the first (crimes of excess) and, to a lesser degree, the second (crimes of initiative) categories. Jäger's subdivision of *Exzesstaten* into additional subcategories further clarifies the nature of these crimes. Of his six subcategories, four are particularly apposite to the Dachau accused: (a) arbitrary crimes; (b) operational excesses; (c) crimes of compliance; and (d) unauthorized commands.

28 On the curious fixation of the Israeli prosecutor on proving that Eichmann had personally murdered a Jewish youth in Hungary, see Hannah Arendt, *Eichmann in Jerusalem: A Report on the Banality of Evil* (New York, 1977), 22; Jäger, *Verbrechen unter Totalitärer Herrschaft*, 297.

29 Jäger, *Verbrechen unter Totalitärer Herrschaft*, 22–75. Jäger's typology of individual perpetration within the overall context of National Socialist criminality bears comparison with the more recent classification of Klaus-Michael Mallmann and Gerhard Paul. In an edited volume containing the biographies of Nazi perpetrators, Mallman and Paul distinguish between five types of perpetrators: (1) "band wagon Nazis," in other words, political opportunists whose crimes were chiefly motivated by a desire to advance their careers; (2) ideological killers (*Weltanschauungstäter*), whose crimes aimed at achieving "the national socialist project of the new racial order of Europe"; (3) "hardcore" killers (*Exzeßtäter*), whose savage crimes required no orders; (4) "bureaucratic killers" (*Schreibtischtäter*), who made administrative contributions to the process of destruction, but did not harm others directly; and (5) a hybrid category of hard-core and bureaucratic perpetrators (*Mischung aus Schreibtisch- und Direkttätern*). The authors caution that each category of perpetrator is an ideal type, and should thus be regarded as descriptive of distinctive features of Nazi criminals without precluding other aspects important to understanding the killers' motives. Klaus-Michael Mallmann and Gerhard Paul, "Sozialisation, Milieu und Gewalt: Fortschritte und Probleme der neueren Täterforschung," in Mallmann and Paul, *Karrieren der Gewalt: Nationalsozialistische Täterbiographien*, 17–18.

a. Arbitrary Crimes. Arbitrary crimes are crimes of excess committed for no apparent motive or for trivial motives. They typically are unaccompanied by clear orders or external pressure; rather, their commission lies squarely within the actor's discretion. The gratuitous practice of forcing naked prisoners to stand outside in winter weather for hours at a time would meet this definition, as would defendant Zisch's weekly habit of forcing sick inmates to perform hours of vigorous exercise and defendant Millenz's extraction of healthy teeth from prisoners' mouths. The pattern of punishing ill and starving prisoners for attending to biological needs – for example, scrounging for grass to eat, or fashioning rags into footwear – also satisfies the definition of an arbitrary crime.

b. Operational Excesses. The operational excess perpetrator commits his crimes as part of an organized scheme aimed at the persecution of others – ghetto clearings, searches of Jewish districts, raids, deportations, prisoner transports. In these situations, the actor's crimes rarely are enforced by concrete orders. As Jäger notes, operational excesses occurred most often in connection with prisoner transports at the end of the war, in the midst of a "collective atmosphere of lawlessness and cruelty."[30] Defendant Hantscharenko's murder of twelve prisoners during the forced march from Buchenwald in April 1945 and defendant Seitz's shooting of eleven prisoners during a similar transport from the Leau subcamp are two notable examples from the Dachau trial series.

c. Crimes of Compliance. This subcategory pertains to crimes perpetrated in situations in which "orders" exist, but are vague or merely suggestive. Such "orders" enabled the higher strata of the Nazi government to steer the criminal enterprise in a desired direction without the need to issue explicit instructions. Rather, they could rest assured that lower-ranking functionaries would "comply" with their ambiguously expressed wishes by translating them into murderous practice. Jäger cites the example of personnel records shipped with some prisoners (especially those unable to work) that bore the inscription, "Return not desired!" or "not desired in the concentration camp," words interpreted by camp personnel as instructions for killing. Although the message in these instructions was clear, it cannot be identified as an explicit order to kill the affected prisoner. A camp guard or administrator who failed to act on it would not face charges for disobedience. Rather, as Jäger points out, "he would only have missed the opportunity to 'prove himself within the spirit of the system.'" The claim by SS guards charged with killing Soviet POWs as part of detail

30 Jäger, *Verbrechen unter Totalitärer Herrschaft*, 33–5.

99 that they acted under the orders of the RSHA to carry out reprisal shootings appears to meet the definition of a "crime of compliance." The order concerned Jewish and Polish saboteurs, yet the SS guards interpreted it broadly to cover Soviet POWs as a class.[31]

d. Unauthorized Commands. This variety of crimes of excess applies to miniaturized killing operations inserted into the overall machinery of destruction governed by command. These smaller operations are conspicuous for being locally administered and independent of orders from a centralized authority. This subcategory includes camp operations to exterminate the "unproductive" in order to create additional space, combat epidemics, or eliminate "useless eaters" – a practice at each of the three main camps we have discussed.[32]

The U.S. Army Dachau trials can be viewed as a struggle between the prosecution and defense over where in this spectrum of perpetration the defendants should be situated. The prosecution sought to persuade the court that they were "excess perpetrators" acting either without orders or "within the spirit" of the criminal camp system. The defense often took the contrary view that the defendants were simply "good soldiers" dutifully following their orders (i.e., their crimes were *Befehlstaten*, the third in Jäger's typology), and thus should not be held criminally liable for the atrocities they had merely carried out.[33] High conviction rates and severe sentences show that the image of the Nazi war criminal endorsed by the military courts – and transmitted via media coverage throughout the world – was of the relatively autonomous, lower-class sadist who inflicted unspeakable agonies and death on helpless victims, with little or no prompting from his superiors.

CONCLUSION

By December 1947, the U.S. Army Dachau trials had run their course; however, they continued to exert a significant influence on German perceptions of Nazi crimes. By the late 1940s, public opinion in West Germany

31 Ibid., 35–6.

32 Ibid., 42–3.

33 Before World War II, international law on the issue of superior orders as a defense to a war crime was inconclusive. The jurisprudence addressing the subject before 1945 – primarily the trials of German military personnel prosecuted by the Reichsgericht at Leipzig after World War I – produced conflicting views. In the Dover Castle case, the court acquitted the defendant on the ground that a subordinate was obliged to obey superior orders; if the result was illegal, then the superior who issued the command, and not the recipient of it, was accountable. The same court returned a different verdict in the Llandovery Castle case, which dismissed the superior-orders defense on the ground that "[the commander's] order does not free the accused from guilt," particularly where, as in the case at bar, the international rule of law was "simple and universally known." *American Journal of International Law* 16 (1922): 707–22. See also the discussion of the defense of superior orders in M. Cherif Bassiouni, *Crimes against Humanity in International Law* (The Hague, 1999), 467–8.

had swung decisively against further war crimes trials. Growing aversion to continued prosecutions led by 1951 to serious discussion within German political circles about a general amnesty for war criminals. Chancellor Konrad Adenauer approved of a more limited amnesty, since, in his words, "among the convicted there was a certain percentage to whom the word 'war criminal' perfectly applies, and whose punishment must be preserved." Although the Allies had convicted many German defendants on political grounds, the "real criminals" would be exempted from any amnesty of convicted war crimes defendants. For German historian Ulrich Herbert, however, Adenauer's identification of "real" Nazi criminality with heartless sadism obscured the vital roles of the "Gestapo Chief or Einsatzgruppen Commander" in the regime's projects of mass extermination. Instead, the chancellor's ascription effectively transformed the plebeian character of Nazism – the "SA brawler and concentration camp guard" – into the essence of its criminality. The lawyer with a doctorate charged with mass shootings on the eastern front, or the general indicted for shooting hostages, went unrecognized as a Nazi perpetrator because he did not fit the profile of the "common" murderer.[34]

The reason Adenauer and many others tended to exonerate the professional, bureaucratized killer may have more to do with deep structures of historical change than with idiosyncratic values. In the historical transition to modernity, the "organization man" emerged as the ideal of bourgeois instrumental rationality: calculating, acting within the dictates of a professional group, objectively scientific, and personally restrained, he readily found his place in increasingly complex bureaucracies as the giver and recipient of orders. Whether in business, government, or organized criminal groups, the organization person became prerequisite to the system's efficient achievement of its purposes. This was, and remains, no less the case when the system served by the organization person pursued monstrously criminal aims. The very fungibility of bureaucratic killers (itself an attribute of modernity) meant that they looked much like professionals in noncriminal settings. When called on to prosecute, convict, and punish their look-alikes, noncriminal professionals tended to hesitate, framing rationales like Adenauer's to mitigate or excuse the bureaucratic killer's actions.[35]

34 Herbert, *Best*, 455–6. In a subsequent essay published with Karin Orth and Christoph Dieckmann, Herbert affirms that "through the press coverage of the first large trials of guards and commandants of the camps this impression [of horror] grew stronger, and the concentration camp now became the symbol for the abhorrent crimes of Nazism as a whole." Ulrich Herbert, Karin Orth, and Christoph Dieckmann, "Die nationalsozialistischen Konzentrationslager. Geschichte, Erinnerung, Forschung," in *Die nationalsozialistischen Konzentrationslager*, Band 1, 18.

35 On the relationship between the rise of modernity and the bureaucratic perpetrator of state violence, see the classic study by Hannah Arendt, *The Origins of Totalitarianism* (New York, 1994), especially

The half-century since the Dachau trials has witnessed an elaboration of this divided mentality that seems ingredient within the process of modernity. In *U.S. v. von Leeb* (1948), the American National Military Tribunal followed the proximity rule of perpetration, holding that a war crime must be directly traceable to a superior before he can be held criminally liable for it. The reasoning of *von Leeb* reappeared in the trial of the commanding officer during the My Lai massacre. In *U.S. v. Medina* (1971), an army court-martial acquitted Capt. Ernest Medina on the ground that he had no "actual knowledge" his subordinates would commit war crimes. One of Medina's lieutenants was not so fortunate: in his 1973 trial, William Calley was convicted on multiple counts of murder. Like many of the Dachau trial defendants, and just as unsuccessfully, he argued that he had merely followed Medina's orders to shoot the victims. Rejecting his defense, the court held that even if Medina had issued the order, Calley knew or should have known it was illegal. In each of these trials, a primary issue was how the court would categorize the defendant on the scale of perpetration: as an excess perpetrator (Calley) or as a facilitator sufficiently removed from the direct violence of the act to escape criminal liability (von Leeb, Medina).[36]

The different treatment accorded excess and bureaucratic perpetrators seems ill-suited to punish the state-organized crimes of the past century. As German historian Jörg Friedrich has observed, the freelancing sadist is inefficient: to commit murder on a grand scale, "a measure implemented bureaucratically and industrially requires agents that conform to it."[37] The thirty-year-old Adolf Hitler, an ingénue to genocide in 1919, seems to have sensed this truth when he distinguished between the anti-Semitisms of reason and emotion: the latter wild, brutal, and ineffectual; the former coldly deliberate, organized, and effective. Each of Hitler's forms of persecution calls forth its own agent of destruction, a grim version of its own

Part Three, "Totalitarianism"; Arendt, *Eichmann in Jerusalem*; Zygmunt Bauman, *Modernity and the Holocaust* (Ithaca, 1989). For recent critiques of the "banality" of administrative evil thesis most forcefully articulated by Arendt, see Yaacov Lozowick, *Hitler's Bureaucrats: The Nazi Security Police and the Banality of Evil* (New York, 2000); Guy B. Adams and Danny L. Balfour, *Unmasking Administrative Evil* (London, 2004), 57; Michael Wildt, *Generation des Unbedingten: Das Führungskorps des Reichssicherheitshauptamtes* (Hamburg, 2003), 16ff.

36 *U.S. v. Wilhelm von Leeb et al.* (Case 12), NARA, RG 238, M898; *U.S. v. Medina*, C.M. 427162 (1971); *U.S. v. Calley*, 46 C.M.R. 1131, aff'd 22 U.S.C.M.A. 534, 48 C.M.R. 19 (1973). General Field Marshall Wilhelm Ritter von Leeb, inter alia Commander in Chief of Army Group North, was acquitted along with his co-defendants of crimes against peace despite their knowledge of Hitler's intention to launch wars of aggression. For the American tribunal, mere knowledge of Hitler's designs, even if accompanied by participation in the plans to wage war, was insufficient to establish criminal liability. Eleven of the thirteen defendants, including von Leeb, were convicted of war crimes and crimes against humanity. Telford Taylor, "The Nuremberg War Crimes Trials," *International Conciliation* 450 (1949): 326–8.

37 Jörg Friedrich, *Die kalte Amnestie: NS-Tater in der Bundesrepublik* (München, 1994), 358.

toxic self. The anti-Semitism of emotion produces the concentration camp thug, a sadist acting within the torturous spirit of Nazi orders yet freely interpreting them, often with demonic inventiveness. The anti-Semitism of reason conjures the cool bureaucrat and scheming *Organisator*, the issuer and transmitter of orders who coordinates railroad timetables and streamlines the industrial macroprocess of annihilation.

In the taxonomy of perpetration, the horrors recounted in the U.S. Army Dachau trials belong to the category of excess and emotion. In these trials, the acts of the indirect perpetrators, those desk-bound facilitators whose instruments of genocide are paper and typewriters rather than guns and poisonous gas, are submerged in the bestial cruelties of the Lager. Of all men's "sinnes," murder alone "shreikes out," as Elizabethan playwright John Webster once wrote. We might expand on Webster's words by adding that murder shrieks loudest when it is sensational and directly committed. In seeking to understand Nazi criminality, however, we are advised to listen to the voices of men's other "sinnes," the arms-length but crucial acts of bureaucratized atrocity. Refined but malefic, these other voices tell the real secret of the Nazis' extraordinary capacity for evil. It resided not in their power to unleash human beings' latent sociopathy within the camp's realm of the unreal, but in their strange success in creating a species of perpetrator made in their own image: fanatical, yet frigidly objective; chimerical, yet administratively realistic; suited to the bland routines of the office suite, yet virulently – and perhaps uniquely – lethal.

5

Perceptions and Suppression of Nazi Crimes by the Postwar German Judiciary

JOACHIM PERELS

"The need to give voice to suffering is the condition of all truth."[1] This statement from Theodor Adorno's *Negative Dialectics* links understanding to moral judgment. The extent to which postwar recognition of Nazi crimes of murder was linked to unequivocal acknowledgment of the role of the perpetrators and the suffering of the victims is evident in the usual decisions of the judiciary. Prosecutors and judges were faced with the task of bringing to light the facts of criminal wrongdoing – above all, acts of murder – and establishing which legal norms had been violated. In the postwar period there existed, I argue, two entirely different and ultimately contradictory approaches to the prosecution and adjudication of the massive crimes of the Nazi state. In the Nuremberg successor trials, the U.S judiciary classified war crimes committed by the Wehrmacht, especially the massacre of civilians, as violations of recognized international laws of war. The same approach was taken in the prosecution of the criminal acts committed by judiciary and the murder of Jews by the Einsatzgruppen.[2] The Einsatzgruppen's systematic killing campaigns, safeguarded by the Wehrmacht,[3] were classified as crimes against humanity under the terms of Article II, 1c of Control Council Law No. 10 of December 20, 1945, which criminalized murder, genocide, and torture alongside other crimes.

The judiciary of the Federal Republic of Germany took a very different approach to war crimes committed by the Wehrmacht and Einsatzgruppen, as well as to Nazi-era destruction of law. In its majority, the West German

1 Theodor W. Adorno, *Negative Dialektik* (Frankfurt/Main, 1966), 27.

2 *Das Urteil gegen das Oberkommando der Wehrmacht* (Berlin, 1960); *Das Urteil im SS-Einsatzgruppenprozess* (Berlin, 1963); Lore Peschel-Gutzeit, ed., *Das Nürnberger Juristenurteil* (Baden-Baden, 1996).

3 Raul Hilberg, *Die Vernichtung der europäischen Juden* (1961), Bd. 2 (Frankfurt/Main, 1990), 298, 315ff, 339, 341; Helmut Krausnick, *Hitlers Einsatzgruppen. Die Truppe des Weltanschauungskrieges 1938 bis 1942* (1981) (Frankfurt/Main, 1985), 179ff.

judiciary did not allow the fact of the suffering of the victims of the Nazi state's machinery of annihilation to come to light. The murder of noncombatants was given legal legitimation. Likewise, the judiciary that had served the Nazi dictatorship was deemed to have acted legitimately. And perpetrators who had commanded the SS killing squads that massacred Jewish civilians largely escaped responsibility.

PUNISHMENT OR JUSTIFICATION OF WAR CRIMES?

The massacre carried out by the Wehrmacht in the Greek town of Kalavryta can serve as an illustration of how American and West German courts dealt with war crimes. The Kalavryta massacre was one of the mass crimes against Greek civilians taken up in the hostage trial conducted by the United States in 1948. The so-called normative command principles governing the Wehrmacht's actions in Greece removed all constraints imposed by international law. The orders issued by the Southeastern Command on December 22, 1943, shortly after the Kalavryta massacre, encapsulate German occupation policy in Greece. The orders removed limits on so-called reprisal measures (*Sühnemaßnahmen*) against communists and explicitly instructed that there was no longer to be a fixed relationship between the number of victims killed by Greek partisans and the Wehrmacht's reprisal. "The Führer has commanded a uniform counteraction against the communist threat in the southeast . . . The previously customary reprisals, punishments, and retaliatory measures must in the future serve the new political objectives. . . . Reprisal quotas are not specified . . . Expiation measures are (a) shooting or hanging; (b) destruction of dwellings . . . If . . . accomplices cannot be found, then it is necessary to fall back on people who, although they have no connection with the individual deed, are nevertheless to be regarded as accomplices. Accomplices are first and foremost those people who show allegiance to communism."[4]

The American judiciary first considered the central question of whether the Wehrmacht's numerous so-called acts of reprisal were justifiable under international law. General Helmuth Felmy, commander of Army Group southern Greece, was sentenced to fifteen years' imprisonment for war crimes against the Greek people, namely the murder of innocent persons. The tribunal, citing specific categories in international law, rejected the argument that Felmy and his men had simply been following orders.

4 Loukia Drouila and Hagen Fleischer, ed., *Von Lidice bis Kalavryta. Widerstand und Besatzungsterror* (Berlin, 1999), appendix, 218ff.

The "Kalavryta undertaking" began on December 6, 1943. As retaliation for the killing of 78 German soldiers, the 117th Division carried out this attack under the command of General von Le Suire. More than 25 villages were destroyed and it has been acknowledged that 696 Greeks were shot as punishment. There is testimony from an eyewitness that approximately 1300 Greeks were murdered in retaliation ... It is hardly even necessary to say that many of these retaliatory killings were exaggerations and that many were illegal because there was no connection between the inhabitants who were shot and the crimes committed. Punishments were meted out to a particular group as well as to "Communists" and "suspected gang members" without establishing a connection with the crimes. The "Kalavryta undertaking" can only be called outright murder and destruction of property.[5]

The West German justice system also took up the Kalavryta massacre. After investigating the role of Franz Juppe, who had been company commander (*Kampfgruppenführer*) in the Kalavryta massacre, the Public Prosecutor's office in Bochum closed the case in 1972 without pressing charges against Juppe. In contrast to the American tribunal, the Bochum prosecutors closed their eyes to the unrestrained use of military terror against civilians. They turned a violation of international law into a legal act. The decisive issue under international law – the relation between defensive military action and partisan attacks – was never even considered: "The partisans violated the basic rules of international law, according to which every combatant must be granted fair and well-mannered treatment. In this situation reprisals were necessary and also a permissible means of international law used to force the opponents, the partisans, to adhere to international law ... Since consequently the reprisals ordered and carried out by the late General von Le Suire cannot be seen as a violation of international law according to the applicable law and they were also not in violation of the criminal law, then participation in them, in whatever form, is not against the law."[6] The murders committed in Kalavryta were coolly disregarded in the Public Prosecutor's decree terminating the investigation. Whereas the U.S. military judges had persuasively refuted the applicability of the concept of retaliation in this case by pointing to the disproportion of the Wehrmacht's response to partisan attacks, the Public Prosecutors in Bochum allowed the term reprisal to conceal the Wehrmacht's unrestricted use of force against civilians. The murders were, in the terminology of Alexander and Margarete Mitscherlich, "de-realized" in order to allow the categories of international law to remain unengaged.[7] The denial of the Wehrmacht's war crimes through the

5 *Das Urteil im Geiselmord-Prozess* (Berlin, 1965), 261f.

6 Eberhard Rondholz, "Rechtsfindung oder Täterschutz? Die deutsche Justiz und die Bewältigung des Besatzungsterrors in Griechenland," in Drouila and Fleischer, *Von Lidice bis Kalavryta*, 253.

7 Alexander and Margarete Mitscherlich, *The Inability to Mourn*, trans. B. R. Placzek (New York, 1975).

creation of the appearance of legality in this instance is anything but an isolated case. Prosecutors at the Central Office for the Investigation of National Socialist Crimes in Ludwigsburg initiated preliminary proceedings against a thousand former Wehrmacht officers and troops suspected of war crimes. All of these proceedings were terminated by local West German public prosecutors.[8] The Wehrmacht's leadership had systematically removed all constraints imposed by international law regarding combatants, prisoners, and noncombatants, but in the Federal Republic there was not a single trial for war crimes committed by the Wehrmacht.[9] The consequences of the West German justice system's suppression of Wehrmacht crimes include, not least, the refusal to give innocent victims the memory that a public trial bringing to light the historical events and violations of rights would have afforded.

CONSTITUTIONAL STATE OR AFFIRMATIVE ASSESSMENT OF NAZI JUSTICE?

In the Nuremberg Judges' Trial of 1947, the role of the Nazi-era justice system was assessed according to the principles of the rule of law.[10] The American laws governing the tribunal had explicitly stated that "political actions in resistance to National Socialism . . . are [not] . . . punishable."[11]

The penalties resulting from the trials of leading Justice Ministry officials, prosecutors, and judges can be seen as standard state administration of justice, punishment for the justice system's role in what Ernst Fraenkel termed the Nazi "prerogative state." The prerogative state, Fraenkel argued, sets aside individual rights and allows arbitrary measures – such as extralegal executions – to serve political and ideological ends. Depending on circumstances, the prerogative state might avail itself of the administrative or judicial apparatus at hand to accomplish its ends, or it might simply disregard prevailing legal norms.[12]

8 Alfred Streim, *Saubere Wehrmacht? Die Verfolgung von Kriegs- und NS-Verbrechen in der Bundesrepublik und in der DDR:* Hannes Heer and Klaus Naumann eds., *Vernichtungskrieg. Verbrechen der Wehrmacht 1941 bis 1944* (Hamburg, 1995), 578.

9 See, e.g., Joachim Perels, *Verpasste Chancen Zur Bedentung der Nürnberger Nachfalgerprozesse, Beiträge zur Geschichte der nationalsozialistischen Verfolgung in Nordwest-Deutschland*, vol. 3 (Bremen, 1997), 32f; Rondholz, "Rechtsfindung oder Täterschutz?" 231; for a comprehensive analysis of the impeded punishment of German war crimes, see Kerstin Freudiger, *Die juristische Aufarbeitung von NS-Verbrechen* (Tübingen, 2003), 126ff, 284ff, 361ff.

10 On this and the following, see Joachim Perels, *Das juristische Erbe des "Dritten Reiches"* (Frankfurt/Main, 1999), 47ff.

11 *Gesetz-Nr. 21 zur Wiedergutmachung nationalsozialistischen Unrechts in der Strafrechtspflege, Bay.* (GVBl., 1946), 180.

12 Ernst Fraenkel, *Der Doppelstaat* (1941) (Frankfurt/Main, 1974).

The defendants in the Judges' Trial actively served the National Socialist prerogative state. Franz Schlegelberger can be considered the personification of the prerogative state. As a state secretary in the Ministry of Justice, the conservative Schlegelberger had, like other representatives of the *Bildungsbürgertum* (educated elite), actively contributed to the erosion of the rule of law in Germany even before Hitler came to power.[13] As the court judgment elucidated, the "Night and Fog" decree came about through the collective efforts of the Justice Ministry, the Gestapo, and the Wehrmacht.[14] In his capacity as acting minister of justice, Schlegelberger played a leading role.

Under this decree, the citizens of German-occupied countries who did not cooperate with the occupation regimes could be secretly deported to Germany and either tried before special courts or simply turned over to the Gestapo for imprisonment in a concentration camp. Those arrested disappeared without a trace: their survivors received no notification of their deaths, and even in the records of executions they were listed not by name but by number.

Schlegelberger was also responsible for drafting and implementing the penal law of December 4, 1941, that made terror against Poles and Jews the norm.[15] A Ministry of Justice memorandum issued on April 22, 1941, had called for a draconian special law for Poles and Jews that would define offenses very broadly and make them punishable by death.[16] The resulting law was without limits: "Poles and Jews will also be punished... if they commit an act that deserves punishment according to the basic idea of a German law, on the basis of reason of state [*Staatsnotwendigkeiten*] in the incorporated Eastern territories."[17]

The law of unconstrained state power meant that the state's own crimes were not subject to punishment. In response to the *Kristallnacht* pogrom of November 9, 1938, for example, the Ministry of Justice decreed:

> The Minister of Justice and Senior Prosecutor Joel have determined that it is, of course, impossible to handle these events in the usual legal manner. If law is suspended from above, it is not possible to prosecute persons who participated... This is legally justified, among reasons, by the fact that the perpetrators were not conscious of the illegality of their action because they were acting on orders.[18]

13 See Eli Nathans, *Franz Schlegelberger* (Baden-Baden, 1990).

14 Heribert Ostendorf and Heino ter Veen, *Das "Nürnberger Juristenurteil"* (Frankfurt/Main, 1985), 176ff, 188ff.

15 Ibid.

16 Ibid., 205.

17 Ingo von Münch, ed., *Gesetze des NS-Staates*, 3rd ed. (Paderborn, 1994), 142.

18 Peschel-Gutzeit, *Das Nürnberger Juristenurteil*, 192.

The same law-rescinding logic lies behind the Ministry of Justice decree of February 12, 1945, allowing ad hoc executions without any legal basis whatsoever. The decree stipulates that "asocial prisoners hostile to the state" held in penal institutions should "be handed over to the police for elimination." On the basis of this order, several prisons and other penal institutions were "emptied out and at least 800 people killed illegally."[19]

It was not only the justice administration but also the judiciary itself that facilitated the state's unlimited power over individuals and provided a veneer of legality. That held above all in the policy of repression enacted in Poland, the first victim of the Nazis' lust for power. The presiding judge at the Nuremberg special court, for example, invoked the sweeping norms of the penal regulations for Poles against a woman who had thrown a stone at a German soldier but had not hit him. The judge sentenced her to death.[20]

At the Nuremberg Judges' Trial, it was not possible to seek exculpation by citing the Nazi regime's prerogative-state norms and command structures. Article 2 Section 1 of Control Council Law No. 10 made juridically facilitated terror subject to punishment. It set out penalties for murder, extermination, deportation, and other inhumane acts inflicted upon civilians as well as for persecution on political, racial, and religious grounds. The charges, as summarized in a commentary following the tribunal's verdict, were "conscious participation in a system of cruelty and injustice that extended across the entire country and was organized by the government, and injustice and violations of the laws of war and the laws of humanity, committed in the name of the law and under the authority of the Ministry of Justice with the help of the courts. The murderer's dagger was hidden under the jurists' robes."[21]

The great majority of the judiciary in the Federal Republic did not take their cue from the affirmation of the rule of law in the verdicts delivered at the Nuremberg Judges' Trial. Instead, they declared the rulings of the Nazi-era judiciary unassailable. In 1956, West Germany's highest criminal court, the Bundesgerichtshof, acquitted Judge Otto Thorbeck for his part in the deaths of several members of the anti-Nazi resistance. Thorbeck, a member of the SS, had sentenced Wilhelm Canaris, Dietrich Bonhoeffer, Hans Oster, and several others to death on April 8, 1945, following a hasty trial. The defendants had not been allowed legal counsel, and Thorbeck was assisted in the proceedings by the commander of the Flossenbürg concentration camp.

19 Ibid., 161ff.

20 Ibid., 211f.

21 Ostendorf and ter Veen, *Nürnberger Juristenurteil*, 140.

The Bundesgerichtshof's explanation of its reasons for acquitting Thorberg adopts the viewpoint of the SS and reads like an implicit rejection of the Nuremberg Judges' Trial. It used the final days of the Third Reich as a positive point of reference. "For the question as to whether through his participation as chair of the court-martial proceedings Dr. T. is guilty of abetting murder or other punishable actions, current knowledge of the events of April 1945 is not decisive," the Bundesgerichtshof explained. "Such a backward-looking valuation would not do the defendant justice. In judging the criminal guilt of the appellant . . . it is more important to keep in mind how his task appears in light of the legal situation and other circumstances at the time of the deed, the mercilessness of the laws at that time, to which he submitted and against which the resistance fighters tried by court martial in Flossenbürg rebelled."[22] The Bundesgerichtshof regarded National Socialist norms as absolutely valid, and it did the resistance members the injustice of casting them in the role of lawbreakers. To place the re-legitimation of National Socialist law on a seemingly unassailable basis despite the evidence of the historical record, the Bundesgerichtshof "normalized" the Nazi regime by regarding it as a state like others: "The starting point . . . is the right of the state to assert itself . . . even the National Socialist state cannot simply be denied the right to make such laws."[23] This statement legitimated the lawmaking power of a regime that was no longer a state, but rather a terror regime that systematically violated the physical integrity of countless individuals. The West German judiciary's refusal to recognize the reality of the Nazi state's rule by terror culminated in the separation of the so-called court-martial proceedings from the political structure of the Third Reich. The actual goal of the proceedings against the resistance fighters – namely, to give the murder of the lawless regime's opponents the appearance of legality – was disregarded, and the Bundesgerichtshof uncritically accepted the SS officials' self-justification.

THE EINSATZGRUPPEN: MASS MURDER WITHOUT PERPETRATORS?

It was with shock that an American military tribunal in 1948 looked upon the incomprehensible efforts of the so-called Einsatzgruppen to exterminate the Jews of Europe. The American judges noted that the crimes of the

22 Christiaan F. Rüter (Hg.), *Justiz und NS-Verbrechen*, vol. 8 (Amsterdam, 1975), 352. This decision in the meantime has been criticized in detail by the president of the Bundesgerichtshof, Günter Hirsch, "Die deutsche Justiz im Unrechtssystem und die Aufarbeitung von Justizunrecht," *Deutsche Richterzeitung*, Issue 6 (2000): 223ff.

23 Rüter, *Justiz und NS-Verbrechen*, 352.

Einsatzgruppen escaped comprehension. "The loss of a single person can only be measured in the consciousness of the living for whom that person is lost forever. Therefore, the annihilation of two million human beings cannot be felt at all. Two million is only a number. No one can grasp the complete, accumulating horror of murder repeated millions of times over."[24]

The judges later elaborated on the nature of the charges: "The first point of the arraignment . . . accuses the defendant of crimes against humanity. Not crimes against a particular country, but against all of humanity. Humanity is the prosecutor . . . In the dark and dreary atmosphere of the region of the innocent dead, a lamp has been lit."[25]

In reconstructing what actually happened, the tribunal did not attempt to portray the acts of murder. Instead, it quoted one of the witnesses at length in its verdict: "The businessman Friedrich Grebe . . . gave a deeply moving report about a mass execution he witnessed in October 1942 in Dubnow, a report that due to its authentic description has earned the right to be added to this opinion of the court in its entirety:

> The people, men, women, and children of all ages, who alighted from the truck had to undress at the order of an SS man, who had a horsewhip in his hand, and put their clothing, sorted in piles (shoes, undergarments, etc.) in particular places. I saw a heap of shoes that contained approximately 8,000 to 10,000 pairs of shoes, huge piles of undergarments and clothing. These people undressed without shouting or crying, stood together in family groups, kissed each other and bade each other good-bye, and waited for the signal from another SS man, who stood by the ditch and also had a whip in his hand . . . An old woman with snow-white hair held a 1-year-old child in her arms, singing to the child and tickling it. The child squealed with joy. The couple looked on with tears in their eyes . . . The ditch was already three-quarters full. According to my estimation, there were already approximately 1,000 people in it. I look around for the sharpshooter, this man, an SS man, sat on the ground at the edge of the ditch, letting his legs hang down into the ditch, had an automatic rifle on his knees and was smoking a cigarette.[26]

The defendants who had commanded Einsatzgruppen, who were all demonstrated to have been staunch Nazis and SS officers, were without exception regarded by the American tribunal as perpetrators of criminal acts. The testimony of SS brigadier general Erich Naumann, the commander of Einsatzgruppe B, made clear that the operational elite of the Central Office for Reich Security themselves thought in terms of perpetration. As the tribunal's verdict notes:

24 *Das Urteil im SS-Einsatzgruppenprozess*, 30.
25 Ibid., 129.
26 Ibid., 68.

On October 17, 1947, he (Naumann) was asked on the witness stand whether he saw anything morally wrong in the Führer's order, and he answered in the negative. He was asked again and he responded emphatically: "I believed the order was correct because in my opinion it was necessary in the course of conducting warfare and achieving the aims of the war." So that there is no doubt about his stance, the court asked whether with his reply Naumann wanted to say that he "saw nothing wrong with the order even though it included the murder of defenseless people" and he replied: "Jawohl."[27]

By and large, the West German judiciary categorized the crimes of the Einsatzgruppen in dramatically different terms than had the U.S. military tribunal. Events were accurately portrayed in the West German proceedings, but the leaders of the SS were systematically absolved of responsibility for the mass murder of Jews. Leaving aside acquittals, almost all of the Einsatzgruppen members tried in West German courts – fully 91.6 percent – were deemed to have been merely accessories rather than perpetrators.[28] They had not acted on their own initiative, the argument ran, in planning and carrying out their murderous operations. In the American Einsatzgruppen trial, the defendants' argument that they had acted on superior orders was refuted by the evidence of their active adherence to Nazi beliefs. In the majority of the West German trials, in contrast, the courts accepted the defendants' claims that they had not acted on their own volition and categorized them, accordingly, as only accessories to murder. These legal findings, which Bettina Nehmer has analyzed in detail,[29] were sharply criticized by a commission of leading lawyers and judges appointed by the Deutscher Juristentag (Association of German Jurists). "The commission has with concern taken note of court decisions in which perpetrators of Nazi violence have received conspicuously low sentences considering the findings in the judgments . . . In a significant portion of these cases, the perpetrators of murder have been convicted as accessories. . . . In the commission's view, however, a perpetrator is, regardless of his motivation, (a) anyone who killed without a specific order [to do so]; (b) anyone who did more than he was commanded to do; (c) anyone who as commander ordered killings on his own decision-making authority or his own discretionary power."[30]

27 Ibid., 155.

28 Bettina Nehmer, "Die Täter als Gehilfen? Zur Ahndung von Einsatzgruppenverbrechen," in Redaktion Kritische Jusitz (Hg.), *Die juristische Aufarbeitung des Unrechts-Staats* (Baden-Baden, 1998), 645.

29 Ibid., 635ff.

30 Barbara Just-Dahlmann and Helmut Just, *Die Gehilfen. NS-Verbrechen und die Justiz nach 1945*, 263. On the widespread application of the category "accessory," see the comprehensive analysis in Freudiger, *Die Juristische Aufarbeitung von NS-Verbrechen*, 143ff; see also Michael Greve, *Der justitielle und rechtspolitische Umgang mit den NS-Gewaltverbrechen in den 60er Jahren* (Frankfurt/Main, 2001), 145ff.

The proceedings against Otto Bradfisch in 1961 illustrate how West German courts transformed major Nazi perpetrators into unwilling accomplices. Bradfisch had joined the Nazi Party in 1931and rose to the rank of major (*Obersturmbannführer*) in the SS. As leader of Einsatzgruppe 8, he was responsible for the murder of 15,000 Jews. The state court in Munich that tried Bradfisch did not call the facts of the case into question. The court, in fact, described both the Einsatzgruppe's campaign of murder and its command structure in detail.

> The EK [Einsatzkommando] 8 arrived in Mogilev on September 9, 1941 . . . There the EK 8 killed a total of at least 4,100 Jewish men, women, and children as well as Russian prisoners of war in at least eight mass shootings [*Erschiessungsaktionen*]. The Jews taken prisoner were held in a factory and brought from there in trucks on the next two days to the execution site, a trench outside of the city. The executions were carried out at several spots along this trench, which was several kilometers long, by members of the EK 8 and the members of Police Battalion 316 and the Belarussian militia [put under the command of EK 8]. . . . All of the executions carried out in Mogilev by the EK 8 were ordered [angeordnet] by the defendant Dr. Bradfisch in fulfillment of Hitler's annihilation order known to him and his subordinates and directed personally by him or by his representative Obersturmführer Koch. . . . At one of the actions in Mogilev, which took place under his personal direction, Dr. Bradfisch also personally shot victims lying in the trench. At the beginning of the execution, he came with several SS leaders to the side of the trench and fired a pistol two or three times in the direction of people lying face-down in the trench.[31]

In summarizing what occurred at Mogilev, the Munich court transformed the person responsible for the crimes into a sort of neutral agent that had nothing to do with Otto Bradfisch's racist beliefs or murderous acts. Bradfisch, the court noted, had in his own defense claimed that "he deplored the execution of Jews and only participated in carrying out the Führer's orders on account of the exigencies of that time, which left him no other way out."[32] The court accepted this self-exculpatory assertion from a career Nazi at face value and without any supporting evidence. "The actions initiated by Dr. Bradfisch were not, however, the expression of a personal interest in carrying out the killing [*Tötungshandlung*] and thus of his own desire to kill independent of the order."[33] Elsewhere in its ruling, the court added: "It is a hallmark of the numerous crimes committed during the Third Reich that the responsible Nazi leaders, who had the state's instruments of power at their disposal, carried out [the crimes] through military or other subordinates in a similar position of obedience [*Gehorsamsverhätnis*],

31 Christiaan F. Rüter (Hg.), *Justiz und NS-Verbrechen*, vol. 17 (Amsterdam, 1997).
32 Ibid., 692.
33 Ibid., 681.

as if they were tools, and that the attitude of the subordinates cannot be judged as the 'intention of a perpetrator' [*Täterwille*]."[34] This premise led the court to make the cynical and bizarre assertion that the individuals who organized the murder of Jews, who had deprived so many people of their right to existence, had not been ill-disposed toward Jews: "There is also no indication of a hostile attitude [toward Jews on the part of the defendant] or of expressions of opinion on the Jewish question."[35] That hostility might find expression in the murder of innocent people apparently did not occur to the court.

The Munich court contradicted its own findings in casting a leading murderer as a simple cog in the machinery of Nazi power. In sentencing Bradfisch to eight years' imprisonment for having been an accessory to murder, the court noted that he had been "transferred to Einsatzgruppe B through no doing of his own and carried out the annihilation order primarily because he approved completely of the state at that time."[36] The court took note of Bradfisch's identification with the Nazi regime and its racial ideology of genocide, but it did so only to lessen his burden of responsibility. For purposes of sentencing, Bradfisch's active agreement with the Nazi regime's goals served to exculpate him even though that agreement was a clear indication of his willingness to participate in acts of murder. The court, in short, adopted a schizoid perspective in order to repress recognition of the actual role of a mass murderer of Jews.

THE CAUSES OF THE REFUSAL TO RECOGNIZE MASS MURDER

The West German judiciary's skewed perspective on the mass crimes of the Nazi era was tied to the problem of legitimacy: West German society was linked in countless ways to the former regime. That was evident, for example, in the persistence, in modified form, of Nazi beliefs among many West Germans, in the attempts to grant amnesty to individuals who had participated in the Third Reich's state-sponsored crimes, and in the continuance of state and judiciary personnel in their previous roles.[37]

That the Wehrmacht's war crimes were essentially reinterpreted as actions legal under international law was clearly connected with the long-prevailing

34 Ibid., 705.

35 Ibid.

36 Ibid., 706.

37 Theodor W. Adorno, "Was bedeutet: Aufarbeitung der Vergangenheit" (1959), in *Eingriffe* (Frankfurt/Main, 1963), 135f; Anna J. Meritt and Richard L. Meritt, ed., *Public Opinion in Occupied Germany* (Urbana, 1970), 295; Perels, *Das juristische Erbe des "Dritten Reiches,"* 79ff.

misperception of the role of the military in the Third Reich. That misperception impeded the prosecution of war crimes. Moreover, the image of a "clean" Wehrmacht was a prerequisite for the establishment of West Germany's army, the Bundeswehr.[38] Prosecuting Wehrmacht war crimes would have damaged that image because of the continuity in leadership from the Wehrmacht to the Bundeswehr. Former Wehrmacht officers would have had great difficulty justifying their role in the Bundeswehr had the Wehrmacht's complicity in Nazi crimes been acknowledged.

The situation was similar for the West German judiciary. The failure to prosecute individuals who participated in turning the law into an instrument of persecution stemmed from the high degree of continuity in personnel. Most of the elite of the Nazi-era justice system were able to continue their careers in the Federal Republic, and they were largely shielded from critical questions about the judiciary's part in sanctioning the Nazi regime's misuse of the law.[39] Unwilling to acknowledge the collapse of the rule of law under the Nazis, West German courts and prosecutors had to "normalize" the administration of justice in the Third Reich and portray the Nazi justice system as an acceptable successor to its constitutional predecessor.[40] The Bundesgerichtshof created the legend of the value-free administration of justice under the Nazis, and it thereby provided a justification for allowing Nazi judges to continue to serve in the Federal Republic – a justification that served its own interests.

The extensive categorization of activist Nazi criminals as "accomplices" was the result of the fundamental assumption that the political leaders of the Third Reich – Hitler, Himmler, and Heydrich were cited most commonly in the Einsatzgruppen trials – bore sole responsibility for the regime's murderous actions. Casting the members of the Einsatzgruppen as accomplices was a tremendous projection that carried over more broadly to the portrayal of Nazi criminals as mere "fellow travelers." As studies carried out at the time by the Institut für Sozialforschung showed, there was a pervasive unwillingness among West Germans in the early 1950s to accept responsibility for the horrors of Nazism, and the West German judiciary gave juridical expression to that unwillingness.[41] The consequences were far-reaching: abolishing the category of perpetrator changed the way victims are

38 Detlef Bald, Johannes Klotz, Wolfram Wette, *Mythos Wehrmacht. Nachkriegsdebatten und Traditionspflege* (Berlin, 2001); Norbert Frei, *Vergangenheitspolitik. Die Anfänge der Bundesrepublik und die NS-Vergangenheit* (München, 1996), 133ff.

39 Perels, *Das juristische Erbe des "Dritten Reiches,"* 181ff.

40 For a critique, see Karl Löwenstein, "Justice," in *Governing Postwar Germany*, ed. Edward H. Litchfield (Ithaca, 1953), 254f; Arnold Brecht, "Personnel Management," in Litchfield, ibid., 263ff.

41 Friedrich Pollok (Bearb.), *Gruppenexperiment. Ein Studienbericht* (Frankfurt/Main, 1955), 150ff.

perceived. When the subjectivity of the horrible murderers disappeared, the victims were made anonymous once again – they suffered only a mechanical death. The tormentors, transformed into accomplices, were nonexistent from a legal point of view.

UNDERMINING THE GERMAN CONSTITUTION TO BENEFIT NAZI PERPETRATORS

The perception of the Nazi crimes carried normative implications. The Federal Republic's constitution specifies in Article 1, Paragraph 3 that the basic rights it outlines "shall bind the legislature, the executive and particularly the judiciary as directly enforceable law." This imperative means that if a constitutional right – above all the right to life (Article 2, Paragraph 2) – is abrogated, the authorities must reestablish that right or at the very least acknowledge the injustice that has occurred.

The commitment of the judiciary to the guarantee of the right to life, which the American military tribunals took as their point of orientation in punishing the mass crimes of the Nazi state, was relativized by the West German judiciary in connection with certain Nazi crimes – with war crimes, with the criminal abuse of law, and with the murders carried out by the Einsatzgruppen. The right to life was abrogated by transformation of genocide into a lawful act and the hollowing out of the concept of the perpetrator by the West German courts' interpretation of military command and the actions of SS killing squads. Because the abrogation of the right to life by the Wehrmacht and Nazi judiciary could not be punished, the West German system of justice failed in upholding its commitment to that right. At the same time, the protective scope of the right to life was systematically circumscribed by the transformation of murderers into accomplices. The hollowing out of the basic constitutional law to the advantage of Nazi perpetrators was a result of the fact that the elite Nazi office holders who continued to serve under the Federal Republic were able, with the support of mainstream West German society, to repress recognition of their participation in the exercise of dictatorial power.

6

Getting Away with Murder

The Täubner Case

DICK DE MILDT

On May 24, 1943, the Supreme SS- and Police Court Munich presided over an unusual case. It concerned the killing of hundreds of Jews by a thirty-three-year-old SS Untersturmführer (second lieutenant) named Max Täubner. Miraculously, the verdict of the SS judges in Täubner's case survived the war and turned up in the course of criminal proceedings against three of his accomplices in the 1970s.[1] To the historian of the legal aftermath of the Nazis' crimes, the Täubner verdict is an intriguing document. Given the genocidal priorities of the Nazi state, the most obvious question that springs to mind is why Täubner was prosecuted. After all, if Täubner had done little more than his colleagues did on official orders, why was he put on trial? And what precisely did the judges have to say about the state's extermination policy and the criminal responsibility of the defendant?

Hardly less interesting than the verdict itself is the postwar sequel to the case. Max Täubner acted as one of the main witnesses in the trials of his former subordinates in the 1970s and 1980s. And even though his performance at these trials was less than sensational, it prompted attempts to re-indict him for his crimes. Those attempts failed, however, and the question we will address below is why.

1 Judgments of LG (state court) Heilbronn, May 24, 1973, Ks 8/72 and of LG Stuttgart, February 15, 1982, IX, Ks5/81. These judgments will be published under Lfd.Nr.793 and Lfd.Nr.877 in the series *Justiz und NS-Verbrechen – Sammlung deutscher Strafurteile wegen nationalsozialistischer Tötungsverbrechen* (Amsterdam and Munich, 1968–) (hereafter: *JuNSV*). In these notes, full references to separate trial judgments will be made only in the first instance. Subsequent references will list only the Lfd. Nr. (case no.) in the *JuNSV* series, plus corresponding pages. If no volume number of the *JuNSV* series is given, the judgments are not yet published and the page references correspond with those in the original judgment; otherwise the page numbers relate to the published *JuNSV* volumes. For more information, go to www.jur.uva.nl/junsv.

The Täubner verdict also had an effect on the postwar court debates on the so-called *Befehlsnotstand* – the defense that one was following orders under duress – and its treatment by the SS courts. And finally, we will see what the author of the Täubner verdict had to say about his decision, his choice of formulations, and the motives behind them. First, however, let us turn to the case itself.

At the early stages of the German assault on the Soviet Union, Max Täubner was placed in charge of a technical supply unit with the First SS Infantry Brigade en route through the Ukraine. As the SS judges noted in the opening lines of their verdict, Täubner was a profound Jew-hater from the very start: "At the beginning of his assignment in the East, he decided to 'wipe out' 20,000 Jews, if given the opportunity."[2] It must have been a disappointment to him, then, that he was put in charge of a mere auxiliary unit, which was not supposed to engage in the systematic killing operations. But that did not stop him from making a serious effort to participate in the killing.

On September 12, 1941, Täubner and his men reached the town of Zwiahel (Novograd Volynsky), about 200 kilometers west of Kiev. The mobile killing squads of Einsatzgruppe C had already decimated the Jewish population of Zwiahel and its surroundings during the initial stages of the German advance into the Soviet Union. Most of those who had survived that onslaught fell victim to the subsequent SS "cleansing operations."[3] Nonetheless, when Täubner and his men reached Zwiahel, there were still Jews alive in the area. Several hundred of them had been incarcerated by local Ukrainian militia in an improvised prison situated close to the town. Entirely on his own initiative, in the belief that the treatment of the surviving Jews by the Wehrmacht was "too sentimental," Täubner decided to shoot the Jewish prisoners with the help of his men. The day after its arrival, Täubner's unit marched off to the prison building, took custody of the prisoners – men, women, and children of all ages – and shot all 319 of them

2 Together with related documents, the text of the trial judgment against Täubner is in part reproduced in *JuNSV*, Lfd.Nr.877, 49ff, and Lfd.Nr. 909, 20ff. It can also be found in Ernst Klee, Willi Dressen, and Volker Riess, eds., *'Schöne Zeiten'. Judenmord aus der Sicht der Täter und Gaffer* (Frankfurt, 1988), 183ff. An English translation is available under the title *The Good Old Days* (New York, 1988), 196–207. The translation here is mine.

3 See the judgments mentioned above and judgment of LG Darmstadt, November 29, 1968, Ks 1/67, *JuNSV*, vol. 31, Lfd.Nr.694. Helmut Krausnick und Hans-Heinrich Wilhelm, *Die Truppe des Weltanschauungskrieges. Die Einsatzgruppen der Sicherheitspolizei und des SD 1938–1942* (Deutsche Verlagsanstalt Stuttgart, 1981), 187ff, 221. Gert Robel, 'Sowjetunion' in Wolfgang Benz, ed., *Die Dimension des Völkermords. Die Zahl der jüdischen Opfer des Nationalsozialismus* (München, 1991), 546.

at a nearby execution pit. On October 17, Täubner and his men carried out another mass execution at the town of Scholochovo, near Nikopol, this time killing 191 Jewish men, women, and children. On Täubner's orders, one of the SS men took pictures of the shootings.

Five days later, Täubner's unit arrived in the city of Alexandria, some 70 kilometers northeast of Kirowograd. Due to heavy rainfall that made further travel impossible, the unit became cut off from the First SS Infantry Brigade. Täubner and his men were stuck at Alexandria for a couple of weeks. To pass the time, Täubner again ordered the shooting of all Jews he could get his hands on. In addition to carrying out large-scale executions in the area, Täubner and some members of his unit also engaged in the brutal torture of Jewish prisoners before they shot them. As the SS court noted in its ruling:

> Jews, who had been ordered to saw wood in the yard of the quarters, were beaten up under the pretext that they did not work in an orderly manner. On this occasion they were also hit with spades, particularly by SS Sturmmann Ackermann. SS Sturmmann Wüstholz induced the Jews to beat each other to death by making the promise that the survivor would not be shot. The Jews did in fact knock each other down, even though not dead. The defendant joined in the beatings and also hit Jewish women with a whip in the face. When a break was held, he played the song *Du bist verrückt, Mein Kind* [You are crazy, my child] on his accordion. . . . On one occasion, a couple of Jews were ordered to tear down a wooden shed. It was arranged so that the shed collapsed on top of them, burying them under the debris. As a result, the Jews were injured but not killed. Also, shootings took place, which were not always orderly; rather, individual Jews were shot on the spot behind the house, after first having been beaten up. On one occasion a Jew was hanged on orders of the defendant.

In the basement of the quarters where Täubner and his men were stationed, Jews who had been randomly picked up from the streets were incarcerated pending execution. One night when Täubner and his men were feasting, he invited the men to join him in abusing the approximately twenty Jewish prisoners, among them women and elderly people, locked up below. Together with six of his men, Täubner went down to the basement, where he started to beat the defenseless and terrified prisoners with a wooden club while his men held the others in check at gunpoint. Alarmed by the cries of the victims and the sound of pistol shots fired, one of Täubner's subordinates came down to the basement to find out what was going on. When he saw the gruesome spectacle, he told Täubner and the others to stop the beatings and leave. Surprisingly, Täubner and the others complied and left the basement, leaving at least two of their victims dead and the others severely wounded. Contrary to custom, Täubner did not have photographs taken on this occasion because of the "unfavorable light conditions" in the basement.[4] The following day, Täubner ordered all prisoners to be shot. A few days later, he had a group of ten to fifteen orphaned Jewish children between the ages of eight and twelve executed, along with the elderly nurse caring for them. All of these killings were photographed and carefully registered in the unit's diary. According to this diary, the "Alexandria killings" involved a total of 969 victims.[5]

After a temporary stay at Konotop in December 1941 – where Täubner had a local Ukrainian militia officer shot – his unit was recalled from the Ukraine in the spring of 1942 and re-stationed, first at Plozk and later at the military training facilities in Arys, East Prussia. While on leave in his home town of Offenburg, the unit's photographer had the photographs of the shootings developed. He took them with him to Arys, and Täubner began to show them around and boast of his "heroic deeds."At the officers' club, he showed them to an officer from the Command Staff of the Reichsführer SS. This landed him in trouble. He and four of his men were arrested shortly thereafter, and court-martial proceedings were started against them. In late 1942, the case was referred to the SS Court Main Office in Munich, together with Himmler's instructions to drop the proceedings against the accomplices and to indict Täubner, *not* for murder but for his "breach of troop discipline."[6]

Even though Täubner was not on trial for murder, the SS court that pronounced judgment on him on May 24, 1943, commented on his killings in a remarkably outspoken manner:

> The defendant should not be punished for the actions against the Jews as such. The Jews must be exterminated; there is no loss in any of the killed Jews. Even though the defendant should have recognized that the extermination of the Jews is the task of Kommandos especially set up for this purpose, it should be assumed in his favor that he may have considered himself authorized to participate in the extermination of the Jews himself. The driving motivation of the defendant has been genuine hatred of Jews.

But if Täubner was not to be blamed for the killings, he was to be seriously punished for the brutal ways in which he had carried them out. Commenting in particular on his actions in Alexandria, the judges said they were "unworthy of a German man and SS officer." Täubner's defense that

4 Cf. the remarks of the Stuttgart court in *JuNSV*, Lfd.Nr.877, 39.
5 *JuNSV*, Lfd.Nr.877, 46, 793.
6 Ibid., 47–8.

his actions were rightful retaliation for the crimes committed by the Jews against the German people was flatly rejected by the court:

> It is not the German way to apply Bolshevist methods during the necessary extermination of the worst enemy of our people. The action of the defendant borders on such [methods] in a doubtful manner. The defendant allowed it to come to such a terrible brutalization among his men that they conducted themselves under his command like a savage horde. The defendant has endangered the discipline among his men in a way that can hardly be imagined worse. Even when the defendant has taken care of his men in any other way, by his conduct he has grossly failed his supervisory duties, among which, according to SS views, is included not to let his men degenerate emotionally.

Täubner's acts of cruelty and brutality were interpreted by the court as an expression of "severe character deficits [and] a far-reaching inner brutalization." That he had pictures taken of the cruelties and the killings – "images conveying the most evil excesses, many are shamelessly revolting" – that he showed to his wife and to acquaintances was a further sign of his degeneracy: "They are the expression of an inferior character. Illustrative of this is that the defendant showed himself particularly pleased with a picture that showed a Jewish woman largely naked."

Täubner was also severely reproached for underestimating the security risks these pictures represented: "How easy would it have been to play them from Southern Germany through Switzerland into the hands of enemy propaganda."

For all of these actions, as well as for the unlawful killing of the Ukrainian militia officer, the court contemplated imposing the death penalty. There were, however, extenuating circumstances in Täubner's case, such as the consideration "that the defendant initially did not act out of sadism but out of genuine hatred for the Jews." Also weighed in his favor was the fact that he had little military training and was therefore unfit as a unit leader. For these reasons, the court abstained from imposing the death penalty and sentenced Max Täubner to ten years' imprisonment. He was also to be expelled from the SS and declared unfit for military duty: "The conduct of the defendant is in the highest degree unworthy of an honor-loving and decent German man."

The Munich SS Court's judgment against Max Täubner was confirmed by Himmler on November 2, 1943. The sixty-nine pictures and negatives of the killings and brutalities by Täubner's unit were destroyed. Max Täubner spent a little over a year in a penitentiary, before being pardoned by Himmler in January 1945.

The outcome of the Täubner case was determined by two precedents involving unauthorized killings of "enemies of the Reich" by members of the military on which both Hitler and Himmler had made some principled decisions.

The first of these cases concerned an army officer by the name of Manfred Blume.[7] Major Blume headed a battalion of the Eighth Infantry regiment during the 1942 summer offensive in the East. In the course of the battalion's advance, Blume, otherwise known as a competent and reliable military commander, suddenly lost his self-control and ran amok. He randomly killed and lethally wounded a number of Soviet prisoners of war by shooting them or by battering them with a spade or the butt of his rifle. He also killed one female prisoner by repeatedly stabbing her with his bayonet. On September 25, 1942, Blume was tried for these killings by a court-martial and convicted of four counts of manslaughter; he was demoted and sentenced to two years' imprisonment. In keeping with regular procedure, the court's president referred the judgment to Hitler for confirmation. Hitler, however, overturned the sentence and terminated the proceedings. The grounds for Hitler's decision were reported to General Field Marshall Keitel by the Chief of the Army's Personnel Office, General Major Schmundt, on October 16, 1942:

> After report, the Führer has ordered that the verdict against Major Manfred Blume is to be annulled. In doing so, the Führer has expressed that one cannot reproach vital natures [*vitalen Naturen*] when they, convinced of the unique fateful struggle of the German people, reject all commands of humanitarianism against the Bolshevik global enemy. Moreover, it should also be held in favor of Major Blume that his brother has been murdered by the Bolsheviks, a circumstance, which necessarily enhanced his hatred for these devils in human disguise. The very favorable review of Major Blume and his performance in battle are mitigating circumstances.

Ten days after Schmundt's report to Keitel, Himmler ruled on a question from the SS Court Main Office in Munich involving the unauthorized killing of a Jew by members of a police unit in Radom.[8] Himmler's response clearly echoed the Führer's position: "Decisive for the question if and what punishment should be given for the shooting of Jews without orders and authorization are the motives." No punishment was to be imposed for "politically motivated" killings unless the maintenance of military discipline was at stake. Only when purely self-seeking, sadistic, or sexual motives were involved were the courts to try such cases as murder or manslaughter.[9]

7 Judgment of the LG Hamburg, January 25, 1966, (50) 24/65 (*JuNSV*, vol. 23, Lfd.Nr.618).
8 Case against Wölfer; see Klee et al., *'Schöne Zeiten,'* 191 and 254.
9 For the text of the order, cf. *JuNSV*, Lfd.Nr.909, 19f, or Klee et al., *'Schöne Zeiten,'* 191.

That Max Täubner was not to be blamed for his private butchery of Jewish men, women, and children was, then, completely in line with Hitler's and Himmler's appreciation for "vital natures" and political warriors in their personal crusades against the archenemies of the Reich. If their zealousness was to be held in check, it was not because they engaged in murders nobody asked them to commit, but because their random killings were often accompanied by excesses and actions that interfered with the orderly and secret implementation of the state's own killing campaigns. Thus, even though the Täubner trial dealt with mass murder, it was, as noted above, not a murder trial. The trial centered on military discipline, against which Täubner had sinned and had to be punished.

That the judges' verdict was neatly tailored to Himmler's directives hardly comes as a surprise. What is surprising is the fact that only a few months earlier those same judges had apparently been at a loss when dealing with similar killings, as their inquiry to Himmler suggests. That matters had to be spelled out to them as late as October 1942 – well over a year after the start of the extermination campaign – shows that there remained considerable confusion about the issue among the SS lawyers. Apparently, they needed time, along with specific instructions from their supreme chief, before they could substitute ideological priorities for legal norms. Or, to put it differently, the period of uncertainty suggests that even within the SS there were lawyers inclined to consider the random killing of innocent and defenseless Jews as plain murder, as, indeed, it would still have been regarded under German law. These lawyers obviously needed some clear advice on how to handle such murders.

By *suspending* punishment for "politically motivated" murders, Himmler effectively told his judges that, where the treatment of Nazism's enemies was concerned, positive law had lost out to the Third Reich's political and ideological agenda. By the time of the Täubner trial, the SS judges had clearly grasped this lesson about the extralegality of the regime's killing campaigns. It is illustrative that Täubner's judges referred to the mass killings of Jews as "the *necessary* extermination of the worst enemy of our people." The choice of adjective here clearly shows that the SS judges did not consider these killings as legal, for there is no doubt that they would have said so if they had thought so. Of course, these legal professionals knew full well that the killing of defenseless and innocent men, women, and children, as committed by Täubner and his men, constituted the crimes of murder and manslaughter as defined in the German criminal code. But they also knew that this understanding of the law had become irrelevant to the political masters they served.

The position taken up by the SS courts with regard to the Nazi state's annihilation program was to play a role in postwar courtroom debates on the so-called *Befehlsnotstand*. At issue were the possible consequences of a straightforward refusal by an SS member or police official to carry out an order to kill within the context of the "Final Solution." Defendants generally argued that refusing such an order would have resulted in severe punishment, possibly even execution. Since all SS and police units on special wartime duty fell under the jurisdiction of the SS and police courts, the question was raised in postwar trials what those courts would have done if a case involving a refusal to carry out orders to kill were brought before them. The formal guidelines of the SS courts explicitly stated that orders were to be followed unconditionally, even when those who received them questioned their legality. Only after executing an order was the subordinate allowed to file a formal complaint. There was one important exception to this rule, however: orders with a *clearly identifiable* criminal intent were not allowed to be followed.[10] This meant that any SS member or police official ordered to shoot defenseless and innocent men, women, and children could and even should refuse to comply on the grounds that doing so would require that he commit a criminal offense.

That was textbook legal theory, however: What about practice? As it turns out, there was no practice. Even after extensive investigations and close scrutiny of all the sources available by historians, prosecutors, defense lawyers, former SS judges, and other "interested parties," not a single example of an SS court dealing with such a case has been found. What might explain this? Given the absence of supporting evidence, the question has not been satisfactorily answered, and the answers suggested by historical experts and former SS authorities acting as trial witnesses (among them many former SS judges) have therefore been largely hypothetical. Still, the basic arguments in the debate are interesting to note as they touch on the image of the SS courts as instruments for the administration of justice.

In brief, the experts have argued that cases involving the refusal to carry out orders were never brought before the SS courts because Himmler did not allow this, for two reasons.[11] First, the implementation of the "Final Solution" was a *Geheime Reichssache*, a highly secretive operation known only to the limited circle of those actively involved in its execution. Even

10 See, e.g., the "Mitteilungen über die SS- und Polizeigerichtsbarkeit," vol. 2, 148ff, cited in the judgment by the LG Münster, February 19, 1962, 6 Ks 1/61 in *JuNSV*, vol. 18, Lfd.Nr. 529, 290ff.

11 See, e.g., judgment of the LG Düsseldorf, September 3, 1965, 8 Iks 2/64 in *JuNSV*, vol. 22, Lfd.Nr. 596, 199; judgment of the LG Oldenburg, September 28, 1966, 2 Ks 1/64, in *JuNSV*, vol. 24, Lfd.Nr. 638, 108ff; judgment of the LG Bochum, June 5, 1968, 16 Ks 1/66, in *JuNSV*, vol. 29, Lfd.Nr. 678, 317ff.

though the trials before the SS courts were not public, allowing cases of refusal to carry out orders to be tried by those courts would have involved disclosing particulars of the Final Solution to an audience outside the circle of so-called *Geheimnisträger* (bearers of secrets). That was to be avoided. Second, with regard to cases of general disobedience and insubordination, the SS courts, which were bound by the German Military Penal Code, acted similarly to regular army courts, considering each case individually and taking account of any mitigating circumstances. In the case of an SS man refusing to comply with an order to kill noncombatants, that procedure would necessarily involve a thorough discussion of the defendant's motives as well as an assessment of the mitigating implications of Section 47 of the Military Penal Code. That section stipulated:

> If the penal law is violated by the execution of an official order, the ordering superior is exclusively responsible. However, the obedient subordinate meets with the punishment of the perpetrator,
>
> 1) when he has transgressed the given order, or
> 2) *when it had been known to him that the order of his superior concerned an activity intended to commit a general or military crime or misdemeanor* [emphasis added].

According to most historians and legal experts, any defendant put on trial before an SS court for refusing an order to kill would undoubtedly have appealed to this section of the Military Penal Code. Consequently, the SS judges would have had to rule on the legality of the Nazi state's extermination policy. Again, for obvious reasons, such a situation was to be avoided.

These arguments helped to give the SS courts a favorable reputation as respectable, law-abiding instruments of justice. They suggest that the SS judges had been kept uninformed of the state's killing campaigns and, moreover, that those judges were upstanding custodians of positive law. Not surprisingly, the former SS judges who served as witnesses in postwar trials did everything possible to uphold this image. It was undoubtedly an unpleasant surprise for them to be confronted with the Täubner verdict, as it showed in rather unambiguous terms the lengths to which the Supreme SS- and Police Court went to endorse Hitler's extermination policies while quite simply glossing over the question of their legality. Moreover, as both the Täubner verdict and Himmler's general directive of October 1942 demonstrate, the Final Solution was by no means kept secret from the SS courts. Obviously, if the courts were to rule on cases like the Täubner case, knowledge of the state's "orderly" extermination campaign was a *conditio sine qua non*. That any SS court or any member of such a court would have dared to identify the killing of Jews as positively illegal and thereby brand its chief organizers – namely, Hitler and Himmler – as criminals is, as one postwar German court noted euphemistically, "hardly imaginable."[12]

As previously mentioned, the Täubner case resulted in two additional trials in the 1970s and 1980s involving three members of Täubner's unit who had participated in the killings. All three defendants were sentenced to prison terms, which ranged from two to twelve years.[13] Obviously, the Täubner verdict played a prominent role in their trials, and so, too, did the original defendant. Max Täubner had survived the war and was living in Bavaria. His performance as a trial witness yielded little, as he claimed he could not remember most of what had taken place during his time in the Ukraine. His discovery by criminal investigators did, however, give rise to attempts to have him re-indicted for his crimes. All of them foundered on the legal status of the original verdict against him.[14] Like the trial verdicts of the military courts, SS and police court verdicts were considered legally valid in the Federal Republic so long as they had been confirmed by their respective supreme judicial authorities.[15] In the case of the military courts, that authority was Hitler; for the SS courts, Himmler. With Himmler's endorsement of November 2, 1943, the Täubner verdict had become *rechtskräftig* (legally valid). Consequently, when prosecutors in Memmingen sought to indict Täubner in the early 1970s for his wartime crimes, they were rebuffed by a district court on the basis of the *ne bis in idem* principle (double jeopardy), which prohibits the renewed prosecution of someone for crimes that had already been duly tried by a German court.[16] Thanks to Himmler's signature on a trial verdict that applauded the Final Solution as "the necessary extermination of the worst enemy of our people," Täubner was protected by German law from standing trial again.

That the signature of a mass murderer could mean the difference between a peaceful retirement and a severe prison sentence was discovered the hard way by Manfred Blume. Ironically, it turned out to be anything but a stroke

12 *JuNSV*, vol. 29, Lfd.Nr. 678, 323–4.

13 Lfd.Nr. 793 and 877.

14 Cf. BGH Urteil vom 24. Mai 1972, 2 ARs 80/72.

15 Cf. in this respect the different opinion of the Hamburg court in an earlier case: "The SS- and Police Courts . . . cannot be considered orderly constitutional courts. They are based on the National Socialist rule of arbitrariness and violence. Their verdicts can therefore not be recognized as legally valid." Judgment of the LG Hamburg, September 21, 1950 (50) 26/50, in *JuNSV*, vol. 7, Lfd.Nr. 240, 443. Obviously, the Hamburg Court was ill-informed.

16 According to article 103, section 3 of the German Grundgesetz. A second attempt by the Memmingen State Attorney's Office to have Täubner's case re-opened was also blocked by the Memmingen court, which ruled that a resumption of the case (*Wiederaufnahmeverfahren*) was only permitted *in favor* of the defendant. A third attempt was undertaken by the Zentrale Stelle in Ludwigsburg with the Bundesgerichtshof. It foundered on procedural grounds. Cf. Decision of the Bundesgerichtshof, May 24, 1972, 2 ARs 80/72.

of good fortune when, as recounted above, Hitler overturned Blume's conviction for manslaughter. In fact, it brought him trouble that would last for the rest of his life. Instead of enjoying the relatively privileged status of a military officer jailed in a German prison for having been somewhat overzealous, Blume had the misfortune shortly after his trial of being put in charge of an infantry battalion stationed in Stalingrad. In early 1943, Blume was taken prisoner by the Soviets and sent to a POW camp near Moscow. In the years that followed, he shared the harsh fate of all the German POWs who had fallen into the hands of the Soviets. After passing through several prison camps across the Soviet Union, Blume stood trial in a Soviet military court in October 1947; it took the court less than thirty minutes to find him guilty and sentence him to twenty years of forced labor. A few months later, Blume was tranfered to the notorious Soviet penal camp in Workuta, north of the Arctic Circle. There, Blume fell victim to typhoid fever and dystrophy. After spending time in a number of other camps and suffering further illnesses, Blume was finally turned over to the West German authorities as a so-called non-amnestied war criminal in January 1956.

Ten years later, Blume – by then living on disability pension – was again put on trial for his unlawful wartime killings. In contrast to Täubner, Blume was not protected against prosecution by the *ne bis in idem* rule. He was not considered to have been punished under German law for his crimes, and his 1947 conviction by a Soviet military tribunal did not stand in the way of a new trial since the *ne bis in idem* article of the Federal Republic's Basic Law applied to German court proceedings only.[17] Of course, the military court that had originally convicted Blume on September 25, 1942, *was* a German court, but its verdict had never become *rechtskräftig*, as Hitler had annulled the conviction. In Blume's case, then, *bis* simply did not apply. On January 25, 1966, a court in Hamburg found Manfred Blume guilty of murder and attempted murder, and sentenced him to fifteen years. He did not receive a life sentence because the court held him only partially accountable for his actions.[18]

Another fascinating story linked to the Täubner case concerns another survivor of the war: Munich SS Court president Günther Reinecke. It was Reinecke who was responsible for the fiercely anti-Semitic phraseology of the Täubner verdict. After the war, the former Standartenführer and deputy chief of the Main Office SS Court was classified as a *Mitläufer* ("fellow traveler," literally; nominal Nazi Party member) by a denazification court and

17 Cf. *JuNSV*, vol. 23, Lfd.Nr.618, 28ff.

18 Ibid. 9ff.

escaped punishment. Thus cleared, Reinecke settled in Bavaria and worked as a lawyer. On several occasions, Reinecke acted as an expert witness in trials against his former colleagues. When his ruling in the Täubner case became publicly known in the early 1970s, the Bavarian Ministry of Justice revoked Reinecke's license to practice law on the grounds that the pronounced racial hatred expressed in the verdict made him unworthy of his profession. To defend his honor as well as his means of livelihood, Reinecke turned to his peers and appealed the ministry's decision. Before the Bavarian Honorary Court of Attorneys, he came up with a rather inventive explanation of his conduct. Had he sentenced Täubner to death, he argued, Himmler would certainly have annulled the sentence. The anti-Semitic phraseology he had used and the endorsement of mass murder in the verdict had been necessary, he contended further, to make the verdict and comparatively harsh sentence acceptable to the SS leader. The members of the Honorary Court considered this defense irrefutable.[19]

We will give the final word on the Täubner case to reporter Peter Henkel. Henkel covered the 1981 trial of two of Täubner's fellow killers for the *Frankfurter Rundschau.* After describing the atrocities committed by the defendants in the 1941 massacres, he noted:

> There is much in this trial which is hard to comprehend. At some point during this fall of 1941, a Ukrainian Jew came to the men of the SS supply unit and pleaded with them to shoot him as they had already killed his entire family. He was told to clear off as they were, after all, no gang of murderers.[20]

19 Peter Henkel, "Selbst der SS war das damals zuviel. Ein schwer fassbarer NS-Prozess in Stuttgart um bekannte Greueltaten," *Frankurter Rundschau*, December 21, 1981.

20 Ibid.

7

"A Great Achievement of German Troops in Mountain Warfare"

Cold War Pressures and the German Prosecution of Wehrmacht War Crimes in the Case of Cephalonia, 1943

NATHAN STOLTZFUS

Communism's demise has unveiled archival records that have undercut German popular memories of the Wehrmacht as a force that had fought honorably and would be judged favorably. It also provided a test for equally enduring claims that pressures of Cold War solidarity with the Western alliance were decisive in turning West German courts away from prosecuting Wehrmacht veterans suspected of war crimes. More than fifteen years on in the new Berlin Republic, in fact, the German judiciary has not proven any more willing to convict and incarcerate Wehrmacht suspects than it had been during any phase of the Cold War.

Germany as a perpetrator country is twice guilty, according to Ralph Giordano – once for committing crimes during World War II and again for turning a blind eye to many of them afterward.[1] This may not comprise the entire story, but nowhere is this appraisal more accurate than in regard to the response of the Federal Republic of Germany (FRG) to war crimes of the Wehrmacht. Even though judges who served in Nazi Germany are no longer active in the FRG, some decisions made quietly during the Cold War are now reiterated publicly and more provocatively.

In 2006, for example, the West German judiciary reached virtually the same conclusion about a Wehrmacht massacre of thousands of Italian troops in September 1943 as it had reached in 1968, but with a more inflammatory rationale and to domestic and international public protest. The

For translations of Greek sources, I owe thanks to my wife Maria Foscarinis, whose uncle, Nikolaos Moshopoulos, was executed by the Germans in June 1942 as a hostage in an "atonement action."

1 Ralph Giordano, *Die zweite Schuld, oder von der Last Deutscher zu sein* (Hamburg, 1987).

Dortmund-based Central Office for Investigation of Nazi-Era Crimes had reopened the investigation of this massacre in 2001 to international fanfare. A main theme in press coverage was the hope that finally, after the demise of the Cold War alliance to contain communism, the perpetrators would be dealt their punishment. The prosecutor himself cited as a reason for reopening the investigation new evidence and sources of evidence that had been out of reach behind the Berlin Wall.

The 2006 judgment, however, not only dismissed the case as definitively as did the 1968 ruling. It did so with a rationale that reflected the perspectives and judgments of Wehrmacht officers implicated in the massacre. While the judiciary had quietly discontinued the case in 1968, its widely publicized judgment in 2006 in effect attempts to shore up the flagging Wehrmacht myth. Its reasoning, more provocative than necessary to sustain the ruling, has offended many, stirring up charges that it reflects a new climate of denial. West Germany's rearmament and membership in NATO had served to promote the Wehrmacht myth and provided various reasons for minimizing the trials of war criminals. Even so, it is fair to conclude at this point that it was not the Cold War, but rather persistent German resistance to trials of Nazi-era criminals, that kept the West German judiciary from adjudicating more World War II war crimes from the beginning, particularly those of the Wehrmacht.

THE COLD WAR EFFECT

Throughout its shifting course, the Cold War had a very considerable impact on efforts to bring war criminals to justice in Germany. Before the end of the 1940s, fear of communism had replaced concern with Nazism in the West. Motivated by the new bipolar international rivalry, the United States, Canada, and other countries pressed into service many thousands of former Nazis. In the occupation zones later united as West Germany, the Cold War brought an early end to the denazification trials carried out by the Allied powers. After West German courts assumed responsibility from the Allies for bringing its war criminals to justice in January 1950, new Cold War alliances allayed the prosecution of war crimes. In East Germany, although trials and purges of war criminals were more extensive than in West Germany, they were skewed toward targeting anticommunists as well as Nazis and allowed little place for adjudicating Nazi crimes specifically against "racial" enemies.[2]

2 Jon Elster, "Introduction," in *Retribution and Reparation in the Transition to Democracy*, ed. Jon Elster (Cambridge, 2006), 4, 7.

West German Chancellor Konrad Adenauer's integration of most elite Nazi functionaries into the public and private sectors in the effort to rebuild Germany met with public approval and Allied cooperation. Postwar surveys from Germany's occupying forces indicated "an enduring presence of Nazi attitudes," with positive images eroded only slowly over time. According to surveys conducted from November 1945 through April 1947, 48 percent agreed that Nazism "was a good idea badly carried out" (there was no expressed support for the mass murder of Jews). In May 1947, 55 percent agreed and the share who held this opinion continued to increase over the following two years. Rather than ruing the Nazi plunder of others all over Europe, most West Germans by the early 1950s "felt more traumatized" by the period from 1945 to 1948 than by the years of relative plenty and national sovereignty from 1933 to 1945. By May 1964, those who considered the Nazi regime criminal still comprised only a slight majority.[3]

This perspective on Nazism provided fertile ground for the myth that the Wehrmacht had acted strictly within the bounds of international law. The Western alliance's preoccupation with containing communism also contributed, if not deliberately, to the minimization or disregard of Wehrmacht crimes. Bowing to public opinion and protests against the continued incarceration of war criminals at Landsberg Prison, the American-run prison for the most serious war criminals, American High Commissioner for Germany John McCloy in January 1951 issued an early release for thirty-one convicted leading Nazis, including all who had been sentenced at Nuremberg to less than fifteen years.[4] McCloy responded to pressures not only from widespread German opinion but to the corollary policies of Adenauer's strategy of democratization through integration into the Western alliance. The release of convicted Wehrmacht generals fit into an evolving pattern of claims that the German army had acted honorably. Such an image was also supportive of Allied demands, especially by the United States, for a reconstructed German army as well as of a common belief in West Germany that the Wehrmacht had nothing to do with the Holocaust or other Nazi war crimes. We are now certain, however, that the Wehrmacht was a "co-perpetrator" of Nazi crimes.[5]

3 Elizabeth Heineman, "The Hour of the Woman: Memories of Germany's 'Crisis Years' and West German National Identity," in *The Miracle Years: A Cultural History of West Germany, 1949–1968*, ed. Hanna Schissler (Princeton, 2000), 21–56, 42; Nick Thomas, *Protest Movements in 1960s West Germany: A Social History of Dissent and Democracy* (Oxford, 2003), 28.

4 Dick de Mildt, *In the Name of the People: Perpetrators of Genocide in the Reflection of Their Post-war Prosecution in West Germany: The 'Euthanasia' and 'Aktion Reinhard' Trial Cases* (The Hague, 1996), 22–3. For an overview of the Federal Republic's prosecution of Nazi crimes, Norbert Frei, *1945 und wir: Das Dritte Reich im Bewusstsein der Deutschen* (Munich, 2005).

5 Wolfram Wette, *The Wehrmacht: History, Myth, Reality*, trans. D. Schneider (Cambridge, MA, 2006 [orig. 2002]), 276. On this myth, see also Klaus Naumann, "The 'Unblemished' Wehrmacht: The

The Wehrmacht cast a long shadow over West Germany's domestic politics and international relations. By 1955, at least a million German POWs had returned from Soviet captivity. Although many were guilty of or had profited from war crimes and mass murder, the returning POWs were seen in West Germany as "victims" of both Hitler and Stalin and "survivors of the enemy" now on the other side of the Iron Curtain.[6] When West Germany established its own army, the Bundeswehr, in 1955, it depended heavily on volunteers who were Wehrmacht veterans. Some of the new army's strategists were former Wehrmacht officers implicated in war crimes. As a result in part of the myth of the honorable Wehrmacht, the Wehrmacht was seen inside and outside the Bundeswehr as a model for the Bundeswehr.[7]

Within an FRG rapidly integrating into and identifying with the Western alliance, members of the Wehrmacht were considered "our soldiers" while in East Germany they were seen as the plundering fascist army. Members of the Wehrmacht comprised 45 percent of those charged with war crimes in the GDR and just 14 percent of those in the FRG, where just three Wehrmacht veterans were found guilty. With a population one-fourth as large, the GDR sentenced forty-nine Wehrmacht soldiers for classical war crimes, all of which were upheld by post-unification FRG courts.[8]

In the FRG, Chancellor Konrad Adenauer negotiated with the Allies for the release of war criminals in return for FRG's integration into the Western alliance against communism.[9] As the FRG began to experience signs of returning prosperity, there was, Theodor Adorno wrote, a public silence surrounding the Nazi past that he regarded as a failure to process the past (*Vergangenheitsbewältigung*).[10] In this context, East Germany, equally

Social History of a Myth," *War of Extermination: The German Military in World War II, 1941–1944* (New York, 2000), 417–29, and in the same volume Omer Bartov, "Whose History Is It Anyway? The Wehrmacht and German Historiography," 400–16.

6 Frank Biess, "Survival of Totalitarianism: Returning POWs and the Reconstruction of Masculine Citizenship in West Germany, 1945–1955," in Schissler, *The Miracle Years*, 57–82, 57–8.

7 Wette, *Wehrmacht*, 265, 296.

8 East German courts acquitted 10 percent of those charged with classical war crimes compared with a 17 percent acquittal rate for accused members of the Wehrmacht. The corresponding results of FRG courts were an abnormally high 48 percent general acquittal and a huge acquittal rate of 88 percent for accused members of the Wehrmacht. Christiaan Frederik Rüter, "Die Ahndung von NS-Gewaltverbrechen im deutsch-deutschen Vergleich," in *Konferenz zum 60. Jahrestag der Befreiung vom Faschismus: Die juristische Aufarbeitung von NS-Verbrechen und deren Widerspiegelung in der Gedenkkultur*, ed. Die Linkspartei.PDS Fraktion im Landtag Sachsen-Anhalt (Halberstadt, 2005), 65–82, 72–3; http://www.linkspartei-pdslsa-lt.de/publikation/konf_reader_web.pdf (August 2, 2006).

9 David Cohen, "Transitional Justice in Divided Germany after 1945," in *Retribution and Reparation in the Transition to Democracy*, ed. Jon Elster (Cambridge, 2006), 59–88, 87.

10 Theodor Adorno, "Was bedeutet: Aufarbeitung der *Vergangenheit*," in Adorno, *Erziehung zur Mündigkeit* (Frankfurt am Main, 1970 [orig. 1959]), 10–28.

interested in silencing its own responsibility for the Nazi past, began a public campaign to reveal continuities between fascist and FRG leaders, illustrated by the GDR Supreme Court's trial of Hans Globke, the former interior ministry official who had helped draft amendments to the infamous 1935 Nuremberg Laws, and became Adenauer's National Security Advisor.[11] The GDR's embarrassing broadcasts about its Cold War rival and Western counterpart spurred the FRG, in its search for legitimacy internationally, to greater efforts to bring Nazi war criminals to justice. Beginning in 1958, a series of trials forced West Germans to confront a more complete picture of both Nazi crimes and their as yet unpunished perpetrators.[12] The most decisive was the Ulm Einsatzgruppen trial of 1958, which opened for public discussion the destruction of Jews in Poland and the Soviet Union, leveraging blame on the SS and Einsatzgruppen mobile killing units while sparing the Wehrmacht.[13]

The huge increase in the number of trials held at the end of the 1950s, together with the FRG's establishment of the Ludwigsburg Central Office for the Investigation (*Aufklärung*) of National Socialist Crimes late in 1958, represent a turn in the FRG's recognition of and response to Nazism. Without the pressure of negative public relations campaigns from the GDR, it is quite likely that West German leaders and prosecutors would not have undertaken either.[14] Moves toward a clean image and satisfactory response to the Nazi past nevertheless put FRG leaders in a bind with continuing political, popular, and judicial opposition to further trials.

Particularly challenging and potentially widely disquieting were results of the Ulm trial establishing that the Wehrmacht was responsible for a significant number of the mass shootings of Jews and communists. In response, the FRG tread a careful path. It established the Ludwigsburg Central Office for the Investigation of National Socialist Crimes as only a processing agency, not a prosecutor's office. It was staffed with just ten judges and prosecutors

11 Jeffrey Herf, *Divided Memory: The Nazi Past in the Two Germanys* (Cambridge, MA, 1997), 183.

12 Devin Owen Pendas, *The Frankfurt Auschwitz Trial, 1963–1965: Genocide, History and the Limits of the Law* (New York, 2006), 18. The agitation for the early release of convicted war criminals may also be considered among German efforts to deal with the Nazi past. See Robert Moeller, "Remembering the War in a Nation of Victims: West German Pasts in the 1950s," in Schissler, *The Miracle Years*, 83–109; and *War Stories: The Search for a Usable Past in the Federal Republic of Germany* (Berkeley, 2001).

13 Detlev Siegfried, "Zwischen Aufarbeitung und Schlußstricht. Der Umgang mit der NS-Vergangenheit in den beiden deutschen Staaten 1958–1969," in *Dynamische Zeiten: Die 60er Jahre in den beiden deutschen Gesellschaften*, ed. Axel Schildt, Detlev Siegfried, Karl Christian Lammers (Hamburg, 2000), 77–113.

14 Annette Weinke, "The German-German Rivalry and the Prosecution of Nazi War Criminals During the Cold War, 1958–1965," in this volume.

to accomplish the enormous task of investigating all Nazi crimes not yet prosecuted. Substantial numbers of potential convicts were exempted from its purview, including those suspected of committing crimes within Germany itself including the *Schreibtischtäter* or desk murderers, some of whom were back in positions of power in the FRG. Also exempted in effect were those who had participated in the arrest and concentration of Jews, and those who were members of killing units. Finally, the Wehrmacht itself was also excluded from Ludwigsburg's scope of action. Not surprisingly, the leader of the Wehrmacht unit implicated in mass murder during the Ulm Trial was soon acquitted.[15] Given its 88 percent rate of acquittal in the case of accused Wehrmacht soldiers, the FRG judicial system was acting primarily as an agency to clear the Wehrmacht's record.

The West German judiciary was a powerful force behind the myth that the Wehrmacht had fought cleanly, with the SS and Einsatzgruppen alone guilty of Nazism's mass killings. Many of those who served Nazi "justice" continued in their roles within the new German democracy.[16] During the 1960s, for example, the official in charge of the director of the Dortmund-based Central Office for Investigation of Nazi-Era Crimes was a Nazi Party member, who had joined the NSDAP in 1933 and had been a member of the SA for four years.[17] In contrast to the GDR's courts, which convicted sixteen Nazi prosecutors and judges, the West German judiciary sentenced none.

The end of the Cold War has provided some basis for testing the extent to which that war had been the critical factor inhibiting the investigation and conviction of suspected Wehrmacht war criminals. Supported by a treasury of photographs available to them only after the end of the Cold War, historians at the Hamburg Institute of Social Research staged the famous Wehrmacht Exhibit that opened in 1995 and dealt a blow to the deeply influential Wehrmacht myth.[18] Although scholars had long since established the Wehrmacht's guilt, as had the Ulm trial itself, photographs showing Wehrmacht units as the often proud mass murderers of Jews and others proved especially adept at challenging popular opinion and stirring

15 Rüter, "Die Ahndung von NS-Gewaltverbrechen im deutsch-deutschen Vergleich," 78, 82, note 54.

16 Ibid., 73. See also Ingo Müller, *Furchtbare Juristen: die unbewältige Vergangenheit unserer Justiz* (Munich, 1987).

17 Georg Bönisch and Frank Hartmann, "'Bäche von Blut,'" *Der Spiegel*, June 2, 2003, 42–6.

18 Wehrmacht war crimes had already been documented by scholars, including Christian Streit, *Keine Kameraden. Die Wehrmacht und die sowjetischen Kriegsgefangenen, 1941–1945* (Stuttgart, 1978); Omer Bartov, *The Eastern Front, 1941–45: German Troops and the Barbarization of Warfare* (London, 1985) and *Hitler's Army: Soldiers, Nazis, and War in the Third Reich* (Oxford, 1991).

up public discussion about the Wehrmacht's role. Research following the end of the Cold War further challenged the mythologized accounts of the military-led July 20, 1944, conspiracy to kill Hitler, which had also acted as a foothold for the Wehrmacht myth. Historians had already faulted the myth's claim about the conspirators' political motives and their stand on Nazi policies, and new work showed that "at the same time" military officers were conspiring to kill Hitler they were "also participating in mass crimes."[19]

The collapse of communism and German unification produced new opportunities for requiting earlier failures to bring Wehrmacht criminals to justice. But the post–Cold War record has only strengthened Norbert Frei's conclusion that, among the reasons the FRG did not expiate more Nazi crimes, "the most important factor of all was the determined German resistance to the legal efforts nigh from the beginning."[20] A case well situated for some analysis of the difference the Cold War made is that of the Wehrmacht massacre of 3,000 to 5,000 Italian soldiers occupying the Greek island of Cephalonia, following the first fall from power of Benito Mussolini. The Central Office for Investigation of Nazi-Era Crimes in Dortmund first opened a preliminary investigation of this massacre in 1964, at the behest of Simon Wiesenthal. After interviewing some three hundred suspects and assembling other eyewitness reports and documents, the court quietly closed the investigation in 1968 for lack of evidence. In 2001, the Central Office reopened the case. Five years later, after rounding up some four hundred suspects and witnesses in several countries and dredging the archives to find documents the 1964–68 investigation had missed, the judiciary again dismissed the case. It went beyond narrow reasoning sufficient for upholding the previous ruling and made statements that victims and survivors consider insulting. The dismissal provoked a furious reaction from Germans, Greeks, and, above all, Italians.

THE CEPHALONIA MASSACRE

When Mussolini's successor, Marshall Pietro Badoglio, declared on September 8, 1943, that the Allies were Italy's new partners, the Wehrmacht demanded that Italian armed forces disarm and surrender to German will or be forcibly disarmed. Since Benito Mussolini's first fall from power on

19 Christian Gerlach, "Men of 20 July and the War in the Soviet Union," in Hannes Heer and Klaus Naumann, *War of Extermination*, 127–45, 128.

20 Norbert Frei, *Adenauer's Germany and the Nazi Past: The Politics of Amnesty and Integration* (New York, 2002), 230.

July 26, Berlin, anticipating Italy's "treason," had prepared for this ultimatum. By the end of August, the Wehrmacht was in position to forcibly disarm Italian forces, and its orders were to do so "as fast as possible" and in the simplest way possible. In the critical early days of September, the attitude of many Germans toward their erstwhile allies had turned to contempt and rage.[21]

Although the Wehrmacht sought cooperation by assuring all Italian soldiers they would be sent home after disarming, the Germans forced most Italian soldiers into labor camps.[22] In retrospect it appears that Hitler and the Wehrmacht High Command (Oberkommando der Wehrmacht, OKW) were in agreement in their intention to allow for an alternative to the internment of disarmed Italians who had been unwilling to fight with the Nazis – an alternative that ended in their massacre. In making determinations about Italian units, German officers paid special attention to Ionian island units since the Wehrmacht wrongly expected the Allies to follow up their invasion of Southern Italy with an attempt to invade the European continent via Greece. Thus the Ionian islands, lying between Italy and the Greek mainland, would be key to resisting an Allied advance and occupying them was an urgent priority.[23]

In September 1943, most Italian forces in Italy and the Italian-occupied portions of France, Greece, and the Balkans disarmed quickly and gave themselves over to the Germans. The most notable example was the Acqui division of the Eleventh Italian Army on the largest Ionian island, Cephalonia, 200 miles southeast of Italy's "heel." There, Lieutenant General Antonia Gandin had some 11,000 soldiers, including more than 500 officers, and a wide array of weapons under his command.[24]

On September 10, the OKW issued an order stating that Italian commanders who refused to disarm were to be shot as "bandits" for their responsibility for "resistance." Lieutenant Colonel Hans Barge, the highest-ranking German on the island, was given corresponding instructions and presented them to Gandin.[25] The following day, Army Group South transmitted orders from the Führer to shoot Italian troops who resisted along

21 Gerhard Schreiber, *Die italienischen Militaerinternierten im deutschen Machtbereich, 1943 bis 1945: verraten, verachtet, vergessen* (Munich, 1990), 87, 95.

22 Manfred Rauh, *Geschichte des Zeiten Weltkriegs*, 3 vols. (Berlin, 1998), vol. 3, 136.

23 Michael Eliot Howard, *Strategic Deception in the Second World War* (New York, 1995 [orig. 1990]), 93.

24 Schreiber, *Die italienischen Militaerinternierten*, 158.

25 *Kriegstagebuch des Oberkommandos der Wehrmacht*, ed. Helmuth Greiner and Percy Ernst Schramm, 4 vols. (Munich, 1982), vol. 3 (2), 1094. Schreiber, *Die italienischen Militaerinternierten*, 110.

with all who collaborated with them. Officers and troops who did not resist were to be taken prisoner and sent to labor camps in the East.[26]

A loyal personal acquaintance of Mussolini, Gandin wished to meet German demands, as his chaplains and senior officers urged him to do. But there was a growing sense of dissension and confusion among his soldiers. Most wanted to quit the war and return home, a sentiment stoked by Greek partisans and encouraged by reassuring German promises. Within days of Mussolini's downfall, Gandin had lost control as his men fell into various factions over the question of whether to disarm and subjugate themselves to the Wehrmacht. The Italian command above Gandin was in disarray as well. Badoglio and King Victor Emmanuel hurried south to the zone of Allied protection while urging the Italian people to resist the Germans.

Added to the growing chaos within the Acqui division were members of the Greek communist-led National Liberation Front (EAM), who exacerbated the discord within Division Acqui in order to spur conflict between the Italians and Germans. They wasted little sympathy on their island's armed occupiers, hoping that the Germans and Italians would weaken each other. Their most urgent goal was to acquire the Italian weapons for themselves. Through personal relationships they had developed with their occupiers over nearly two and a half years, they fed the Italians' desire to combat the Germans (for example, by claiming inside information supporting the notion that the Allies would support Acqui resistance). The release of Italian-held Greek prisoners followed a noisy Greek demonstration in the square of the island capital, Argostoli, on September 9, organized by an EAM eager to arm and integrate them into its partisan forces.[27]

While the German resolution to subjugate the Italians grew firmer by the day, the command structure of the Italian occupation force on Cephalonia deteriorated rapidly. The division's artillery unit led the move to confront the Wehrmacht. On September 13, it fired on German ships nearing the port of Argostoli, sinking one and forcing another to surrender and a third to turn back. The Wehrmacht's losses included five dead and a number of heavy weapons.[28]

As it became clear that some of his men were agitating to resist the Germans, General Gandin conducted a survey of opinion among his troops

26 Greiner and Schramm, *Kriegstabebuch*, vol. 3, 1094.

27 Author's interview with EAM member and eyewitness, Angelo-Dionysis Debonos, July 26, 2004, Argostoli, Cephalonia. Debonos gives considerable credit to Greek resisters for acting as a catalyst in Acqui's decision to resist the Wehrmacht.

28 Gerhard Schreiber, "Kephalonia 1943," in *Orte des Grauens: Verbrechen im Zweiten Weltkrieg*, ed. Gerd R. Ueberschär (Darmstadt, 2003), 92–101, 92, 3.

that indicated many wanted to resist the Wehrmacht.[29] The smoldering Italian resentment against the Germans was fanned when a commander of the Italian artillery division showed that there were specific reasons for mistrusting German promises that Italian soldiers would be sent home upon disarming. He therefore suggested that Gandin require a guarantee from the German command that it would stick to the agreements it had made.[30]

According to Wehrmacht sources, Gandin reported to Lieutenant Colonel Barge on September 14 that his men had refused his orders, a stance the Italian government reinforced that day, according to historian Gerhard Schreibo. Gandin, however, promised to have his division disarm in three successive stages by September 16 – on condition of German honesty. His division would maintain its position as long as it was given guarantees that "preclude every double entendre" and could retain its "weapons and ammunition, handing the artillery over to the Germans only in the instant they boarded the ship." Gandin's conditions add to the evidence that a key reason his men were willing to confront the Wehrmacht was that they did not put much faith in the German promise of being returned home upon disarmament. It is clear in any case that a common sentiment among the soldiers was that they wanted to return home and forget the war. But were the Germans really going to help them? If the German command did not guarantee the return home of his men, Gandin said, his "division would rather fight than suffer the ignominy of disarmament." Gandin concluded with a warning that Acqui would resist any further Wehrmacht advances toward his base in Argostoli,[31] and he refused a German request for the names of Italian officers and commanders who had opened fire against German marines the day before.[32]

29 This "plebiscite" has become a focal point of controversy in the postwar interpretation of the meaning of the Cephalonia massacre for the Italians. Was this a true plebiscite in the sense that everyone had a vote and everyone's vote was counted, as the Italian Left, for whom Cephalonia represents resistance to fascism, had claimed early in the postwar period? According to this version, everyone was asked and, many heroically, wanted to fight German fascism. For example, Greek EAM resister and historian Spyros Loukatos wrote that Gandin consulted with all the men of his division on the evening of September 13 and found that many wanted to resist rather than either surrendering to the Germans or fighting with them; in the artillery, men prepared to arrest Gandin, should he insist on disarmament, and a shot was fired at the general. Spyros D. Loukatos, *Ta chronia tēs Italikēs kai Germanikēs katochēs kai tēs ethnikēs antistasēs stēn Kefalonia kai Ithakē (The years of the Italian and German Occupation in Cephalonia and the National Resistance in Cephalonia and Ithaca)*, vol. 2, 43 (Athens, 1981).

30 Staatsanwaltschaft Dortmund, 45 Js 34/64, *Verfahren gegen Barge u.a. wegen Mordes bzw. Beihilfe zum Mord* (hereafter *Barge*) 1, 45, citing Chaplain Father Romualdo Formato, who as a prisoner witnessed the mass executions and published his wartime record of events on Cephalonia in 1946.

31 Gerhard Schreiber, *Deutsche Kriegsverbrechen in Italien: Taeter – Opfer – Strafverfolgung* (Munich, 1996), 78; *Barge*, 13, 18–20, citing Gandin's message to Barge on September 14, 1943.

32 *Barge*, 9, 20.

General Hubert Lanz of Army Group Southeast flew to Cephalonia to meet with Gandin in an effort to minimize German costs in taking control of the island. Lanz was reassuring and created a relaxed atmosphere, according to Father Rumualdo Formato, an Italian chaplain and Gandin confidant. The division must disarm, Lanz told Gandin, but officers could keep their hand weapons – an incentive for initial compliance that in practice represented just a brief stage on the way to total disarmament once Italian forces had weakened. Following his reassurances to Gandin, Lanz wrote to General Alexander Löhr, the chief of Army Group F, who had commanded over southeast Europe, that Gandin's troops would now proceed "smoothly." He noted ominously, however, that Gandin's infantry had committed an "unmistakable act of hostility."[33]

General Lanz's promises to Gandin told him what he wished to hear: If the Acqui disarmed without conflict, the division "like all other Italian divisions" would be "transferred to Italy." Gandin, however, now requested that the Wehrmacht remove its troops from the island by the following morning (September 16), adding that he awaited orders from Badoglio or the king. This declaration led General Lanz to conclude that Gandin could never be of use to the Wehrmacht[34] – so in essence it became the general's death sentence.

The Wehrmacht deftly petitioned Gandin to extend his deadline for removing their troops until two o'clock the next day. Gandin readily agreed. The Wehrmacht, however, used Gandin's extension to land "abundant" reinforcements on Cephalonia. Gandin then forbade further German reinforcements from arriving, and Italian artillery subsequently shot down a German plane. An hour later, German Stukas filled the skies over Argostoli, dropping bombs that "suddenly turned the ground near the city into "an inferno of whistles, explosions, and flames."[35]

In retrospect, the Italians were ill-advised to tell the Germans that their plans had changed and conflict was inevitable, rather than allowing the Germans to find that out for themselves. Were the Italians tied to a notion of honor that required them to attempt to level with the Germans? Was their deception due to indecision or naïveté? Gandin, whose most trusted advisors were the chaplains, was more capable of goodwill gestures than wily stratagems.

Meanwhile, hundreds of Wehrmacht First Division Mountain Troops (*Gebirgstruppen*) arrived in Cephalonia. By the evening of September 17,

33 Lanz to Gandin, September 13, 1943, *Barge*, 18, 125.

34 Lanz to Oberbefehlshaber of Army Group E (FS-KR-Blitz), September 13, 1943, *Barge*, 13, 16, 17.

35 *Barge*, 1, 49, citing Formato.

the last Mountain Troops had reached the island, as still more German companies and officers were on their way. The previous month, the company of Mountain Troops that had arrived under the command of Richard Klebe had just participated in the massacre of everyone they found in the Greek village of Komeno. Many were women and children; men often slept in the hills away from the village, fearing a reprisal that would target men (but not women and children). Many women were raped before being murdered; soldiers stuffed gas-soaked rags in the mouths of children and then burned them to death. After the war, several soldiers recalled the abject cruelty – physical mutilations of bodies, and "some soldiers made fun of the corpses and cracked jokes." One said he had not realized until then "that there were sadists in [his] 12th company."[36]

On September 18, Hitler ordered that Wehrmacht Southeast should no longer take Italians as prisoners, due to their "cowardly and treasonous" (*gemein und verraeterish*) behavior on Cephalonia. By some accounts, the OKW itself issued this order in Hitler's name, and evidence shows that Löhr did not need orders from Hitler before undertaking mass murder.[37] To be sure, the Germans closest to Cephalonia probably had the greatest thirst for revenge. And while the Wehrmacht thought it had to prepare to thwart an Anglo-American invasion through Greece from Italy via the tiny Ionian islands, Hitler at that time expected the invasion in the Netherlands because German forces were weakest there, while the Dutch people would be most likely to lend their support for a successful Allied invasion.[38]

At one front of the German attack on September 18, Reinhold Klebe's troops, including companies of Mountain Fighter Regiment III.98 and Battalion 54, apparently committed many atrocities.[39] The important recently published diaries of Alfred Richter, who served in Klebe's Battalion 54, characterize the victims as "brutally annihilated [*vernichtet*]." Italian ammunition carriers, still in their positions, had been "shot, clobbered, and smashed with hiking boots. . . . It must have happened just minutes before.

36 Mark Mazower, "Military Violence and the National Socialist Consensus: The Wehrmacht in Greece, 1941–1944," in Heer and Naumann, *War of Extermination*, 146–74, 165. H. F. Meyer has also published important works on Wehrmacht crimes in Greece, including *Von Wien nach Kalavryta. Die blutige Spur der 117. Jäger-Division durch Serben und Griechenland* (Mannheim, 2002) and *Blutiges Edelweiß. Die 1. Gebirgs-Division im Zweiten Weltkrieg* (Berlin, 2007).

37 *Kriegstagebuch*, Greiner and Schramm, eds., vol. 3, 1119; Schreiber, *Deutsche Kriegsverbrechen in Italien: Taeter – Opfer – Strafverfolgung*, 79.

38 *Die Tagebücher von Joseph Goebbels*, Elke Fröhlich, ed., pt. II, *Diktate* 1940–45, 15 vol. (Munich, 1993–96), IX, entry for September 9, 1943. Expressing the National Socialist conviction that popular support, armed or unarmed, is a key element of government and even military success, Hitler considered the element of local support for an Allied invasion important, apparently more so than the Allies themselves did.

39 *Barge*, 21, 16–17.

Under the bloodied corpses "someone still jerked and breathed, beside another the eyes lie next to the skull stomped flat."[40]

The Italians expected air force support that never materialized, and Stukas cut them down in their positions at will. After brief combat, Italian troops raised white flags. The Wehrmacht massacred upwards of 5,000 Acqui men, including Gandin and hundreds of other officers who had surrendered.[41]

Waldemar Taudtman, Richter's comrade in Klebe's 54th Mountain Troop battalion, noted in his diary the morning of September 20: "No prisoners will be taken, everything we see before us will be cut down." Two days before Klebe's Eleventh company of Mountain Troops had "annihilated" Italian infantry regiment 317, according to Major Harald von Hirschfeld, who had replaced Barge as the Wehrmacht's top officer on Cephalonia.[42] Hirschfeld's cursory description puts emphasis on his troops' mettle: Klebe's fighters had marched for twenty hours with only three hours of rest before their attack, he wrote.[43] He neglected to mention that Klebe's men brought the captured Italians to a quarry, gathering other Italian prisoners along the way until there were 900 or more who had surrendered. Thinking they were being temporarily imprisoned, many of the Italian troops "threw themselves on the ground to rest." An Italian eyewitness reported that,

> suddenly from all sides, from walls and fences, horrible machine gunfire began. There was no escape . . . all ran instinctively toward the middle of the glen. They hung themselves on each other, tried to get away, fell, stepped on each other all at the same time, and constructed finally a twitching pile. From it sprayed blood and guts. It flowed around a slope on either side, and joined again in a scarlet red stream. Screams filled the air . . . Until this pile of 900 tormented human bodies grew still . . . After a time of silence one heard moaning. The Germans . . . climbed onto the heap and shot their machine pistols deep into it. But not even through that did all die. The bullets didn't reach those covered with many bodies. One could still hear harsh gasping and groaning. Then the Germans thought of a gruesome trick. They cried: "The medics are here. Whoever is still alive, come out. He will be allowed to live and taken to a military hospital." After a while about 20 persons wormed their way out with the greatest difficulty, bloody, wounded, and scared. The murderers bent over in laughter and with one last machine gun salvo the last survivors were killed.[44]

Explanations for the German troops' actions include the common one of compulsory superior orders. One squad of Bavarians who were "none

40 *Barge*, 21, 3–4, citing *Tagebuch Richter*.

41 Schreiber, *Deutsche Kriegsverbrechen in Italien*, 85. See also *Barge*, 13, 43.

42 Major Hirschfeld, Combat report for the period September 16–22, 1943 on Cephalonia, dated 20.9.1943, *Barge*, 4, 37.

43 Hirschfeld, Combat Report, September 22, 1943, *Barge*, 4, 40.

44 *Barge*, 13, 46, 47.

too soft" objected to the slaughter, Richter wrote, only to be "silenced by an officer with the threat that they themselves would be put up against the wall."[45] If an officer did make such a threat, it stands in contrast to the experience of uniformed Germans who asked not to participate in mass shootings elsewhere, none of whom were executed according to extant records.[46] Illustrative is the case of Lieutenant General Ulrich Kleemann, commander of the Wehrmacht's assault troops on the Greek island of Rhodes, who had refused orders to shoot Italian officers for resisting that same month and went on to receive two further promotions before the war's end.[47]

Richter wrote that a German officer threatened the lives of soldiers who objected to the mass slaughter of Italian troops who had already surrendered and thrown down their weapons. He does not say that the men who raised objections were forced to carry out the slaughter, although he does imply that they had no choice. On the other hand, these men may have never had an opportunity equal to this one for being acknowledged by the Führer, whose attention had been drawn to the battle: Hitler bestowed the "Führer's letter of recognition" on a soldier present at one of the bloodiest sites of the Cephalonia massacre: "My special recognition of lieutenant Sigwart Goeller for his outstanding service on the battlefield of Dilinata on September 21, 1943."[48]

Compulsory orders are, in any case, too simple to explain the brutality of the Cephalonia mass murders. According to an Italian testimony, for example, about twenty captured Italians who feared execution were put to work instead. That evening they made friends quickly with their German captors, "and on every evening there was common festivity . . . The work lasted six days and at the end they sat down together at a banquet (festessen), provided by the Germans, and prepared by a Neapolitan chef. Afterwards the officer [who in particular had befriended the Italians] explained that he unfortunately had to do his duty, and that the execution squad was already waiting . . . the young Italians, who had worked and celebrated so happily, had to accept their totally unexpected and horrible end."[49]

45 *Barge*, 21, 144, citing *Tagebuch Richter.*

46 See Christopher Browning, *Ordinary Men: Reserve Battalion 101 and the Final Solution in Poland* (New York, 1992); Daniel Goldhagen, *Hitler's Willing Executioners: Ordinary Germans and the Holocaust* (New York, 1996).

47 Schreiber, *Deutsche Kriegsverbrechen in Italien*, 76. For a brief account of Kleeman's career in the Wehrmacht, see Samuel W. Mitchen, *Rommel's Desert War: The Life and Death of the Afrika Korps* (Mechanicsburg, 2007), 23, 222.

48 Hitler's signed letter was dated November 17, 1943, Barge, 21, 5, citing Franz Thomas and Guenther Wegmann, eds., *Die Ritterkreuzträger der Gebirgstruppe*, vol. 1 (A–K) (Osnabrück, 1993), 205–14.

49 *Barge*, 13, 51, 52, citing an eyewitness.

Richter identified a motive for the slaughters as "a delirium of omnipotence."[50] The order to "take no prisoners" was a euphemism used in the *Vernichtungskrieg* since the first days of the war against the USSR.[51] If Cephalonia is used as an example, "take no prisoners" indicated that soldiers had free rein with the victim who was in any case to be killed. Reports from a variety of sources indicate that the Germans eagerly robbed Italians, before or after murdering them, of everything from money to rings, watches, knapsacks, armbands, and even the "paltry things they had given to the priests before the shootings."[52]

Given the testimony of survivors and relatives of victims more than sixty years later, the case also illustrates how much more difficult it is for victims to deal with such brutality than it is for perpetrators. After the massacre, one Mountain Troop commander wrote of how he relished his days on the island directly following the killing spree, calling them "among the most beautiful of the summer."[53]

THE WEST GERMAN RESPONSE

Signs of German memory of the Cephalonia massacre during the first five decades after the war were sparse. The U.S. Military Tribunal in Nuremberg did sentence General Hubert Lanz to twelve years in prison in 1948; although the prosecution raised the issue of his responsibility for the murders on Cephalonia, the court seems to have accepted Lanz's claim that he had tried to hinder Hitler's orders, thereby saving Italian lives. Lanz was released in 1951, although it is likely that he had in fact sought to fulfill Hitler's orders.[54]

By 1956, the West German Foreign Ministry probably urged its Italian counterpart to drop preparations for prosecuting Wehrmacht suspects, including those from Cephalonia. The Italian Foreign Ministry requested that the Italian Defense Department's military tribunal set aside documents

50 Mazower, "Military Violence and the National Socialist Consensus," 146–74, 164–5. Richter cited in Nicholas Farrell, *Mussolini: A New Life* (London, 2003), 425.

51 Christian Gerlach, "Men of 20 July and the War in the Soviet Union," in Heer and Naumann, *War of Extermination*, 127–45, 133.

52 *Barge*, 1, 58, citing Formato.

53 Lieutenant Christoph Huber, "Eine Analyse der Kriegsverbrechen des XXII. Gebirgsarmeekorps auf der Insel Kephalonia im September 1943," Diplomarbeit zur Erlangung des Grades eines Diplom-Staatswissenschaftlers, July 31, 2001, Die Universität der Bundeswehr München, 124.

54 Schreiber argues that Lanz's orders allowed him to execute only a handful of officers, not thousands. Schreiber, *Kriegsverbrechen in Italien*, 83–4; *Trials of War Criminals Before the Nuremberg Military Tribunals Under Control Council Law No. 10. Vol. 11: United States of America v. Wilhelm List, et al.* (Case 7: "Hostage Case") (Washington, DC, 1950), 1088–1110.

its prosecutors were preparing in anticipation of trying Germans for war crimes, including the Cephalonia massacre. In a 1956 letter to Defense Minister Emilio Taviani (Christian Democrat), Foreign Minister Gaetano Martino (Liberal Party) called the Cephalonia massacre a barbaric act, but stressed that prosecutions would promote criticism of Wehrmacht behavior and, in turn, undermine German rearmament.[55]

Like West Germany, however, Italy possessed reasons of self-interest in this case that had nothing to do with the Cold War. At the time, Italy was refusing to meet foreign demands, mostly from Yugoslavia, for the extradition and trial of suspected Italian war criminals. Furthermore, Italian officials did not wish to increase critical, sometimes jeering scrutiny of the country's wartime military. Illustrative is the 1953 military tribunal conviction of two journalists, Renzo Renzi and Guido Aristarco, under criminal statutes that outlawed vilifying Italy or national political institutions. Even though the law stipulated that vilification did not occur if allegations were factual, the court found Renzi and Aristarco guilty of "insulting the armed forces" for a publication about Italy's disastrous military experience in Greece during World War II.[56]

In 1955, as the Federal Republic began building an army, it relied on many Wehrmacht veterans, including several associated with the Mountain Troops' atrocities, notably Lanz, Klebe, and Karl-Wilhelm Thilo. As Chief of Staff of the First Division of Mountain Troops, Thilo had signed orders for mass murder in Greece and Yugoslavia, but he nonetheless went on to become a three-star general and deputy inspector of the Bundeswehr. Lanz, who would be the only member of the Wehrmacht's Mountain Troops to serve a sentence, went on to serve as honorary president of the Bundeswehr's Mountain Troop division and as an advisor to the FDP (Free Democratic Party) on military matters. Rheinhold Klebe, who admitted to giving the order for the execution of General Gandin on Cephalonia, was put in charge of reestablishing the First Mountain Troop Division and became a lieutenant colonel in the Bundeswehr. The Mountain Troops established the largest postwar association of German veterans, the *Kameradenkreis* or Comrades' Circle, which has ties to FRG's power elite beyond the military. Meeting on Bundeswehr property, transported to the site by the Bundeswehr, the

55 Michael Braun, "Italien öffnet 'Schrank der Schande': Parlamentarischer Untersuchungsausschuss in Rom soll klären, warum 50 Jahre lang die Gräuel von SS und Deutscher Armee im 2. Weltkrieg vertuscht wurden," *Die Tageszeitung*, December 12, 2003.

56 Angelo Piero Sereni, "Community Security vs. Man's Right to Knowledge: Italy," *Columbia Law Review* 54, no. 5 (1954): 800, 801; Richard Bosworth, "Film Memories of Fascism," in *Italian Fascism: History, Memory and Representation*, ed. R.J B. Bosworth and P. Dogliani (London, 1999), 109.

Mountain Troops from the Wehrmacht and their younger collegues from the Bundeswehr have celebrated their tradition and their wartime activities in annual meetings of their *Kameradenkreis* since 1957. They gather at Mittenwald, a Bavarian village with strong ties to the Wehrmacht's Mountain Troops located near the Austrian border, celebrating their history and honoring fellow fallen soldiers, apparently without apology for their many innocent victims.

Klebe, Lanz, and Thilo were by no means the only former Wehrmacht officers or Nazi functionaries who filled important positions in West Germany (and a number of other countries as well). Still, rather than acknowledging their crimes, they praised the Wehrmacht's Mountain Troops, as indicated by Lanz's testimony in the German judiciary's first investigation of the Cephalonian massacre. That investigation began in 1964 following a letter from Simon Wiesenthal to the Office for the Prosecution of Nazi-Era Crimes in Dortmund. The famous Nazi hunter was at first surprised that German prosecutors had overlooked such a crime. Then "little by little" it occurred to him that the Wehrmacht, not the SS or Gestapo, was the culprit and "in the FRG influential forces strove to keep the Wehrmacht out of all war crimes trials."[57] Prosecutor Johannes Obluda duly interrogated hundreds of witnesses, and almost all claimed they had not heard or seen anything of the massacre. Even former Major Wilhelm Spindler, the commander of the soldier-diarists Richter and Taudtmann's battalion, claimed to have heard and seen nothing. He testified to having heard only talk at a dinner with Lanz on September 22 against an order to shoot Italian officers.[58]

Lanz himself testified in 1965 that the battle on Cephalonia had been similar to others, although the possibility that "individual lower ranking officers" went further than they should have (*Uebergriffe*) in the course of battle "cannot be precluded." To the extent that this was true, according to Lanz it resulted from understandable "testiness" (*Gereitzheit*) due to the deep-rooted sense that the Italians had acted like "traitors." They believed that the Italians had brought upon themselves whatever massacre may have taken place. Throughout Lanz's various statements to the court in 1965, a central theme was the claim that he had abridged Hitler's order and saved Italian lives.[59]

Rather than disregarding Hitler's orders, the record shows that the OKW may well have led the way in the development of Hitler's murderous orders.

57 Bönisch and Hartmann, "'Bäche von Blut.'" 58 *Barge*, 13, 96.

59 Lanz testimony, April 7, 1965, in *Barge*, 3, 114–23, 120. See also related testimony, *Barge*, 2, 144ff.

Löhr had given orders for antipartisan "atonements" in Greece to First Division Mountain troops who, under the command of General Hubert Lanz, had formed the northern wing of General Munstein's Army Group South in the eastern front in early 1942. Without orders from above, Löhr "secretly ordered all the German units in the Balkans to be ready to disarm the Italian forces there."[60] Anticipating the Komeno massacre, Löhr demanded in August 1943 that the Mountain troops carry out "atonement measures" against Greeks "with the most rigorous means.[61] In Greece, as in Yugoslavia, these tactics for suppressing partisan resistance dated back to the first half of 1941.

In the summer of 1941, German troops provided the "impetus toward a more radical procedure" for mass murder of "political unacceptables" because this appealed to them – even though it went against the will of superiors and the "principle of obedience to higher authority."[62] On Cephalonia, rather than stopping their men, officers following the massacre praised them, rewarding them with a twenty-four-hour period to do whatever they wanted with, and take whatever they wanted from, the local Greeks.[63] This is similar to Hannes Heer's explanation of the Wehrmacht's mechanisms of mass murder on the eastern front: "the imperative 'you must' is now joined by the potential 'you may'; the pressure of obligation is compensated for by the pleasure of permission . . . orders prepared the ground for . . . a heightened form of combat morale within the German ranks, the morale of annihilation which Hitler needed to pursue his war." After all, "limitless terrain for war" and "increased scope for action" maximizing chances for killing and minimalizing the threat of being killed "made victory seem inevitable."[64]

In 1965, Obluda stopped actively pursuing the investigation of Wehrmacht veterans suspected of mass murder in Cephalonia.[65] Three years later,

60 Mark Mazower, *Inside Hitler's Greece: The Experience of Occupation, 1941–1944* (New Haven, 1993), 147.

61 Mazower, "Military Violence and the National Socialist Consensus," 146–74, 152–3.

62 Christian Streit, "Soviet Prisoners of War in the Hands of the Wehrmacht," in Heer and Naumann, *War of Extermination*, 80–91, 86.

63 Hirschfeld, the highest ranked military official on the island, issued the following reward after the massacre: "Men, the next twenty-four hours belong to you." Barge, 1, 59. A Greek eyewitness remembers German soldiers going door to door in Argostoli upon their arrival, announcing they could do anything or take anything they wanted during the next 24 hours. Interview with Frosini Lucatos, Washington, DC, April 22, 2006.

64 Hannes Heer, "The Logic of the War of Extermination: the Wehrmacht and the Anti-Partisan War," in Heer and Naumann, *War of Extermination*, 92–126, 102–3, 117.

65 Christiane Kohl, "Ermordete Frauen, verbrannte Kinder," *Süddeutsche Zeitung*, March 24, 2001. See also the collection of Kohl's essays on Wehrmacht crimes against Italians, *Der Himmel war strahlend blau: Vom Wüten der Wehrmacht in Italien* (Vienna, 2004).

the Central Office for Investigation of Nazi-Era Crimes formally, quietly, discontinued the investigation for lack of evidence, a decision that was not above suspicion. As a 1995 investigation made public, Obluda's supervisor (*Abteilungsleiter*) had been a member of the SA who had joined the Nazi Party in 1933. Lawyers had likely prepared the witnesses on how to avoid indictment, and, according to one of Obluda's successors, the prosecutors made no effort to confiscate materials (for example, through house searches).[66] Wehrmacht suspects were spared the rigorous questioning that suspects should undergo in a holding so dependent on witness testimony. At the same time, the prosecutor showed disdain for the testimony of Italian and Greek eyewitnesses. "It must be taken into account that the Italian and Greek descriptions contain a considerable number of obvious or provable errors and mistakes," the Central Office for Investigation of Nazi-Era Crimes wrote in justifying its discontinuance dated September 17, 1968.[67]

This may have been accurate, but the most glaring unsatisfying aspect of the proceedings was evident in suspect statements given by Wehrmacht veterans. Routinely, each former soldier blamed the executions on some unit beside his own; each suspect pointed the finger of guilt at someone else who in turn pointed back. Yet the prosecutor relied on these contradictions to conclude that establishing blame was not possible and instead spoke only of mistakes and errors the accusers made. Furthermore, the history of the Wehrmacht encounter with the Acqui Division, even in the documents on hand for the prosecutor's decision not to press charges, amply indicate that while the Italians had naively continued to attempt straightforward negotiations with the Germans as if they were still allies, Wehrmacht men spoke with a forked tongue if they thought this would give them the upper hand. Could these Wehrmacht men, so superior to the Italian army in lying to get their way in war, be more trustworthy than their victims in these postwar statements when they stood to lose so much more personally?

To be sure, considering the international alliances of the Cold War as well as domestic politics, it would have been difficult even for the Office for the Prosecution of Nazi-Era Crimes to convict a member of the Wehrmacht in the mid-1960s. Yet surely the prosecution could have made a "lack of evidence" ruling without casting aspersion so blatantly on the testimony of its traumatized survivors, or neglecting to consider that Germany itself in a crime against the peace was the war's primary aggressor.

66 Bönisch and Hartmann, "'Bäche von Blut'"; author's interview with Maaß, March 10, 2003, Dortmund.

67 *Barge*, 13 (Decision) 41, signed Dr. Nachtweh, Oberstaatsanwalt.

Following the discontinuance of the Cephalonia massacre case, a minor drama ensued between Rome and Bonn at diplomatic levels, out of public view. In the fall of 1969, the Italian embassy requested a copy of the judiciary's discontinuance of the case "in view of the particular sensitivity" to it in Italy. One year later, West Germany fulfilled the request. In 1973, an Italian TV station (RAI) was denied its request for an interview with the state attorney in charge of the case. The West German Foreign Ministry was against the interview; as one diplomat said, one would never be able to make the Italians understand why the case had been discontinued. In any case, airing dirty laundry like that could lead to polemics from ill-willed groups that could threaten the German-Italian relationship.[68]

In 1987, a documentary aired on a West German TV network introduced its audience to the Cephalonia massacre. Klebe wrote in response that "the struggle for Cephalonia can be seen, militarily-tactically, as a great achievement of German troops in mountain warfare." Partisans were dastardly breakers of war customs, he maintained, and when the Italians turned treasonous, just as they had done in World War I, German "exasperation" (*Erbitterung*) was great. The Italians brought it on themselves with their "treacherous, deceitful [*truegerische*] behavior." He concluded indignantly that, "we soldiers don't need to allow ourselves to be upbraided as the murderers of Cephalonia."[69]

Shortly after communism's collapse and the demise of Cold War alliances, Italy resumed prosecution of German war criminals. While searching for documents to make the case, Italian military prosecutor Antonino Intelisano uncovered hundreds of American documents, including materials on the Cephalonia massacre, that had been used in the preparation of more than one hundred cases and given to Italy in 1945. Four decades after Italy agreed to stop its preparations for prosecuting Germans for war crimes, Intelisano found the treasury of records in a locked safe with its door turned to the wall, soon dubbed the "poison cabinet." Former Italian Defense Minister Emilio Taviani at that point explained that in 1956 he had followed the Italian Foreign Ministry's request to put aside further preparations for war crimes trials because the Soviets had just invaded Hungary, and a trial "about the horrendous crimes of Cephalonia could have stirred up public opinion possibly making impossible a resurrection of the German military from the ashes of National Socialism for years to come."[70]

68 Kohl, "Ermordete Frauen, verbrannte Kinder." In 1969, an article on the massacre drew some attention to it: "Kriegsverbrechen Wehrmacht: Härter als üblich," *Der Spiegel*, December 8, 1969.

69 Reinhold Klebe, "Das Unternehmen Kephalonia im September 1943," *Die Gebirgstruppe* 37, no. 1 (1988): 6–11.

70 Thomas Götz, "Italienische Hilfe zur deutschen Wiederbewaffnung," *Berliner Zeitung*, January 2, 2001.

A wind in the sails of the notoriety of the massacre was Louis de Bernières' 1994 international bestselling novel, *Captain Corelli's Mandolin*, and the Hollywood film that followed in 2001. While many hailed this international attention as the end of a conspiracy of silence by German officials, others believed that the events in Cephalonia had been "copiously researched" and neither "concealed nor covered up."[71] But important revelations soon followed that dealt an important blow to claims like those of Klebe that the Wehrmacht had performed honorably and cleverly on Cephalonia. The *Süddeutsche Zeitung* published excerpts from the diaries of Alfred Richter, following his death, along with those of his fellow soldier Waldemar Taudtman, on March 24–25, 2001. Richter, a diarist since the age of twenty-six, had been charged with keeping a daily account of his unit's operations.

In March 2001, President Ciampi visited Cephalonia to honor murdered Acqui soldiers, saying they had written "one of the most honorable chapters in Italian history." The value of the Cephalonia massacre for twentieth-century Italian national identity was soaring as: Division Acqui's "conscious decision [to resist the Wehrmacht] was the first act of resistance by an Italy freed from fascism . . . They preferred to fight and die for their fatherland."[72] Ciampi also apologized to Greece for Italy's actions and inferred that Italy would like to receive a similar gesture from Germany.

During the same year, the Mountain Troops' war crimes became a focal point of activists concerned about the honest commemoration of World War history. As awareness of the Cephalonia massacre and the leading role that the Wehrmacht's Mountain Troops had played there became more widespread, German, Italian, and Greek activists began an annual protest in Mittenwald coinciding with the annual reunions of the Mountain Troops' *Kameradenkreis*. Dozens of veterans deployed to Cephalonia at the time of the massacre were among the thousands attending the annual *Kameradenkreis* meetings, according to protest organizers, AK Angreifbare Traditionspflege and the Organization of those Persecuted by the Nazis (Vereinigung der Verfolgten des Naziregimes-Bund der Antifaschistinnen und Antifaschisten).[73] Bavarian Minister-President Edmund Stoiber, a member of the *Kameradenkreis*, greeted and formally addressed the association on several occasions. In 2002, the first year activists protested the Mountain Troops'

71 Christiane Kohl, "Vertuschte Massaker," *Süddeutsche Zeitung*, November 13, 2000; Ranier Blasius, "Umfassend erforscht und dokumentiert: Das Massaker auf Kephalonia 1943 wurde weder verheimlicht noch vertuscht," *Frankfurter Allgemeine Zeitung*, November 14, 2000.

72 Christiane Kohl, "Italiens Staatspräsident und ein Wehrmachtsverbrechen," *Süddeutsche Zeitung*, March 5, 2001; Tony Paterson, "Germans face charges over Massacre on 'Corelli island,'" *The Sunday Telegraph* (London), September 28, 2002.

73 See, for example, the VVN's "Dokumentation zu Wehrmachtsverbrechen, u.a. zu dem Mord von Kephalonia," *Barge*, 22.

annual reunion, they observed veterans wearing medals adorned with the swastika, a criminal act in Germany. The judiciary began an investigation but discontinued it for lack of evidence.[74]

Protesters went to Mittenwald to confront veterans with the crimes of their Wehrmacht units and to provide opportunities for survivors to speak publicly and present their narratives. But protesters who confronted veterans at the hotel where the meeting was taking place were driven out forcibly amid insults ("garbage filth"), arrested, and charged with "disturbing the peace" and "defamation." The protesters have nonetheless continued their efforts.[75]

At the Central Office for the Investigation of Nazi-Era Crimes, meanwhile, senior prosecutor Ulrich Maaß, Obluda's successor, had reopened the Cephalonia investigation as the stakes were escalating and the press was eager to report his progress. Reporters from different European countries wrote that the Cold War had hindered efforts to bring German suspects to justice. According to Maaß, however, documents newly available from the former GDR provided a new "information base." Two hundred suspects who had lived "out of reach" behind the Berlin Wall, including nine officers and a non-commissioned officer, could now be "held accountable." No one was to escape justice any longer. The question, he said in 2001, was whether the men who carried out the massacre knew that they were following an order "aimed at military crime or malfeasance." That would establish guilt according to the old German military criminal code from the time.[76] Two years later, stating that the investigation could well bring some ten persons under indictment, Maaß noted that the statute of limitations had long since eliminated the possibility of charges for "manslaughter," and proving charges of "murder" would not be easy. The Mountain Troops still "have a good lobby," he added.[77]

Nevertheless, in May 2004, Maaß reported that his preparations for the indictment of two suspects were "about to conclude" (*abschlussreif*).[78] Having collected thousands of pages of evidence, including testimony from Wehrmacht veterans and eyewitnesses, written reports, and archival documents, Maaß had prepared materials for the indictment of two former soldiers. Since they lived in Bavaria, Maaß passed his materials on to Senior

74 Joachim F. Tornau, "NS-Orden stören den soldatischen Schulterschluss in Mittenwald nicht," *Frankfurter Rundschau*, May 21, 2002.

75 Author's interview with arrested protester Markus Mohr, May 17, 2007, Washington, DC.

76 Christiane Kohl, "Angst vom dem Kriegsgericht," *Süddeutsche Zeitung*, December 11, 2001.

77 Author's interview with Senior Prosecutor Ulrich Maaß, June 21, 2006, Dortmund.

78 Joachim F. Tornau, "Prozess über Massaker von Kephalonia steht kurz bevor," *Frankfurter Rundschau*, May 27, 2004.

Prosecutor August Stern of Munich, but one of the two soldiers died before Stern decided whether to pursue prosecution.

In July 2006, Stern issued an eight-page statement on the surviving suspect Ottmar Mühlauser, a former lieutenant in the Wehrmacht who had admitted giving orders to execute Italian troops. There was no evidence to charge Mühlhauser with murder, according to Stern, and the statute of limitations on manslaughter had already expired. According to German law, murder is defined as killing for base (*niedrig*) motives, such as killing someone for belonging to a particular political, social, or ethnic group. Stern found that the Wehrmacht had executed thousands of Acqui soldiers and officers without "political motive" and that "military needs" (*Belange*) led to the shootings. Thus the suspect could claim "human weakness" (*menschliche Schwäche*) in his defense.

Had Stern stuck to the argument that there was insufficient evidence to try Mühlhauser for murder, his decision would have caused less outrage. But he also cited Italy's alliance with Germany in the 1939 "Pact of Steel" and maintained that the massacred Italian troops were roughly equivalent to German soldiers who deserted and sided with the enemy: turning from their alliance they became "fiercely fighting enemies and thus, in the parlance of the military, 'traitors.'" The greatest outcry arose over Stern's use of the word "traitor," which pushed any surviving, guilt-ridden soldiers back into the state of denial that characterized the postwar era, while at the same time insulting Wehrrmacht deserters.

Stern's decision and its rationale caused a storm of protest from Italians, Greeks, and highly energized groups of activists in Germany, where, in glaring contrast to the much trumpeted reopening of the case a few years earlier, it received little notice. Across Italy, thousands protested publicly. The daily *La Repubblica* denounced Stern, accusing him of whitewashing history, trampling the memories of a fellow NATO and EU country, and legitimizing one of the "most atrocious" Nazi massacres of Italians, which could give confidence to neo-Nazis. Marcella De Negri, the daughter of one of the Wehrmacht's Cephalonia victims and an organizer of the campaign to protest Stern's decision, said it insulted her father and his fellow soldiers.[79] Fifty-one senators and fifty-five members of Italy's parliament signed a letter of protest, and on December 8, 2006, some traveled to Munich to protest in person a decision that "throws out the window" the

79 Andrea Tarquini, "A Cephalonia erano traditori – sentenza choc in Germani," *La Repubblica* [Rome], September 22, 2006.

decisions of the Nuremberg trials. Senator José Luís Del Roio, who pointedly repudiated the aggressive wars launched by Fascist Italy and thus in his name, said that Stern was perpetuating Nazi ideas. Senator Claudio Brassi called Stern's decision "reason for shame" and his rationale for it "unacceptable." The Italian Foreign Ministry formally expressed indignation to its Berlin counterpart about Stern's rationale and his use of the words "traitor" and "deserters."[80]

Stern's decision not to prosecute and the protests against it have cast a spotlight on the efforts of survivors and protesters to draw attention to this war crime and a Wehrmacht unit that was implicated in more than a few. Activists have drawn attention to the Mountain Troops' still unpunished crimes and may well play a critical role in determining public memory of this branch of the Wehrmacht in the future. In 2007, in the wake of Stern's decision, the Cephalonia massacre was the focal point of the protest in Mittenwald as the Mountain Troops' *Kameradenkreis* met to celebrate its fiftieth anniversary.

Judged by the stability of its democracy and rejection of extreme right political movements, the Federal Republic of Germany's confrontation with the Nazi past has been a success. Recent German political leaders have acted to soothe rather than inflame survivors and activists. Speaking to Bundeswehr commanders in November 1995, Defense Minister Volker Rühe (CDU) said that the Wehrmacht's role in World War II precluded it, as an institution, from serving as "the founder of traditions." His speech "marked an end to decades of debate" about that matter within the Bundeswehr.[81] In April 2000, German President Johannes Rau (SPD) traveled to the Greek village of Kalavryta to apologize for the massacre the Mountain Troops had committed there.

If the myth that the Wehrmacht was unblemished had at one time served to democratize, as some have argued, Germany's democracy is now strong enough to dispatch with that service.[82] The present democratic strongholds in turn present opportunities for reversing missed opportunities to convict Wehrmacht soldiers. For, as a German political scientist argues in this

80 Statement of Vittorio Craxi, Deputy Secretary of State for Foreign Policy, Stenographical Report of Parliament Assembly, December 12, 2006, p. 93 (legxv.camera.it/_dati/lavori/stenografici/sed083/s330.htm). PDS-Munich, "Italienische Delegation protestiert am 8.12. in München gegen Einstellung des Verfahrens gegen einen Kriegsverbrecher," *mitLinks* Nummer 17, December 14, 2006: www.gegen-krieg-und-rassismus.de.

81 Wette, *Wehrmacht*, 276.

82 Klaus Naumann's concise social history of the myth of "The 'Unblemished' Wehrmacht" argues that it has served democratizing purposes: "The 'Unblemished' Wehrmacht: The Social History of a Myth," in Heer and Naumann, *War of Extermination*, 417–29.

volume, because the FRG judiciary was unwilling to acknowledge the collapse of the rule of law under Nazism, it had to "normalize" the Nazi administration of justice, thereby justifying the continued work in the FRG of judges who had served the Nazi regime. The judiciary categorized Nazi perpetrators as accomplices and thus as not culpable, transforming genocide into a seemingly lawful act, and abrogating the right to life as a basic right guaranteed by the FRG constitution.[83]

The current German judiciary's verdict on Wehrmacht crimes is no longer cast from a society that lived virtually in consensus about Hitler as during the early postwar period, and Cold War pressures no longer apply. Generations after the crimes, members of the FRG judiciary who had served Nazi "justice" have finally retired. Why has the FRG judiciary's reasoning not changed in step? Many of its critics today may well have understood a judgment of Mühlhauser that did not require the octogenarian to go to jail. Yet the judiciary could avoid a continuing castigation and disdain for the Wehrmacht's innocent victims, a posture that Klebe's wartime letters to his wife reveal was his attitude toward populations around the Balkans and the Mediterranean.[84]

During the Cold War, the wave of trials that would have been necessary to bring all war criminals in the FRG to justice would have been political "suicide" at home and hardly feasible internationally as well, according to Friedrich Rüter.[85] Does this mean that more should be expected of the post–Cold War FRG judiciary? If so, Ralf Giordano's verdict of the "second guilt" of perpetrator-countries in their failure to deal justice to agents of mass murder has never been more accurate in relation to Wehrmacht crimes.

83 Joachim Perels, "Perceptions and Suppression of Nazi Crimes by the Postwar German Judiciary," in this volume.

84 Author's interview with Senior Prosecutor Ulrich Maaß, June 21, 2006, Dortmund.

85 Rüter, quoted in Ulrich Sander, "Die Strafverfolgung Mörderischer Gebirgstruppler wird wieder Möglich, *Neues Deutschland*, December 5, 2002. Barge 22, 29.

8

The Trials of Nazi War Criminals in Austria

WINFRIED R. GARSCHA

Some of the worst Nazi butchers and a considerable number of those responsible for the major atrocities of the Holocaust were Austrians. A few examples will suffice:

(1) Odilo Globocnik, Hans Höfle, and Ernst Lerch, the men in charge of "Operation Reinhard," the killing of about 1.8 million Jews and Gypsies in the extermination camps of eastern Poland during 1942 and 1943;[1]
(2) Franz Stangl, commandant of the Treblinka extermination camp and onetime deputy to the senior supervisor of the "euthanasia" killing center Hartheim in Upper Austria;[2]
(3) Siegfried Seidl, commandant of the Theresienstadt ghetto in Bohemia;
(4) Franz Murer, who was responsible for the supply of the Vilnius ghetto in Lithuania; his name was preserved in the songs of the starving Jews of the ghetto.[3]

The list could be continued. In addition, we should not forget that 70 percent of Adolf Eichmann's staff were Austrians.

The fact that thousands of Austrians had been part of the Nazi extermination machine was hardly acknowledged in Austria itself until the onset of the Waldheim debate in the 1980s. That conflict shook Austrian society and changed Austrian attitudes toward the Nazi past.[4] In 1991, the Austrian government assumed responsibility for acts Austrians had committed during the Nazi period.[5] Until that point, all Austrian governments had maintained

1 See Adalbert Rückerl, *NS-Vernichtungslager im Spiegel deutscher Strafprozesse* (Munich, 1977).

2 Henry Friedlander, *The Origins of Nazi Genocide: From Euthanasia to the Final Solution* (Chapel Hill, 1995), 204–6.

3 Florian Freund, Franz Rutter, and Hans Safrian, *Ess firt kejn weg zurik . . . Geschichten und Lieder des Ghettos von Wilna, 1941–1943* (Vienna, 1992), 157.

4 See Richard Mitten, *The Politics of Antisemitic Prejudice: The Waldheim Phenomenon in Austria* (San Francisco, 1992).

5 Austrian government declaration, July 8, 1991. The complete text was published in *Wiener Zeitung*, July 9, 1991.

that Austria could not be held responsible for crimes committed between 1938 and 1945 because Austria had been part of the German Reich during that period and the state had therefore not existed.

During the vehement debates over the Waldheim affair and Austria's Nazi past, a certain Martin Bartesch arrived in Vienna. A native of Romania who had been a member of the Nazi Party and had served in the SS, Bartesch had emigrated from Austria to America after the war and became a citizen of the United States by hiding his Nazi past. In May 1987, to avoid a trial and eventual deportation, Bartesch came to an agreement with the U.S. Office of Special Investigations whereby he would voluntarily leave the United States and give up his U.S. citizenship. He departed for Austria in June 1987; his denaturalization became final in 1989. After Bartesch arrived in Vienna, former inmates of the Mauthausen concentration camp recognized him and identified him as the murderer of Alfred Oxhorn, a popular and respected Jewish camp inmate. The Mauthausen survivors called for judicial proceedings to punish the killer, and they erected a memorial to Oxhorn in a market square of one of Vienna's old Jewish quarters.

Austrian authorities initiated proceedings against Bartesch, but the state attorney did not charge him. The statute of limitations had expired because Bartesch had been a minor at the time he committed the murder. During the discussion of the handling of this case by the Austrian authorities, some Austrian officials criticized the U.S. government for not transmitting the records of its investigation of Bartesch – as if there never had been any Mauthausen trial in Austria itself. In this way, Austrian authorities reinforced the widely held belief that Austria had made no serious attempt to proceed against Nazi war criminals.

At the time of the Bartesch affair, more than a decade had passed since the last Austrian trial of a Nazi criminal. That had been the trial of Johann Vinzenz Gogl, a former guard at the Mauthausen concentration camp. Gogl had been acquitted in 1972 by a jury in Linz, although the evidence against him was overwhelming. The verdict was subsequently overturned, and the Supreme Court ordered a retrial in Vienna. In 1975, Gogl was acquitted again. It would be twenty-five years before another accused Nazi murderer stood trial in Austria.

During the 1960s and 1970s, even as major trials of suspected Nazi criminals were under way in West Germany, Austrian society seemed almost willing to grant mass murderers immunity. The few trials that did take place in Austria in these years were often the result of private investigations undertaken by Holocaust survivors like Simon Wiesenthal. And often the juries at these trials refused to convict defendants even when the evidence against them was conclusive. Some of these trials provoked international scandals:

(1) Franz Murer was acquitted by a jury in Graz (Styria). During the trial, the judge had allowed the defense and the courtroom audience to mock Jewish witnesses; the verdict was welcomed enthusiastically by the audience when it was announced.
(2) The state attorney in Klagenfurt (Carinthia) dropped the charge against Ernst Lerch two days into the trial.[6] Lerch had been Odilo Globocnik's adjudant at the time of the mass murders of Operation Reinhard; he had also been responsible for killing hundreds of partisans in and near Trieste.
(3) A Viennese jury acquitted Robert Jan Verbelen, a former officer of the Flemish SS in Nazi-occupied Belgium, of five charges of murder. Verbelen, having fled to Austria from Belgium, had been sentenced to death in absentia in Brussels in 1946 for atrocious war crimes. In Austria, he worked for the U.S. Army's Counter Intelligence Corps and eventually acquired Austrian citizenship. Austria's Supreme Court partially overturned Verbelen's acquittal, but he was never again brought to trial.[7]
(4) It required four trials over a period of eight years to reach a verdict on Franz Novak, Adolf Eichmann's infamous "station master of death," that was not overturned by the supreme court. One of the rejected verdicts was an acquittal.[8]
(5) A Viennese court acquitted two Austrian engineers, Fritz Ertl and Walter Dejaco, who had constructed the gas chambers of Auschwitz.[9]

This list could go on. After another Auschwitz trial in Vienna ended scandalously with a second acquittal in 1972,[10] Austrian state attorneys ceased to issue indictments for Nazi crimes. By 1978, all pending cases had been abandoned. In public debate, the minister of justice argued that

6 On Murer and Lerch, see Eva Holpfer and Sabine Loitfellner, "Holocaustprozesse wegen Massenerschiessungen und Verbrechen in Lagern im Osten vor österreichischen Geschworenengerichten: Annäherung an ein unerforschtes Thema," in *Holocaust und Kriegsverbrechen vor Gericht: Der Fall Österreich*, ed. Thomas Albrich, Winfried R. Garscha, and Martin F. Polaschek (Innsbruck, Vienna, and Bolzano, 2006), 87–126; Marion Wisinger, "Über den Umgang der österreichischen Justiz mit nationalsozialistischen Gewaltverbrechen," Ph.D. diss., University of Vienna, 1991.

7 Winfried R. Garscha, "'Taten, die den allgemein anerkannten Grundsätzen des Völkerrechts und des Kriegsrechts widersprechen.' Prozesse wegen Verletzung des Kriegsvölkerrechts," in Albrich et al., *Holocaust und Kriegsverbrechen*, 262–78.

8 Winfried R. Garscha, "Holocaust On Trial: The Deportation of the Viennese Jews Between 1941 and 1942 and the Austrian Judiciary After 1945," in *Austria and the European Union*, ed. Günter Bischof, Anton Pelinka, and Michael Gehler, *Contemporary Austrian Studies* vol. 10 (Somerset, NJ, 2002), 288–97; Eva Holpfer, "Ich war nichts anderes als ein kleiner Sachbearbeiter von Eichmann": Die justizielle Ahndung von Deportationsverbrechen in Österreich, in Albrich et al., *Holocaust und Kriegsverbrechen*, 151–82.

9 Sabine Loitfellner, "Auschwitz-Verfahren in Österreich: Hintergründe und Ursachen eines Scheiterns," in Albrich et al., *Holocaust und Kriegsverbrechen*, 183–97.

10 Winfried R. Garscha, "'My memory hasn't faded. I wish it would have!' Foreign Witnesses in Nazi Crimes Trials in Austria and the Austrian Judicial System of the 1960s and 1970s," in *Beyond Camps and Forced Labor*, ed. Johannes-Dieter Steinert and Inge Weber-Newth (Osnabrück, 2005), CD-ROM.

further trials would be fruitless. The state attorneys stopped all preliminary proceedings at an early stage, like the above-mentioned proceedings against Martin Bartesch.

It was not until 1992 that Austrian authorities investigated a Holocaust-related case. Emil Sabukoschek, a well-known dentist in Graz (Styria), turned out to be identical with a young ethnic German SS officer in occupied Serbia who had been involved in the mass deportation of Jews from Belgrade in 1942. But soon after the start of the preliminary investigation, Sabukoschek died of a stroke. There was no trial.

It became known in the late 1970s that Heinrich Gross, one of Austria's foremost experts on mental illness, had been involved in the Nazis' so-called euthanasia program. Ruling in a defamation case in 1982, a Viennese appeals court noted that Gross had been responsible for the deaths of a "great number" of children. Nonetheless, state attorneys refused to indict him on the grounds that participation in the Nazi euthanasia program constituted manslaughter, not murder, and the statute of limitations on manslaughter had expired. The minister of justice ordered a new investigation and asked the state attorneys to leave it to the jury to decide whether the killing of mentally ill children was murder or manslaughter. Gross was indicted for murder in 1999, but his trial in 2000 lasted less than one hour. He pretended not to be able to follow the proceedings, but shortly after leaving the courtroom he gave a press conference in a nearby café. The trial never resumed, and Gross died in 2005.

Although a few cases are still pending, it is unlikely that any of the suspected Nazi murderers still alive will have to stand trial in Austria. Half a century of investigations of Nazi crimes by the Austrian judiciary led to thirty-five trials against forty-eight defendants. The proceedings against forty-three of the forty-eight defendants concluded with verdicts: twenty were convicted and twenty-three acquitted. Five of the convictions were for charges arising from the mass murder of Jews in Galicia. Four involved the murder of Poles and Jews in central Poland. One of the convicted defendants had been an adjutant to Amon Göth, the infamous commandant of the Plaszow concentration camp on the outskirts of Cracow who later became a well-known figure as a result of Steven Spielberg's movie *Schindler's List*. The state attorneys focused their investigations on Austrians who had been involved in Operation Reinhard (more than 300 SS men), who had served as guards or SS officers in the Auschwitz-Birkenau extermination camp (roughly 60 men), or who had served in police battalions (several hundred men). Only seven out of these perpetrators had to stand trial, and not one was found guilty by a jury.

These figures do not tell the entire story, however. Attitudes toward Nazi criminals had been very different in Austria during the immediate postwar period. The trials of war criminals during the 1960s and 1970s actually had very little in common with the trials conducted between 1945 and 1955 in the so-called people's courts (*Volksgerichte*).[11]

The people's courts were established under the *Verbotsgesetz,* the Nazi Prohibition Act, which was promulgated on May 8, 1945, by the Austrian provisional government established twelve days earlier. Until the surrender of the German Reich, the Austrian provisional government's jurisdiction extended only about 25 miles to the west and 40 miles to the south of Vienna. The provisional government had been established under Soviet auspices, but, the initial skepticism of the Western Allies notwithstanding, it was not a Soviet puppet. It included members of the conservative People's Party, the Socialist Party, and the Communist Party. On October 20, 1945, the Western Allies also recognized the Austrian provisional government, which served as both executive and legislature until the parliamentary election of November 1945.

On June 26, 1945, the provisional government promulgated the War Criminals Act (*Kriegsverbrechergesetz*). The following eight articles of this law defined the crimes and the conditions under which they were to be tried before the people's courts. In brief, the War Criminals Act addressed:

(1) War crimes and crimes against the "natural demands of humanity";
(2) Incitement to launch wars of aggression;
(3) Torture and acts of cruelty (such offenses were assumed to have been committed by members of the Gestapo, the SS Secret Service (SD), and concentration camp staff);
(4) Violation of human dignity;
(5) Superior orders: this article ruled out superior orders as a defense for offenses under Articles 3 and 4, and it stipulated that those who ordered actions covered by those articles should be punished more severely than those who carried them out;
(6) Illegal enrichment (this article covered cases of "Aryanization" of Jewish property);
(7) Acts of denunciation;
(8) High Treason against the Austrian nation, including propaganda and other forms of agitation in favor of the 1938 *Anschluss* by individuals in influential

11 Albrich et al., *Holocaust und Kriegsverbrechen*. The first scholarly analysis of the people's courts was published by Dieter Stiefel, *Entnazifizierung in Österreich* (Vienna, 1981); the first statistics were published by the Ministry of Justice: Karl Marschall, *Volksgerichtsbarkeit und Verfolgung von nationalsozialistischen Gewaltverbrechen in Österreich: Eine Dokumentation*, 2nd ed. (Vienna, 1987). See also Winfried R. Garscha and Claudia Kuretsidis-Haider, "Justice and Nazi Crimes in Austria, 1945–1955: Between Self-Purge and Allied Control," *Bulletin du comité international d'histoire de la deuxième guerre mondiale* 27–28 (1995): 245–55.

> positions, membership in the illegal Nazi movement prior to 1938 as well as sponsorship of the movement by nonmembers (applied also against cabinet members and members of the senior civil service whose actions prepared the way for the *Anschluss*). The most famous case under this article was the trial against the last pre-1938 minister of foreign affairs, Guido Schmidt, who was acquitted of high treason against the Austrian nation in June 1947 after a trial that lasted nearly four months.[12]

The most significant articles, especially for historians, were the three concerning crimes against humanity, acts of cruelty, and violation of human dignity. Most of the people indicted under the War Criminals Act, however, were charged with violations of Article 7 involving denunciation.

In late 1945, an amendment to the War Criminals Act, Article 5a, expanded the scope of the law. Article 5a, covering the crimes of expulsion, expropriation, evacuation, and resettlement, was designed to penalize those who participated in the deportation of Austrian Jews to the extermination camps. This article was added after delegates from the southern Austrian province of Carinthia demanded that amendment at the "conference of the provinces."[13] Article 5a was originally intended to make possible the prosecution of those who had taken part in the resettlement and dispossession of the Slovenian minority in Carinthia, not those who organized the Holocaust. The fact that the members of the Austrian provisional government did not really comprehend what had happened to the Jews was first brought to Austrian public attention by the British historian Robert Knight, who published extracts from the minutes of the provisional government's cabinet meetings in 1988.[14]

Like similar laws passed after the war in other European countries in both the East and West, most articles of the Austrian War Criminals Act were retroactive. They also preceded the London Charter of the Nuremberg International Military Tribunal of August 8, 1945.

The people's courts were composed of two professional judges and three lay judges, with one of the professional judges serving as the court's presiding judge. The Department of Justice (as the Ministry of Justice was called until the end of 1945) selected the three lay judges from a list of eligible candidates

12 See *Der Hochverratsprozess gegen Dr. Guido Schmidt vor dem Wiener Volksgericht: Die gerichtlichen Protokolle mit den Zeugenaussagen, unveröffentlichten Dokumenten, sämtlichen Geheimbriefen und Geheimakten* (Vienna, 1947).

13 The so-called *Länderkonferenz* of September 1945 was a meeting of representatives from each Austrian province, including those occupied by the Western Allies, to negotiate the extension of the provisional government's jurisdiction to include the whole of Austria's territory; as mentioned above, the provisional government had until that time been recognized only by the Soviets.

14 Robert Knight, "Ich bin dafür, die Sache in die Länge zu ziehen," *Wortprotokolle der österreichischen Regierung von 1945–52 über die Entschädigung der Juden* (Frankfurt, 1988).

compiled by the three parties that formed the provisional government. Finding professional judges presented a problem because the overwhelming majority of them had served in the Nazi judicial system, which meant that they were no longer eligible to perform judicial duties.[15]

The most distinctive feature of the rules governing trials before the people's courts was the abrogation of the right to object to an indictment, the right of appeal. Judgments delivered by the people's courts were to be carried out without reprieves. However, the presiding judge of the supreme court could bring a case before a commission of supreme court judges if he had reasonable doubts about the lawfulness of a sentence. This commission could reverse judgments (both convictions and acquittals) and refer the case for another trial before a different people's court. Soon it became the most important task of the defense to convince the presiding judge of the supreme court that reasonable doubts existed. After 1948, a great number of convicted Nazi war criminals successfully demanded a retrial.

Four people's courts functioned in Austria – one in each Allied occupation zone – with seats in Vienna (Soviet zone), Graz (British zone), Linz (American zone), and Innsbruck (French zone). The Western Allies did not authorize Austrian courts, including the people's courts, to operate until early 1946. The earliest trials before a people's court were thus held only in the Soviet zone. The first trial of the Viennese people's court opened on August 14, 1945.

In the ten years of their existence, the Austrian people's courts launched investigations of 137,000 individuals suspected of committing crimes covered by the *Verbotsgesetz* and the War Criminals Act. As 550,000 Austrians had been members of the Nazi Party, the figures indicate that one out of four party members was interrogated by an investigating magistrate; 108,000 of them were under formal investigation by early 1948. These proceedings resulted in trials against 28,000 suspects. Of those tried, about 40 percent were indicted for crimes covered by the War Criminals Act as well as for crimes under the *Verbotsgesetz*; the remainder were charged only with crimes set out in the *Verbotsgesetz*, such as high treason.[16] Of those tried, 13,600 (48 percent) were convicted and sentenced. The courts imposed forty-three death sentences, and thirty of those were actually carried out;

15 This was true only for the criminal jurisdiction. A considerable number of ex-Nazi judges served in the civil law jurisdiction.

16 See the official statistics in Manfred Schausberger, "Die Verfolgung von NS-Gewaltverbrechen in Österreich," in *Nationalsozialismus und Justiz: Die Aufarbeitung von Gewaltverberchen damals und heute*, Agenda Geschichte 3 (Münster, 1993), 198–220; an updated version had been published under the same title in Claudia Kuretsidis-Haider and Winfried R. Garscha, eds., *Keine "Abrechnung." NS-Verbrechen, Justiz und Gesellschaft in Europa nach 1945* (Leipzig and Vienna, 1998), 25–31.

two convicts sentenced to death committed suicide before they could be executed. Twenty-nine of the defendants found guilty were sentenced to life imprisonment, and 350 received prison sentences of ten years or longer.

The people's courts did not impose death sentences after 1948 and sentenced only six defendants to life imprisonment after that year. In the 1950s, the majority of convicted war criminals were granted pardons. Many of those who were not pardoned were granted new trials; retrials usually resulted in dismissal, acquittal, or a reduced sentence.

Dismissals and acquittals had also occurred during the early trials in the people's courts, especially when the defendant was a judge or a state attorney. Still, unlike the courts in the Federal Republic of Germany, the Austrian people's courts did convict a few jurists, including the presiding judge of the appeals court for Styria and Carinthia and the attorney general for Vienna.

The people's courts also treated physicians rather gently. Consequently, the court records show doctors to have been much more deeply involved in the "destruction of unworthy life," as the murder of the handicapped was termed, than the verdicts the courts handed down might suggest.[17] Physicians did receive harsh sentences, however, if the state could prove that they personally had played an active part in committing murder. In April 1946, the permanent senate in Klagenfurt, Carinthia, of the people's court in Graz, imposed four death sentences. The convicted defendants were Franz Niedermoser, the director of the lunatic asylum in Klagenfurt who was responsible for between 500 and 600 murders, and three nurses; only Niedermoser was executed. In July 1947, Ernst Illing, who was responsible for the murder of at least 250 children in Vienna, was sentenced to death by the Viennese people's court. Another physician was sentenced to fifteen years' imprisonment, and a third physician received a prison sentence of ten years. The fifteen-year sentence was later reduced to six and a half years in a retrial, however, and the physician who was sentenced to ten years' imprisonment was again practicing medicine in Vienna in the 1950s.

In December 1955, six months after the conclusion of the State Treaty between Austria and the four Allied powers, the parliament abolished the people's courts.[18] Thereafter, the prosecution of Nazi war criminals became

17 The best survey is Peter Malina and Wolfgang Neugebauer, "NS-Gesundheitswesen und Medizin," in *NS-Herrschaft in Österreich. Ein Handbuch*, ed. Emmerich Tálos, Ernst Hanisch, Wolfgang Neugebauer, and Reinhard Sieder (Vienna, 2000), 696–720; on the postwar trials, see Martin Achrainer and Peter Ebner, "'Es gibt kein unwertes Leben': Die Strafverfolgung der 'Euthanasie'-Verbrechen," in Albrich et al., *Holocaust und Kriegsverbrechen*, 57–86.

18 On the connection between the State Treaty and abolition of the people's courts, see Brigitte Bailer and Winfried R. Garscha, "Der österreichische Staatsvertrag und die Entnazifizierung," in

the duty of the standard Austrian courts – with dismal results. Between 1956 and 1975, only forty-eight individuals were charged with Nazi-era crimes, and only twenty of them were convicted. As noted above, no suspected Nazi war criminal has been brought to trial in Austria since 1975 except for the physician Heinrich Gross, whose trial was quickly suspended.

Although the thousands of trials before the postwar people's courts were of great significance in Austria, only a few received international attention. The main reason for this was timing: the people's courts were only active during the immediate postwar years when the Allies themselves were prosecuting the major Nazi war criminals and other prominent Nazis were assuming new identities to escape justice. The United States, for example, tried numerous Austrian war criminals before military commissions. Austrians involved in the murder of U.S. pilots were tried in Salzburg,[19] for example, and those who had served in the concentration camps were tried at Dachau.[20] Other Austrians were tried before the military courts of the other Allies. Austrian authorities had to supply the Allies with lists of all arrested Nazi war criminals on a regular basis. Furthermore, many Austrian war criminals were extradited to the countries in which they committed their crimes. For instance, the Austrian Gestapo officer Maximilian Grabner, who had served as chief of the political department at Auschwitz, was extradited to Poland. There, he was tried, convicted, and executed.

The Austrians did bring some relatively prominent war criminals to trial. One was Siegfried Seidl, who had served as commandant of the Theresienstadt ghetto. Seidl had been jailed in Vienna in September 1945. Although Seidl was supposed to be extradited to Czechoslovakia, the people's court in Vienna did not turn him over because the Austrians wanted a chance at a high-profile trial. Seidl's trial started in Vienna just as the trial of the major war criminals ended in Nuremberg. Seidl's trial lasted a week and resulted in his conviction. He was sentenced to death on October 4, 1946, and executed in Vienna on February 4, 1947.

Anton Brunner was another leading Nazi criminal tried by the people's courts. He had been one of the so-called Eichmann Men responsible for the

Der österreichische Staatsvertrag 1955. Internationale Strategie, rechtliche Relevanz, nationale Identität/The Austrian State Treaty 1955. International Strategy, Legal Relevance, National Identity, ed. Arnold Suppan, Gerald Stourzh, and Wolfgang Mueller (Vienna, 2005), 629–54.

19 Kurt Tweraser, "Amerikanische Kriegsverbrecherprozesse in Salzburg: Anmerkungenzur justitiellen Verfolgung von Kriegsverbrechern in der amerikanischen Besatzungszone in Österreich, 1945–1955," in Kuretsidis-Haider and Garscha, *Keine "Abrechnung,"* 66–101.

20 On the Mauthausen trials at Dachau, see Florian Freund, "Der Dachauer Mauthausenprozess," in Dokumentationsarchiv des österreichischen Widerstandes, *Jahrbuch 2001* (Vienna, 2001), 35–66.

deportation of Austrian Jews to the extermination camps in the East.[21] He is often referred to as Brunner II to avoid confusion with Alois Brunner, Adolf Eichmann's most important colleague in Vienna. Alois Brunner survived in hiding and in 1954 managed to escape to Syria. Anton Brunner was tried before the people's court in Vienna in 1946, convicted, and sentenced to death.

The first trial before a people's court of Vienna concerned the killing of Hungarian Jewish slave laborers in Engerau, a village south of Brattislava. Toward the end of the war, more than 500 Hungarian Jews died of starvation and ill treatment at the small labor camps in Engerau; more than one hundred were killed in March 1945 during the evacuation of the camps. The first of an eventual six Engerau trials took place in August 1945 and resulted in three death sentences, which were carried out in November 1945. Another five trials were conducted over the next nine years.[22] The second Engerau trial started in Vienna in November 1945 and resulted in two death sentences, which were carried out in February 1946. The third Engerau trial took place in October and November 1946 and resulted in four death sentences, which were carried out in July 1947.

The torture and murder of Hungarian Jews along the Austro-Hungarian border during the last days of the war was linked to the German effort to stop Soviet troops by a system of trenches and mounds, the so-called Southeast Rampart (*Südost-Wall*). The rampart was primarily built by slave laborers, including many Jews from Hungary.[23] After the war, legal proceedings were instituted against hundreds of individuals suspected of having committed crimes during the construction and the evacuation of the Southeast Rampart. In addition to the convictions in the Engerau trials, death sentences were handed down for the murder of Hungarian Jews in Güns (Köszeg), Ödenburg (Sopron) in Hungary, and in Reinersdorf, a village in the southern part of the Austrian province Burgenland.[24]

Two of the largest Southeast Rampart trials dealt with massacres carried out in the small Burgenland villages Rechnitz and Deutsch-Schützen.[25] In

21 See Hans Safrian, *Die Eichmann-Männer* (Vienna, 1993).

22 Claudia Kuretsidis-Haider, *"Das Volk sitzt zu Gericht": Österreichische Justiz und NS-Verbrechen am Beispiel der Engerau-Prozesse 1945–1954* (Innsbruck, 2006).

23 See Szabolcs Szita, "The Forced Labor of Hungarian Jews at the Fortification of the Western Border Regions of Hungary, 1944–45," in *Studies on the Holocaust in Hungary*, ed. Randolph L. Braham (New York, 1990), 175–93.

24 For a survey of the trials for crimes in the last phase of the war, see Susanne Uslu-Pauer, "'Vernichtungswut und Kadavergehorsam': Strafrechtliche Verfolgung von Endphaseverbrechen am Beispiel der so genannten Todesmärsche," in Albrich et al., *Holocaust und Kriegsverbrechen*, 279–304.

25 Eva Holpfer, "Der Umgang der burgenländischen Nachkriegsgesellschaft mit NS-Verbrechen bis 1955 am Beispiel der wegen der Massaker von Deutsch-Schützen und Rechnitz geführten Volksgerichtsprozesse," M.A. thesis, University of Vienna, 1998.

Deutsch-Schützen, the individuals responsible escaped; their accomplices, who were minors at the time of the killings, were arrested at school a year later and did stand trial. In the mid-1950s, one of those most responsible for the massacre was caught, but he benefited from the trend toward more lenient treatment of Nazi war criminals; he was acquitted in 1956.[26]

The largest trial before an Austrian people's court concerned the mass murders in the Stein an der Donau Prison on April 6, 1945. On that day, several prison guards, together with members of the SS and the Volkssturm, killed more than 300 inmates, mostly Austrian, Czech, and Greek political prisoners. Five senior prison officials, including the prison director Franz Kodré, were also murdered because they had ordered the prisoners freed. The trial of fifteen defendants before the people's court of Vienna lasted four weeks in August 1946. It concluded with five death sentences and five sentences of life imprisonment; one defendant was sentenced to three years in prison, and the remaining four defendants were acquitted. The death sentences were carried out in February and March 1947, after the defense was unable to get the proceedings reopened and the defendants' clemency petitions had been rejected. Four Nazi prison guards and the commander of the Volkssturm unit were executed. The commander of the SS unit escaped to Germany; he lived untroubled under his own name there, working as the director of tourism in a Bavarian summer resort near the Austrian border, until his death in the 1980s. The Nazi functionary most responsible, the Nazi Party district leader for Krems, had committed suicide before he could be arrested, as had his superior, the Gauleiter for Lower Austria.

The people's court of Vienna carefully documented the events of April 6, 1945 at the Stein an der Donau Prison. The court's ruling is an important historical document. On the fiftieth anniversary of the massacre, the Austrian Ministry of Justice and the Documentation Center of Austrian Resistance (Dokumentationsarchiv des österreichsichen Widerstandes) published the ruling together with a historical analysis and a foreword by Nikolaus Michalek, the then Austrian minister of justice.[27]

The records of the proceedings of the people's courts and of the Nazi war crimes trials before regular courts in Austria have been classified in the country's archives as material of permanent historical value; already the courts marked each folder "to be kept forever." There are virtually no restrictions on access to the records, but defendants' names may not be published until

26 In 1995, the mass graves of the victims of the massacre were discovered near Deutsch-Schützen. The mass grave of the victims of the Rechnitz massacre has not yet been found; in 1994, the futile search for this mass grave served as the theme of the touching Austrian film *Totschweigen* (A Wall of Silence), Directors: Margareta Heinrich and Eduard Erne (Austria/Germany, 1994).

27 Gerhard Jagschitz and Wolfgang Neugebauer, eds., *Stein, 6. April 1945: Das Urteil des Volksgerichts Wien (August 1946) gegen die Verantwortlichen des Massakers im Zuchthaus Stein* (Vienna, 1995).

fifty years after the end of the proceedings against them without a judge's approval. Thereafter, access to the records is controlled by the archives. The only real difficulty in using these documents for historical research is the insufficient cataloguing system. This is probably the reason historians had scarcely made use of this important source material until recently.

In 1999, the Austrian Research Center for Postwar Trials began to compile databases and other search aids (e.g., registers of all records concerning crimes in camps such as Mauthausen).[28] For the people's court of Linz, which had jurisdiction over the U.S. zone, a complete database is available at the Upper Austrian regional archive. Between 2002 and 2006, several Austrian academic institutions sponsored a research project on the court proceedings concerning Nazi crimes in which victims died (murder and manslaughter as well as other crimes, such as denunciation, that might result in the victim being killed). The teams of young historians and lawyers found 561 such trials involving 845 defendants. By comparison, there were 915 trials for such offenses in the Federal Republic of Germany, whose population is ten times larger than Austria's.[29] Of the 561 Austrian trials, 526 were held before people's courts.[30]

28 Peter Eigelsberger, "'Mauthausen vor Gericht.'" Die österreichischen Prozesse wegen Tötungsdelikten im KZ Mauthausen und seinen Aussenlagern," in Albrich et al., *Holocaust und Kriegsverbrechen*, 198–228.

29 C. F. Rüter and D. W. de Mildt, eds., *Die westdeutschen Strafverfahren wegen nationalsozialistischer Tötungsverbrechen 1945–1997. Eine systematische Verfahrensbeschreibung mit Karten und Registern* (Amsterdam, 1998). For updated versions, see http://www1.jur.uva.nl/junsv/.

30 Albrich et al., *Holocaust und Kriegsverbrechen*, 8.

9

The German-German Rivalry and the Prosecution of Nazi War Criminals During the Cold War, 1958–1965

ANNETTE WEINKE

In the spring of 1968, the West German Bundestag passed a seemingly inconspicuous amendment, known as the EGOWiG,[1] to the country's criminal code. Thanks to later court rulings, this provision retroactively established a de facto statute of limitations that barred the prosecution of most alleged perpetrators of Nazi crimes if they had not already been under investigation before 1960. This consequence was not yet clear in December 1968 when the right-wing conservative commentator Winfried Martini held a long lecture criticizing the entire practice of prosecuting Nazi crimes. Martini's lecture was later published under the title "The Nazi Trials in the Context of the East-West Conflict."[2] Before 1945, Martini had worked in the Foreign Office under Paul Carl Schmidt, the head of the Information and Press Division in Berlin. In the years after the war, he was a freelance contributor to *Rheinischer Merkur*, *Christ und Welt*, *Die Zeit*, and *Die Welt*.[3] In his talk, Martini raised fundamental objections to the idea of dealing with Nazi injustices through criminal law – thereby rejecting the course the Federal Republic had set out upon ten years earlier. Warning against a recent

I want to thank Nicholas E. Levis for his skillful translation of this essay; David Lazar of the German Historical Institute, Washington, DC, for his many thoughtful suggestions and fine editing; and, last but not least, the conveners and participants in the conference "Nazi Crimes and the Law" organized by the German Historical Institute, Washington, DC, and the University of Amsterdam for their valuable comments on my paper.

1 EGOWiG: Einführungsgesetz zum Ordnungswidrigkeitengesetz.

2 Winfried Martini, *Die NS-Prozesse im ost-westlichen Spannungsfeld* [The Nazi Trials in the Context of the East-West Conflict] (Pfaffenhofen, 1969).

3 Christina von Hodenberg, *Konsens und Krise. Eine Geschichte der westdeutschen Medienöffentlichkeit 1945–1973* (Göttingen, 2006).

United Nations resolution that lifted the statute of limitations on war crimes and crimes against humanity,[4] and looking ahead to yet another Bundestag debate on a statute of limitations for Nazi crimes, Martini appealed to West German legislators not to bend to "foreign pressure" for a second time. He argued that the internal consolidation of the Federal Republic instead required that "legal peace and quiet" finally be achieved and, for that reason, there should be an amnesty for Nazi perpetrators.[5] He also argued that an amnesty law was necessary because the Eastern bloc states were exploiting and promoting trials of suspected Nazi perpetrators as a means of defaming and isolating West Germany on the international stage. By selectively releasing documents and sending witnesses to such trials, the communist states intended "to gradually persuade the Western world, consciously or unconsciously, to identify West Germans with Nazi perpetrators and the Third Reich with the Federal Republic," Martini said. The Eastern bloc strategy was also meant to shake the political and social foundations of West Germany by creating a condition of "permanent domestic insecurity." Martini raised the frightening prospect that continuing the investigation and prosecution of Nazi-era crimes in West Germany would give "aid to the motives" of the Eastern bloc, subjecting the Federal Republic to "a process of gradual decay."[6]

Martini's overly dramatic plea for amnesty was overtaken by reality a few months later. In a May 1969 decision, the Federal Supreme Court (Bundesgerichtshof) ruled that the EGOWiG revision of Paragraph 50 II of the criminal code was applicable to Nazi perpetrators, with fatal consequences for investigations against high-ranking *Schreibtischtäter* (desk-bound perpetrators).[7] But the decisive stimulus for the public interventions by Martini and others did not really lie in the actual workings of the West German justice system. These commentators were more concerned with the overarching symbolism of attempts to address the Nazi past via the courts and with what they saw as the emblematic significance of the Nazi crimes trials within West German political culture. This is evident in the

4 Convention on the Non-Applicability of Statutory Limitations to War Crimes and Crimes against Humanity from November 26, 1968, 754 U.N.T.S. 73.

5 Martini, *NS-Prozesse*, 19.

6 Ibid., 12.

7 On the so-called cold amnesty, see Jörg Friedrich, *Die kalte Amnestie. NS-Täter in der Bundesrepublik* (Frankfurt/Main, 1985); Michael Greve, *Der justitielle und rechtspolitische Umgang mit den NS-Gewaltverbrechen in den sechziger Jahren* (Frankfurt/Main, 2001); Michael Wildt, *Generation des Unbedingten. Das Führungskorps des Reichssicherheitshauptamtes* (Hamburg, 2002); Marc von Miquel, *Ahnden oder amnestieren? Westdeutsche Justiz und Vergangenheitspolitik in den sechziger Jahren* (Göttingen, 2004).

rhetoric they repeatedly employed: the characterization of the Nazis' policy of genocide as an "excess" of modern mass society; the charge that the Allies had propagated the notion of German "collective guilt";[8] the contrast of "Germans" and "Jews"; the barely concealed resort to Nazi terminology;[9] and a crude anti-communism that saw any and all Eastern bloc assistance to West Germany in Nazi-related matters as an especially perfidious attempt to undermine the West German polity.

The Federal Republic's attempt to achieve retroactive "self-purification"[10] through criminal charges against alleged Nazi perpetrators began in the late 1950s within a narrow framework of political and legal provisos. This effort increasingly became the subject of controversy within the Federal Republic during the 1960s. The most radical and pronounced critiques came from those who fundamentally rejected the liberal strategy of a limited, legalistic approach for coming to terms with the past. Foremost among them were the ideologues of the "Free West," who saw themselves as front soldiers in a "Cold Civil War" and some intellectuals within the New Left.[11] Beyond the legal controversies surrounding the investigations of Nazi crimes and the body of court decisions, such critiques and the controversy surrounding the prosecution of suspected Nazi perpetrators, together with the press coverage of important court proceedings like the Auschwitz trial, gave rise to the notion of the "unmasterable past" (*unbewältigte Vergangenheit*) that still confronted the Federal Republic more than a decade after its founding.[12] On a pragmatic level, discussion of coming to terms with the Nazi past centered on the terms and scope of a legal response to the mass crimes of the Nazi regime. On the meta-level, it is clear that the conflicts

8 Norbert Frei, "Von deutscher Erfindungskraft oder: Die Kollektivschuldthese in der Nachkriegszeit," in *Hannah Arendt Revisited: "Eichmann in Jerusalem" und die Folgen*, ed. Gary Smith (Frankfurt/Main, 2000), 163–76; Jeffrey K. Olick, *In the House of the Hangman. The Agonies of German Defeat, 1943–1949* (Chicago, 2005).

9 Compare Michael Geyer, "War, Genocide, Extermination: The War against the Jews in an Era of World Wars," in *Shattered Past: Reconstructing German Histories*, ed. Konrad Jarausch and Michael Geyer (Princeton and Oxford, 2003), 111–48.

10 Martin Broszat, "Siegerjustiz oder strafrechtliche 'Selbstreinigung.' Vergangenheitsbewältigung der Justiz 1945–1949," *Vierteljahreshefte für Zeitgeschichte* 29 (1981), 477–544.

11 For the different media reactions, see Detlef Siegfried, "Zwischen Aufarbeitung und Schlußstrich. Der Umgang mit der NS-Vergangenheit in den beiden deutschen Staaten," in *Dynamische Zeiten. Die 60er Jahre in beiden deutschen Gesellschaften*, ed. Axel Schildt, Detlef Siegfried, and Karl Christian Lammers (Hamburg, 2000), 77–113; Devin O. Pendas, "'Auschwitz, je ne savais pas ce que ć était'. Le Procès d'Auschwitz à Francfort et Í opinion publique allemande, " in *Le génocide des Juifs entre procès et histoire 1943–2000*, ed. Florent Brayard (Brussels, 2000), 79–111.

12 On the analytical potential of terms like *Vergangenheitsbewältigung* [coming to terms with the past] and *Vergangenheitspolitik* [politics of the past], see Peter Reichel, *Vergangenheitsbewältigung in Deutschland. Die Auseinandersetzung mit der NS-Diktatur von 1945 bis heute* (München, 2001).

were bound up with the omnipresent issue of defining a postwar German identity and its political-ideological orientation.[13]

The practice of confronting Nazi injustices through criminal law that began in 1958–59 was intended to bolster the legitimacy of the otherwise seemingly well-established Federal Republic.[14] In the state's early years, West Germany's political, governmental, and judicial elites tried to overcome the obstacles to legitimation by denying the "violation of civilization known as Auschwitz" and refusing to take responsibility for bringing the perpetrators of Nazi crimes to justice.[15] This was followed, starting in 1958, by a "long wave" of a limited confrontation with the past that focused on criminal prosecution.[16] Like the "fundamental liberalization" West Germany was then undergoing,[17] the ever broader confrontation with the specifics of Nazi crimes and with individual perpetrators did not proceed from a coherent strategy. Rather, the process was shaped to a large extent by contingencies, unexpected events, and unpredictable factors. One highly unpredictable factor was the Eastern bloc's campaign against certain notable West Germans, which initially helped spur the process.

Both scholarly and public discourse long viewed the investigations and trials of Nazi crimes as the litmus test for "success" or "failure" in "coming to terms with the past." In West Germany, this genre of "quantified historical '*Bewältigung*' research," as Norbert Frei termed it, really got going in the 1980s largely in response to Hermann Lübbe's provocative thesis that a veil of silence must necessarily be cast over the past and, on the other side, to Ralph Giordano's postulate of the "second guilt" of postwar West German society for its failure to deal with Nazi perpetrators.[18] Only in more recent years have we seen a movement away from the attempt to measure the success of West Germany's approach to the past. Surely, it is no coincidence

13 Mary Fulbrook has pointed out that the public representation of the Nazi past, as manifested in films, theater plays, exhibitions, and also in court proceedings and related discussions, reflects both present politics and historical realities; Fulbrook, *German National Identity after the Holocaust* (Cambridge, 1999), 49.

14 This motive was similar to that underlying the "politics of the past" of the early Adenauer era as explored by Norbert Frei, *Vergangenheitspolitik: Die Anfänge der Bundesrepublik und die NS-Vergangenheit* (München, 1996).

15 Dan Diner, *Beyond the Conceivable: Studies on Germany, Nazism, and the Holocaust* (Berkeley, 2000).

16 Helmut König, *Die Zukunft der Vergangenheit. Der Nationalsozialismus im politischen Bewusstsein der Bundesrepublik* (Frankfurt/Main, 2003), 30.

17 This term was initially coined by Jürgen Habermas.

18 Norbert Frei, "NS-Vergangenheit unter Ulbricht und Adenauer," in *Die geteilte Vergangenheit: Zum Umgang mit Nationalsozialismus und Widerstand in beiden deutschen Staaten*, ed. Jürgen Danyel (Berlin, 1995), 125–32; Hermann Lübbe, "Der Nationalsozialismus im deutschen Nachkriegsbewußtsein," *Historische Zeitschrift* 236 (1983): 579–99; Ralph Giordano, *Die zweite Schuld oder von der Last ein Deutscher zu sein* (Hamburg, 1987); Manfred Kittel, *Die Legende von der "Zweiten Schuld": Vergangenheitsbewältigung in der Ära Adenauer* (Berlin, 1993).

that the latest change in perspective and the related shift in political and moral standards coincided with the demise of the German Democratic Republic and the end of the East-West conflict. It seems that both the treatment of the Nazi past and the ways historians viewed that process were strongly influenced by the East-West conflict.[19] As the ideological paradigm of quantification began to fade, so, too, did the habit of trading accusations. The focus of research shifted instead to issues that had not been studied. Not only the Nazi past, but also the way it was treated after the fact became an object of historical and political analysis, and scholars turned their attention increasingly to the criminal-law approach to Nazi crimes – to the political and social frameworks in which Nazi crimes were investigated and prosecuted and to public responses to the pursuit of Nazi criminals.

The issue of the prosecution – or failure to prosecute – Nazi perpetrators in the two German states has become a major topic in contemporary historical research, as a great many interesting publications attest.[20] This research has received important impetus from recent work on the history of the Federal Republic,[21] from the "new" perpetrator research of the 1990s,[22]

19 Jürgen Danyel, "DDR-Antifaschismus: Rückblick auf zehn Jahre Diskussion, offene Fragen und Forschungsperspektiven," in *Vielstimmiges Schweigen. Neue Studien zum DDR-Antifaschismus,* ed. Annette Leo and Peter Reif-Spirek (Berlin, 2001), 7–19.

20 While the majority of new publications on the issue still take a traditional approach, concentrating on institutions and (political) events, alternatively, a couple of recently published studies adopt an interdisciplinary design, pursuing questions of social history, "New" Cultural history, and Gender Studies; for examples, see Ulrich Brochhagen, *Nach Nürnberg: Vergangenheitsbewältigung und Westintegration in der Ära Adenauer* (Hamburg, 1994); Claudia Kuretsidis-Haider and Winfried R. Garscha, eds., *Keine "Abrechnung." NS-Verbrechen, Justiz und Gesellschaft in Europa nach 1945* (Leipzig/Wien, 1998); Matthias Meusch, *Von der Diktatur zur Demokratie. Fritz Bauer und die Aufarbeitung von NS-Verbrechen in Hessen (1956–1968)* (Wiesbaden, 2001); Kerstin Freudiger, *Die juristische Aufarbeitung von NS-Verbrechen* (Tübingen, 2002); Norbert Frei, ed., *Karrieren im Zwielicht. Hitlers Eliten nach 1945* (Frankfurt/Main, 2001); Annette Weinke, *Die Verfolgung von NS-Tätern im geteilten Deutschland, Vergangenheitsbewältigungen 1949–1969 oder: Eine deutsch-deutsche Beziehungsgeschichte im Kalten Krieg* (Paderborn, 2002); Claudia Moisel, *Frankreich und die deutschen Kriegsverbrecher. Politik und Praxis der Strafverfolgung nach dem Zweiten Weltkrieg* (Göttingen, 2004); Bernhard Brunner, *Der Frankreich-Komplex. Die nationalsozialistischen Verbrechen in Frankreich und die Justiz der Bundesrepublik Deutschland* (Göttingen, 2005); v. Miquel, *Ahnden oder amnestieren?*; Rebecca Wittmann, *Beyond Justice: The Auschwitz Trial* (Cambridge, 2005); Devin O. Pendas, *The Frankfurt Auschwitz Trial, 1963–1965. Genocide, History, and the Limits of Law* (Cambridge, 2006).

21 For current tendencies in historiography, see Ulrich Herbert, ed., *Wandlungsprozesse in Westdeutschland. Belastung, Integration, Liberalisierung 1945–1980* (Göttingen, 2002); Schildt, Siegfried, and Lammers, *Dynamische Zeiten*; Hanna Schissler, ed., *The "Miracle" Years: A Cultural History of West Germany, 1949–1968* (Princeton, 2001).

22 Gerhard Paul, ed., *Die Täter der Shoah. Fanatische Nationalsozialisten oder ganz normale Deutsche?* (Göttingen, 2002); Klaus-Michael Mallmann and Gerhard Paul, "Sozialisation, Milieu und Gewalt. Fortschritte und Probleme der neueren Täterforschung," in *Karrieren der Gewalt. Nationalsozialistische Täterbiographien* (Darmstadt, 2004), 1–32; Harald Welzer and Mitarbeit von Michaela Christ, *Täter: Wie aus ganz normalen Menschen Massenmörder werden* (Frankfurt/Main, 2005).

from "dual German history,"[23] and from "transition research."[24] Historians in the field are focusing in particular on three sets of problems.

First, new studies on Nazi extermination policy have shown that the number of persons directly and indirectly involved in the killings was much higher than previously thought. Scholars now generally assume that certain behavioral and attitudinal patterns within the Nazi "national community" were much more strongly anchored in German society than was previously believed. These two realizations suggest that, in its early years, the Federal Republic was saddled with an extraordinarily difficult personal and mental burden, which in turn made a prerequisite of the pose of "decency" assumed after 1949. This raises a decisive question in the history of anti-Nazi prosecution: How was it possible that a social consensus for a limited judicial approach to the Nazi past arose despite the integration of Nazi perpetrators into society and the early years of de facto inaction?

Second, the decision by West Germany's state and federal governments in 1958 to create an agency to investigate Nazi crimes, the Zentrale Stelle der Landesjustizverwaltungen, embodied a particular strategy of coming to terms with the past that was characterized, on the one hand, by a certain defensiveness and, on the other, by an eagerness to see action taken on prosecuting suspected Nazi criminals. What were the reasons underlying this development? What factors influenced subsequent developments?

The third set of questions concerns the connection between the criminal-law strategy of dealing with the past and the ways Nazi perpetrators were perceived and discussed. To what extent did a strategy of confronting the past based in criminal law influence West German conceptions of Nazi perpetrators? How did this promote or block a broader confrontation with the Nazi past?

In the pages that follow, I will argue that there was a close – indeed constitutive – relationship between the division of Germany into two states and the West German project of criminal prosecution as the means of addressing the Nazi past. This argument might not meet with unanimous agreement among historians, especially since most of the specialist literature to date has concentrated on the Federal Republic and treated the German Democratic Republic as peripheral. Nevertheless, a more exacting look at the "asymmetrical" history of the division of Germany and the dialectic of the

23 See for example the essays in Arnd Bauernkämper, Martin Sabrow, and Bernd Stöver, eds., *Doppelte Zeitgeschichte. Deutsch-deutsche Beziehungen 1945–1990* (Bonn, 1998).

24 Neil Kritz, ed., *Transitional Justice: How Emerging Democracies Reckon with Former Regimes*, 3 vols. (Washington, DC, 1995); Gary Jonathan Bass, *Stay the Hand of Vengeance: The Politics of War Crimes Tribunals* (Princeton, 2000).

"dual coming to terms with history"[25] shows that the West German strategy of dealing with history in the courts and the East-West confrontation on the politics of the past did not merely influence each other; they were in fact interdependent, at least during the 1950s and 1960s. Many aspects of the prosecution of Nazi perpetrators are incomprehensible outside of the context of the German-German rivalry. Giving attention to the Cold War context has the additional advantage of revealing not only the inner-German aspects of the process of coming to terms with the Nazi past but also the hitherto neglected transnational connections and influences that decisively affected that process. To illustrate this thesis, I will examine two facets of the history of West Germany's prosecution of suspected Nazi criminals: first, the decision to resume investigation and prosecution of Nazi suspects in the late 1950s and, second, the connection between the West German debate over the statute of limitations on Nazi crimes and the German-German competition for access to Nazi files in Poland.

THE RESUMPTION OF PROSECUTION IN WEST GERMANY

A look at the history of the prosecution of Nazi criminals in divided Germany inevitably raises the question of why investigations against suspected perpetrators were suspended for several years during the 1950s in West Germany. The years immediately following the founding of the two German states in 1949 were characterized by a "let's get over it" attitude in both West and East Germany. The number of investigations and convictions in the West declined steadily after 1949, dropping to almost zero by the mid-1950s. In their treatment of the past, both German states employed a strategy aimed at "universalizing" the criminal history of the Third Reich. Despite their ideological differences, politicians in both the East and the West were devoted to the idea of integrating the millions of collaborators. This legal, political, and moral rehabilitation was one of their first tasks, and it was tackled almost simultaneously in the two German states. In the Federal Republic, a powerful lobby of church representatives and legal experts came together soon after the first Bundestag elections of 1949 with the goal of eliminating the consequences of what they called the "Nuremberg System," namely, the prosecutions and denazification procedures carried out

25 Martin Sabrow, "Die NS-Vergangenheit in der geteilten deutschen Geschichtskultur," in *Teilung und Integration. Die doppelte deutsche Nachkriegsgeschichte,* ed. Christoph Klessmann and Peter Lautzas (Bonn, 2005), 132–51; Ulrich Herbert and Olaf Groehler, *Zweierlei Bewältigung. Vier Beiträge über den Umgang mit der NS-Vergangenheit in den beiden deutschen Staaten* (Hamburg, 1992).

by the Allies. They sought a comprehensive reversal of the Allied investigative project, to regain national confidence. In East Germany, by contrast, the letter and spirit of the Allied legal norms were appropriated by the Socialist Unity Party (Sozialistische Einheitspartei Deutschlands, SED) to serve its own political purposes. One especially drastic example of the SED's abuse of the legal framework the Allies established was the Waldheim mass show conducted from April through June 1950; 3,432 prisoners at "special camps" who had not yet stood trial were tried during the Waldheim proceedings.[26]

The two German states were conspicuously similar in their collective silence about the question of responsibility for the Nazis' crimes and in their disregard of the Nazi past. The culture of leaving the Nazis' crimes unpunished had, however, different roots in the two Germanys. In the East, political considerations dictated a cautious approach to the fact that the whole society was in some way implicated in the former regime. The Western lack of interest in prosecution, by contrast, followed directly from the policy of reintegration adopted under Chancellor Konrad Adenauer. In their engagement on behalf of the war criminals imprisoned in Landsberg, Werl, and Lech, the elites of the Federal Republic showed a nearly pathological identification with serious criminals – with individuals whom the Allies would have preferred to send to the gallows. In a position paper of 1953, the Allied High Commission described the West German attitude toward the "war criminal question" as an expression of a national psychosis that could not be "banished from the world by rational argument."[27]

Once the laws imposed by the Allies during the occupation were lifted in 1955, most perpetrators in West Germany might have felt it was safe to assume that the era of criminal trials was over. This changed in the second half of the decade when the SED increasingly began making a public issue of the "anti-totalitarian" consensus in the Federal Republic and exposing its internal contradictions. The evidence suggests that the SED leadership did not really view the campaign against unpunished West German "Nazis and war criminals" as a "vision of the politics of the past"[28] or as a matter of conviction. The background to the SED's new course seems, rather, mainly

26 Annette Weinke, "Die Waldheimer 'Prozesse' im Kontext der strafrechtlichen Aufarbeitung der NS-Diktatur," in *Die Waldheimer "Prozesse" – fünfzig Jahre danach*, ed. Norbert Haase and Bert Pampel (Baden-Baden, 2001), 27–48.

27 Quoted from Brochhagen, *Nach Nürnberg*, 93.

28 Jürgen Danyel, "Die beiden deutschen Staaten und ihre nationalsozialistische Vergangenheit. Elitenwechsel und Vergangenheitspolitik," in *Deutsche Vergangenheiten – eine gemeinsame Herausforderung. Der schwierige Umgang mit der doppelten Nachkriegsgeschichte*, ed. Christoph Kleßmann, Hans Misselwitz, and Günter Wichert (Berlin, 1999), 128–38, 137.

to have been tactical calculations. Even after the Soviet Union proposed a two-state solution to the German question, the GDR remained committed to the goal of a unified German state. But the East German elites adapted to the changed situation in that they made the elimination of all "war criminals" from the West German government a precondition of German reunification under socialist auspices.[29]

This demand was articulated by way of "antifascist" actions to expose high-ranking representatives of the West German system. The SED's campaigns against Konrad Adenauer, Chancellery head Hans Globke, Expellee Minister Theodor Oberländer, and the "blood judges" in the West German judiciary were both simple and persuasive. The GDR gradually recovered many Nazi records from the Soviets during the early 1950s.[30] Starting in about 1956, these documents were subjected to "political-operative" analysis; in other words, East German functionaries went through the files in search of incriminating information about West German politicians, civil servants, and public figures. Given the number of prominent West Germans who had held positions of authority in the Third Reich, it is not surprising that the East Germans had an easy time finding what they were looking for.

One of the most successful of these campaigns was the "Major Action Against the West German judiciary."[31] From 1957 to 1960, the "Committee for German Unity" led by SED chief propagandist Albert Norden published the names of West German jurists and ministerial staff members who were implicated in delivering death sentences against political and "racial" prisoners of the Third Reich. These lists were issued roughly every six months and eventually totaled about 1,000 names in all. Although the "blood judges" brochures were apparently based on authentic documents, their effect in the West was at first limited. This was partly because of the still-widespread "self-immunizing" effect of the anti-communism that held sway throughout West German society. It did help the SED campaign that

29 Michael Lemke, "Instrumentalisierter Antifaschismus und SED-Kampagnenpolitik im deutschen Sonderkonflikt 1960–68," in Danyel, *Die geteilte Vergangenheit*, 61–86.

30 Henry Leide, *NS-Verbrecher und Staatssicherheit. Die geheime Vergangenheitspolitik der DDR* (Göttingen, 2005); Christian Dirks, *"Die Verbrechen der anderen." Auschwitz und der Auschwitz-Prozeß der DDR: Das Verfahren gegen den KZ-Arzt Dr. Horst Fischer* (Paderborn, 2006).

31 Brochhagen, *Nach Nürnberg*, 229; "Klaus Bästlein, Nazi-Blutrichter als Stützen des Adenauer-Regimes. Die DDR-Kampagnen gegen NS-Richter und -Staatsanwälte, die Reaktionen der bundesdeutschen Justiz und ihre gescheiterte Selbstreinigung 1957–1968," in *Die Normalität des Verbrechens. Bilanz und Perspektiven der Forschung zu den nationalsozialistischen Gewaltverbrechen*, ed. Helge Grabitz, Klaus Bästlein, and Johannes Tuchel (Berlin, 1994), 408–43; Annette Weinke, "Die Selbstamnestierung der bundesdeutschen Justiz 1957–1965: der Fall West-Berlin," in *Zeitschrift für Geschichtswerissenschaft* 46 (1998): 622–37.

Norden favored a rather heavy-handed presentation of the evidence that even some within the SED party apparatus found crude.[32]

The antifascist agitation did gradually succeed in putting pressure on the West German government, thanks to a number of mutually reinforcing factors. During the early months of the blood judges campaign, the West German judiciary was already facing a crisis of legitimacy on account of controversial rulings on Nazi crimes cases and several scandals concerning judges with Nazi backgrounds.[33] Moreover, the second half of the 1950s saw an upturn in neo-Nazism and anti-Semitism in West Germany. The Bonn government attempted to counteract both of these phenomena with a cautious press campaign at home and abroad. This backfired, however, by spurring interest in the still-festering issues of the Nazi past.[34] The West's almost unrestricted policy of integration and amnesty also backfired, and the negative effects were compounded by the West German press's tendency to distance certain groups of perpetrators from the population at large by portraying them as pathological or even almost demonic.[35]

Half a decade after its founding, the Federal Republic found itself, despite its impressive political and economic success, under considerable "suspicion of guilt and continuity from abroad,"[36] to the dismay of many West Germans. The general perception of a loss of credibility crystallized around the issue of the former Nazi judges. The judiciary received the brunt of the criticism because of the role it played in the Nazi regime and because of the higher-than-average proportion of former Nazi officials within its ranks. The question now was how the West German government and judiciary should deal with the problem of former Nazis in positions of authority – which, I again emphasize, was a general problem and by no means restricted to the judiciary. In October 1958, the federal and state justice ministers decided at a meeting in Bad Harzburg to create a central office to investigate Nazi mass crimes, the Zentrale Stelle in Ludwigsburg. This decision came in response to a complaint from the attorney general of

32 Members of the working group within the Central Commitee considered the term "blood judges" as inappropriate and counterproductive for the overall objectives of the campaign; compare Norbert Podewin and Albert Norden, *Ein Rabbinersohn im Politbüro* (Berlin, 2001), 296.

33 Examples are the trials against the SS general Max Simon and the Huppenkothen case; see Reichel, *Vergangenheitsbewältigung*, 144ff.

34 See Brochhagen, *Nach Nürnberg*; Weinke, *Verfolgung von NS-Tätern*.

35 On the media images of Nazi perpetrators see Habbo Knoch, *Die Tat als Bild. Fotografien des Holocaust in der deutschen Erinnerungskultur* (Hamburg, 2001).

36 Agnes Blänsdorf, "Die Einordnung der NS-Zeit in das Bild der eigenen Geschichte. Österreich, die DDR und die Bundesrepublik Deutschland im Vergleich," in *Schwieriges Erbe. Der Umgang mit Nationalsozialismus und Antisemitismus in Österreich, der DDR und der Bundesrepublik Deutschland*, ed. Werner Bergmann, Rainer Erb, and Albert Lichtblau (Frankfurt/Main and New York, 1995), 18–45; 32.

Baden-Württemburg about the handicaps prosecutors faced in an ongoing trial in Ulm of members of an SS unit, one of the so-called Einsatzgruppen, that was implicated in mass killings in Lithuania.

Historians are unanimous in viewing the establishment of the Ludwigsburg agency as a fundamental turning point in West Germany's approach to dealing with the Nazi past. They usually account for it with the explanation that the justice ministers, shocked by the details of the mass murder of Jews brought to light by the Ulm trial, were moved to create an agency for systematic criminal investigations. That, in turn, prompted West German society as a whole to confront the Nazi past.[37] This interpretation is in part based on the historical narratives West German legal and law enforcement institutions have created for themselves, and it has been repeated without critical reflection for many years. But given the difficult historical and political contexts, we must ask whether the resumption of anti-Nazi prosecution can really be explained by this simple formula of a sudden and cathartic awakening.[38]

Without denying the importance of these events for the West German culture of memory, an examination of the written record makes clear that the motives and expectations behind the establishment of the Zentrale Stelle were not quite as pure as they are usually said to be. First, Bonn and the states agreed with remarkable speed to restructure their investigatory jurisdictions in late 1958. Separate plans for the new central investigative agency were submitted by the Justice Ministries of Bavaria and Baden-Wurttemberg, both within a few weeks after the state attorney general in Stuttgart, Erich Nellmann, first made the case for centralizing investigations of Nazi crimes. While Nellmann originally advocated running the investigations through the Office of the Federal Attorney General, the Bad Harzburg summit of justice ministers approved only the creation of an interstate agency that could conduct investigations but not issue indictments or make arrests. This was because of the opposition to the entire plan raised by Federal Minister of Justice Fritz Schäffer (CSU) and the wait-and-see position of Federal Attorney General Max Güde. The minutes of the justice ministers' conference make clear that only a small number of the officials gathered at

37 For a recent treatment of this theme, see Bernd Stöver, *Die Bundesrepublik Deutschland* (Darmstadt, 2002), 68.

38 Recently the adequacy of this narrative has been put under intensified scrutiny, for example by Brochhagen, *Nach Nürnberg*, 254; Annette Weinke, "Die Verfolgung von NS- und SED-Unrecht in der Bundesrepublik als Gegenstand historischer Forschungen, *Zeitschrift für Geschichtswissenschaft* 44 (1996), 127–39; Norbert Frei, "Die Rückkehr des Rechts. Justiz und Zeitgeschichte nach dem Holocaust – eine Zwischenbilanz," in Bauernkämper, Sabrow, and Stöver, *Doppelte Zeitgeschichte*, 417–31.

Bad Harzburg had a clear vision of what the new agency was supposed to investigate; most had only very vague ideas. Consequently, there was a marked disparity between the broad resolution the justice ministers issued at Bad Harzburg[39] and the administrative agreement reached a few weeks later.[40] Under the latter, the new central investigative agency's jurisdiction was to be limited to crimes committed in concentration camps and by Einsatzgruppen outside of the territory of the Reich. At the Bad Harzburg meeting, the justice ministers also agreed to coordinate the ongoing investigations against former Nazi criminal judges but to keep them under the jurisdiction of state authorities.

One year later, in a further decision with wide-reaching consequences, the justice ministers agreed not to take the initiative in securing Nazi-era documents in possession of governments on the other side of the Iron Curtain. This decision was the result in large part of the ambiguous position of the Adenauer government. Off the record, government officials were willing to tolerate the use of documents provided by Eastern bloc governments as a matter of necessity. In public, however, they held to the official line, consistent with the Hallstein Doctrine, of categorically refusing any contact with governmental representatives of communist countries except the Soviet Union.[41]

The rush to create the Ludwigsburg agency and the lack of reflection on its actual investigative mission point, I would argue, to a higher level of causation. These events mark the beginning of a gradual withdrawal from the previous dual strategy of normative distancing from National Socialism while generously exculpating the individuals responsible for Nazi crimes.[42] The Bad Harzburg resolution also attests to continuing mental blocks toward confronting the Nazi past and a defensiveness about West Germany's record on Nazi criminals, suggesting that 1958 represents less a decisive turning point than the start of a period of transition. In the strategy of a selective criminal prosecution with a continuing general apologia adopted in 1958, we see the dilemma in the memory politics the Federal Republic faced. It was forced by growing criticism to confront its "unmastered past" but, at

39 Niederschrift über die 27. JuMiKo vom 1.–4.10.1958 in Bad Harzburg; SfJ Generalia 3131-I/A.1, Sonderband 14, Bl. 26.

40 Entwurf einer Verwaltungsvereinbarung über die Einrichtung einer zentralen Stelle der Landesjustizverwaltungen zur Aufklärung nationalsozialistischer Verbrechen [o.V.; o.D.]; Generalia Ludwigsburg 41–1/2.

41 Protocol of the 28th Conference of the Justice Ministers on October 13–15, 1959 in Hamburg; SfJ Generalia, [special] vol. 3131-I/A, 135.

42 Frei, *Vergangenheitspolitik*; see also Helmut König, *Die Zukunft der Vergangenheit. Der Nationalsozialismus im politischen Bewußtsein der Bundesrepublik* (Frankfurt/Main, 2003), 24.

the same time, it sought to fend off the East German propaganda attacks. This situation encouraged the "judicialization" of discourse on the past and contributed to a top-down approach to addressing the Nazi past by means of criminal law. The new strategy seemed to serve the nation's conflicting needs – to remember and to forget – equally well.

THE STATUTE OF LIMITATIONS CONTROVERSY AND THE STRUGGLE OVER THE POLISH-HELD RECORDS

The extent to which the politics of the past in the two German states was linked became clear in 1964 when West Germany took up the issue of the statute of limitations on Nazi murders. A symbolic and propagandistic form of addressing the Nazi past was still dominant, as was evident in the plans both German states made at the time to gain improved access to Nazi-era German documents held in Eastern bloc countries. Each sought to improve its image on the international stage. It was typical of their entanglement that the deadline imposed by the statute of limitations spurred Bonn to become more active in trying to gain access to archival materials in Eastern Europe and the Soviet Union, whereas East Berlin became increasingly secretive about the materials in its possession.

The approaching expiration of statute of limitations on Nazi murders on May 8, 1965,[43] created a variety of domestic and foreign policy problems for Chancellor Ludwig Erhard's governing coalition. On the one hand, the government had to plan for likely protests from other Western countries if the statute of limitations was allowed to expire and had to be ready to defuse those protests as quickly as possible. On the other hand, West German voters were largely opposed to continuing the prosecution of suspected Nazi perpetrators. In the spring of 1964, Federal Justice Minister Ewald Bucher (FDP) told the press that he intended to allow the statute of limitations to expire. That summer, officials at the Justice Ministry and Foreign Office scrambled to develop a public relations strategy to counter the expected protests. They arrived at the idea of coupling a cabinet decision upholding the statute of limitations with an international appeal to all countries to provide the Federal Republic with any evidence relevant to Nazi crimes in advance of the deadline imposed by the statute of limitations.

43 On the legal situation in the Federal Republic, see Heribert Ostendorf, "Die – widersprüchlichen – Auswirkungen der Nürnberger Prozesse auf die westdeutsche Justiz," in *Strafgerichte gegen Menschheitsverbrechen,* ed. Gerd Hankel and Gerhard Stuby (Hamburg, 1995), 73–97; the Eastern side is covered by Günther Wieland, "Die Nürnberger Prinzipien im Spiegel von Gesetzgebung und Spruchpraxis sozialistischer Staaten," in ibid., 98–123.

The Erhard government issued this appeal on November 20, 1964, shortly after its official announcement that it would allow the statute of limitations to expire. The appeal was nominally directed to the "international community," but for all practical purposes it was aimed at the socialist states of the Eastern bloc, which held most of the still unexamined documents.[44] Western governments that might be in possession of relevant materials were given official notification; the governments of Poland, Hungary, Romania, and Bulgaria were informed by the West German trade missions operating in those countries. The GDR, which held a substantial number of documents, was not notified because West Germany did not maintain any sort of formal or informal representative office there.

Bonn miscalculated in its strategy. Despite information to the contrary from its embassy and consulates in the United States, it had assumed that the SED was the driving force behind the international protests to the West German statute of limitations on Nazi murders and that appealing to other nations to provide evidence of Nazi crimes would be sufficient to defuse the protests. Officials in Bonn were thus startled when it became clear that this strategy, far from quelling criticism, served only to increase opposition to the West German statute of limitations. Erhard's cabinet had by then decided to hold to the statute of limitations, but the chorus of protest, both at home and abroad, was growing louder by the day. The only solution was a forward retreat. In late 1964, the Justice Ministry, in collaboration with the Zentrale Stelle in Ludwigsburg, began to try to improve contacts as quickly as possible with law enforcement agencies in Poland and Czechoslovakia, which played a pivotal role in the debate on the statute of limitations. Officially, the new diplomatic feelers were intended to help West German authorities gain access to the documents necessary to file new indictments in anticipation of the expiration of the statute of limitations. In fact, this initiative, like the international appeal that preceded it, was little more than an empty act of political symbolism meant to convince the skeptical "international community" that Bonn was still willing to support the law enforcement agencies in their difficult task.

West Germany and Poland's quasi-official cooperation in investigating Nazi crimes began in December 1964 with two important events. The international media were invited to cover the visit by members of a Frankfurt court and jury to the "Black Wall" at Auschwitz on December 12. This visit, the first ever of a West German judicial delegation, was the initiative of Henry Ormond, a co-plaintiff in the Frankfurt Auschwitz case. Ormond

44 File "Verjährung," Generalia Ludwigsburg, 41–60/40, 5.

had filed a motion calling for the visit in June.[45] The following week, on December 18, State Attorney Erwin Schüle, the head of the Zentrale Stelle in Ludwigsburg, arrived in Warsaw to discuss the future use of the Nazi archives stored in Poland with representatives of the Polish Ministry of Justice. These two visits to Poland marked a decisive break in the history of West German memory politics and opened the way toward putting the informal, "cold" cooperation between the Zentrale Stelle and the Warsaw Main Commission initiated in 1959 on official footing. At the end of 1964, it seemed for the first time as though the West German government would no longer allow the prosecution of Nazi crimes to be hampered by its foreign policy – which was itself moving toward greater flexibility vis-à-vis the Eastern bloc.[46]

This encouraging situation was, however, overshadowed by the reality that Bonn was only acting under pressure. In early December, the Social Democrats and renegades from the CDU and CSU had submitted a resolution in the Bundestag calling for the use of evidence from the "Soviet-occupied zone" – in other words, East Germany – and the Eastern European countries in prosecuting suspected Nazi perpetrators and to allow research in Eastern bloc archives in investigating "normal" Nazi crimes.[47] Moreover, Bonn was motivated less by a desire to normalize relations with Warsaw than by the hope of justifying the controversial statute of limitations.

Much as it had during a controversy over the statute of limitations for manslaughter in 1959–60, the Zentrale Stelle played an important strategic role in the controversy of 1964–65. When the West German government issued its international appeal for evidence on November 20, it made the Ludwigsburg agency responsible for analyzing whatever documents foreign governments provided. Erhard's cabinet was willing to include the Zentrale Stelle in its strategy because Schüle had argued forcefully in public in support of Justice Minister Bucher's general position on the statute of limitations. Although Schüle did not agree with Bucher on all points, he provided the convenient argument that because his agency had already initiated investigations of all the major Nazi mass crimes and suspected perpetrators, the expiration of the statute of limitations would have little practical effect.

45 Compare Sybille Steinbacher, "'Protokoll vor der Schwarzen Wand.' Die Ortsbesichtigung des Frankfurter Schwurgerichts in Auschwitz," in *"Gerichtstag halten über uns selbst. . . ." Geschichte und Wirkung des ersten Frankfurter Auschwitz-Prozesses*, ed. Irmtrud Wojak (Frankfurt/Main and New York, 2001), 61–89; Werner Renz, "Auschwitz als Augenscheinobjekt. Anmerkungen zur Erforschung der Wahrheit im ersten Frankfurter Auschwitz-Prozeß," *Mittelweg* 36, 1 (2001): 63–72.

46 Manfred Görtemaker, "Die Ursprünge der 'neuen Ostpolitik' Willy Brandts," in Bauernkämper, Sabrow, and Stöver, *Doppelte Zeitgeschichte*, 44–57.

47 BT-Drucksache IV/2823, 5.

Schüle was critical of the West German media coverage, which he contended reinforced the impression that many Nazi criminals still remained unidentified despite his agency's systematic work. According to Schüle, the figures on open investigations reported in the press were "far too high" and did not, therefore, justify an extension of the statute of limitations. In a newspaper interview a few days after his first visit to Poland, Schüle delivered his fateful prediction that he did not expect the Poles would find "significant new incriminating documents" of use to his agency.[48]

Given the standoff between the two German states since the building of the Berlin Wall, it is no surprise that the cautious rapprochement between the West German and the Polish authorities on the issue of prosecuting Nazi criminals exacerbated German-German tensions. Schüle's plan to visit Warsaw and the prospect that West German prosecutors might soon have regular access to the archives in Poland triggered nervousness and discomfort in East Berlin. The East German intelligence service, which had become the primary agency for securing and analyzing Nazi files, undertook an effort to sabotage the planned talks between West German and Polish officials. Within the SED and intelligence service, it was assumed for ideological reasons that West Germany's declaration of interest in the Polish files was intended to serve as an alibi for allowing the statute of limitations on Nazi murders to expire. It was also believed in East Berlin that the West German investigations of suspected Nazi criminals were meant to distract attention from the *Schreibtischtäter* who still held positions of authority in the Federal Republic. The fact that the Polish authorities were prepared to work officially with West German law enforcement agencies raised doubts in East Berlin about the loyalty of the GDR's Warsaw Pact ally and the cohesiveness of the "antifascist" alliance. The East Germans assumed, not without reason, that Poland would help West Germany with its investigations in order to establish relations with the Federal Republic outside of the framework of its Warsaw Pact obligations. Finally, East Berlin saw that improved Western access to the Polish files would have a negative effect on its own "antifascist" campaign and possibly cause serious damage to East Germany's own image, given the likelihood that the West Germans would discover unexposed Nazi perpetrators in the GDR. That concern was decisive in spurring the East German intelligence and security service to try to establish a monopoly on research in and analysis of the Polish-held records.

What measures did the East Germans employ in trying to block West German investigators' access to the Nazi files in Polish possession? The

48 *Die Welt*, December 22, 1964.

announcement on December 17 that Schüle would be traveling to Poland the next day came as a complete surprise to East Germany's notoriously well-informed Ministry for State Security (Stasi), which learned of the trip from a wire-service story. Stasi head Erich Mielke lost no time in trying to intervene directly with the new Polish minister for the interior and state security, Mieczyslaw Moczar.[49] Mielke had little trouble convincing his Polish counterpart that the largely unread Nazi files in Polish possession were of extremely high "political-operative" value. He then tried to persuade the Polish authorities to rescind their invitation to Schüle.

Only after this attempt had failed did the East Germans decide to try to get into the Polish-held files before the West Germans did. The Stasi chief was assured by his Polish counterpart that the investigators from Ludwigsburg would not be given access to any materials potentially embarrassing to East Berlin. In the weeks that followed, East German agents were dispatched to begin sifting through the major groups of Nazi documents in Polish possession. During this operation, code-named *Konzentration* (concentration), Stasi personnel worked their way through approximately 34,000 files in the possession of the Warsaw Main Commission, the Ministry of the Interior, the Jewish Institute in Warsaw, and numerous regional archives. With the help of Polish archivists, legal experts, and secret police personnel, Stasi agents gained an overview of the material. They prepared an inventory of the Polish-held records and sent some 200,000 pages of copies back to East Berlin, where most were preserved in the Ministry for State Security's secret archive of Nazi-era documents.

The East Germans involved in operation *Konzentration* told their Polish colleagues that the materials they were collecting would be used to continue the campaign exposing former Nazis in positions of authority in West Germany in order to force an extension of the statute of limitations. But the working notes they sent back to East Berlin tell a different story: the announced goal of uncovering as yet undiscovered crimes or identifying Nazi criminals was merely an excuse to gain access to the Polish archives. The Stasi's main interest was, however, to find materials for its propaganda campaigns and other operations. One of the most important products of the operation was the *Baunbuch* ("brown book"), a *Who's Who* of alleged Nazi perpetrators in West Germany, published in July 1965. It was based primarily on information the Stasi had found in Eastern bloc archives.

49 On the planning and conduct of intelligence operations like *Konzentration* and others, see Weinke, "Der Kampf um die Akten. Zur Kooperation zwischen MfS und osteuropäischen Sicherheitsdiensten bei der Vorbereitung antifaschistischer Kampagnen," *Deutschland-Archiv* 4 (1999): 564–77.

How did Poland respond to this German-German competition and what were its motives? Polish Interior Minister Moczar, as noted above, accommodated the Stasi's investigation while at the same time refusing to snub the West German delegation by calling off their visit at the last minute. There has been no research as yet on Poland's calculations in its legal cooperation with West Germany, so we can only speculate about the reasons behind Moczar's decisions. The Stasi files note that Moczar himself hoped to use the Nazi material to gain politically useful information from the time of the German occupation of Poland. An ardent communist and nationalist, Moczar had been carrying out a purge of Jews and politically unreliable personnel in the Interior Ministry and the military since the beginning of the decade.[50] Moreover, he saw in Mielke's offer an opportunity to solidify East German–Polish cooperation in exposing former Nazis in West Germany, which could in turn provide Poland with useful arguments in the event it felt compelled to launch a campaign against German "revanchism." This collaboration soon paid off not only in the campaign branding President Heinrich Lübke of the Federal Republic as a "concentration camp builder"[51] but also in a 1966 agreement formalizing the cooperation between the Polish and East German security services. It is, finally, very likely that Moczar was motivated by the possibility of using the issue of prosecuting Nazi criminals to score against Minister of Justice Marian Rybicki and securing control of Poland's Main Commission.[52]

The journey of the Ludwigsburg delegation to Poland led to a propaganda campaign against Schüle which culminated in the eventual professional dismantling of the Ludwigsburg chief prosecutor, a parliamentary triumph for the opponents of the statutory limitation, and the early resignation of Justice Minister Bucher. Apart from this surprising denouement to the West German legislative controversy, the visit from Ludwigsburg served

50 Compare Jerzy Holzer, "Nationalismus, Ressentiment und Manipulation. Die deutsche Frage im kommunistischen Polen," in *Sozialismus und Kommunismus im Wandel. FS für Hermann Weber zum 65. Geburtstag,* ed. Klaus Schönhoven and Dietrich Staritz (Köln, 1993), 535–47; Feliks Tych, "Prag und Warschau 1968," in ibid., 567–81; Beate Kosmala, "'Die jüdische Frage' als politisches Instrument in der Volksrepublik Polen," in *Die Vertreibung der Juden aus Polen 1968. Antisemitismus und politisches Kalkül* (Berlin, 2000) 49ff; an insight into current Polish debates provides the article "Antisemitismus in der polnischen Armee," *Frankfurter Allgemeine Zeitung*, March 10, 2001.

51 During the Second World War, Lübke was employed as an engineer by the Baugruppe Schlempp, a company from Berlin which conducted many building projects for Albert Speer's Ministry for Armaments and Munitions. In this position, Lübke also became responsible for the recruitment and exploitation of so-called Eastern workers and Jewish slave laborers; Jens-Christian Wagner, "Der Fall Lübke," *Die Zeit*, July 19, 2007.

52 Apparently, Moczar eventually managed to gain control over the Warsaw Main Commission in spring 1966, when its former leader Janucz Gumkowski was replaced by Czeslaw Pilichowski, a former member of the Ministry for State Security.

as an important confidence-building measure in the relationship between Poland and the Federal Republic. These are especially surprising results, when one recalls that the original point of Schüle's trip was to strengthen the CDU/FDP position on statutory limitations. The German-German struggle over the Polish-held files was an unequal one: the West Germans were at a huge disadvantage.[53] This raises the question of how Poland exploited the German-German conflict as a means of presenting itself as a reliable partner to both sides. How did the Polish officials succeed in giving the East German Stasi the impression of reliable cooperation in the personal campaign against Schüle, while at the same time convincing the West Germans that they were neutral actors on this issue?

During Schüle's first visit to Warsaw in December, it had been agreed that a delegation of Ludwigsburg prosecutors would travel to Poland in February 1965 to examine the relevant Polish archival records. When Schüle and his team returned to Warsaw on February 4, 1965, he was suddenly obliged to respond to a carefully arranged campaign against him. A troop of journalists swarmed around him to ask about ADN's report that he had been a Nazi. What ADN and the leading East German newspaper *Neues Deutschland* presented as scandalous revelations were in fact just the opposite. Already back in January 1959, the GDR had publicized information about Schüle's former NSDAP and SA membership, but without creating the hoped-for scandal.[54] Overwhelmed by this unexpected situation, Schüle unwisely denied he had ever belonged to the party. Later he reconsidered and, on the orders of his superior, Baden-Württemberg Justice Minister Wolfgang Haussmann, issued a written statement on the accusations through the West German trade consulate in Warsaw. Soon thereafter, Schüle met with the head of the Polish Main Commission, Janucz Gumkowski, who assured him that the East German campaign was viewed in Warsaw as an "internal matter" between the two German states and would in no way hinder Polish-West German cooperation in prosecuting Nazi criminals.[55]

In the days that followed, the Polish authorities engaged in behavior that confused Schüle greatly. First, the Polish media reported the details of the continuing GDR campaign against Schüle. Second, the Polish archivists denied all requests from the West German investigators. This tactic was suddenly reversed on February 12, the day that Schüle left Warsaw for a visit

53 On the other hand, in their reports to the East Berlin headquarters, Stasi officers relativized the success of their "antifascist" mission by pointing to the fact that their Polish partners had not fully complied with the previous agreements; see Weinke, *Verfolgung von NS-Tätern*.

54 Brochhagen, *Nach Nürnberg*, 257.

55 On the first Poland trip of the Ludwigsburg investigative office, see Weinke, *Verfolgung von NS-Tätern*.

to Prague. Right after his departure, Polish Main Commission employees began to supply the investigators from Ludwigsburg with files documenting previously undisclosed crimes, thereby laying the foundation for the opening of new cases against suspected perpetrators. This abrupt shift caused a fundamental change in the West Germans' view of the value of the Polish-held files. Schüle's deputy, Adalbert Rückerl, submitted Ludwigsburg's official report on the Polish-held files on February 28. Contradicting Schüle's earlier conclusions, Rückerl estimated that there were at least 200–300 new cases involving perpetrators of different ranks to be investigated. Given the wealth of material available, it would be "completely impossible" to initiate proceedings against all suspected perpetrators before the expiration of the statute of limitations on May 8, 1965.[56]

This unusually clear conclusion had a decisive influence on the parliamentary debate on the statute of limitations. When Bucher presented the Justice Ministry's report on the results of West German prosecution of Nazi criminals at the end of February, he had to admit for the first time that new material had been found in archives in the "Soviet area of control" and that it would be impossible to adequately evaluate this evidence before the expiration of the statute of limitations. For that reason, he could no longer guarantee that "as-yet unknown major crimes or unknown perpetrators in important positions" would not come to light *after* May 8, 1965.[57] The opponents of the statute of limitations in the Bundestag, led by the Social Democratic expert Gerhard Jahn and West Berlin Christian Democrat Ernst Benda, took this late confession as a confirmation of their earlier objections to the form and content of the Erhard government's resolution on the statute of limitations. After the presentation of what became known as the "Bucher Report," there was no doubt that what the defenders of the statute of limitations had unanimously claimed up to that point was false. Anyone who still supported allowing the statute of limitations to expire, for whatever reason, would have to take into account that serious Nazi crimes would go unprosecuted and unpunished.

The Erhard government finally lost the parliamentary battle over the statute of limitations on March 25, 1965, as a direct consequence of Bucher's manipulative information policy with regard to Allied and West German prosecutions of Nazi crimes. Bucher did not want to bear the burden of blame alone. Schüler's eventual resignation was preordained when the press

56 Report of the Archival Working Group of the Ludwigsburg Investigative Office from March 2, 1965 on their visits to Warsaw and Lublin in January/February 1965; *Generalia Ludwigsburg*, 9–1, vol. 1.

57 BT-Drucksache IV/3124.

reported at the time of the government's setback that officials in the Justice Ministry were quite "disappointed" about the way he had handled information pertaining to the issue of the statute of limitations.[58] In the scholarly literature on the subject, the suspension of communication between East German law enforcement and the Ludwigsburg investigative office in 1965 is still seen as following directly from the GDR's release of information about Schüle's Nazi past.[59] But this thesis overlooks the fact that Schüle's fall had nothing to do with the accusations against him, but was actually the result of his dismissive and premature assessment of the Polish files. In the end, his willingness to support the Erhard government's questionable political decision undermined his credibility and eventually led to his professional isolation.

CONCLUSION

Michael Kohlstruck has written that all attempts to come to terms with the Nazi past are "inappropriate by definition."[60] Even if that is true, scholars still must ask under what conditions and in what stages the process of getting away from National Socialism was achieved. It is, accordingly, useful to view the history of the prosecution of Nazi crimes in West Germany not only as an indicator but also as a *medium* of "transformative politics."[61] Just as it is impossible to draw a sharp contrast between the apologetic interpretations of the Nazi period during the 1950s and later perspectives,[62] so, too, is it impossible to distinguish clear-cut strategies in coming to terms with the Nazi past. Addressing the Nazi legacy by means of criminal law combined elements of amnesty, integration, normative distancing, and selective punishment. Each of those strategies was in turn marked by a particular mix of confession and silence, of suppression and confrontation, and the emphasis shifted over the years. This observation is not meant to gloss over the serious failures in the West German prosecution of Nazi perpetrators, but rather to show the importance of viewing them from a historical perspective.

58 *Frankfurter Allgemeine Zeitung,* March 12, 1965.

59 Adalbert Rückerl, *Die Strafverfolgung von NS-Verbrechen 1945–1978. Eine Dokumentation* (Heidelberg and Karlsruhe, 1979), 173; Günther Wieland, "Die deutsch-deutschen Rechtsbeziehungen zur Ahndung von NS-Verbrechen zwischen Mauerbau und Wiedervereinigung," in Grabitz, Bästlein, and Tuchel, *Die Normalität des Verbrechens*, 386–407, 398ff.

60 Michael Kohlstruck, "Der Umgang mit dem Nationalsozialismus. Zu einigen neueren Untersuchungen," *Politische Vierteljahreszeitschrift* (1997): 346ff.

61 Wilfried Loth and Bernd-A. Rusinek, eds., *Verwandlungspolitik. NS-Eliten in der westdeutschen Nachkriegsgesellschaft* (Frankfurt/Main, 1998).

62 Herbert, *Wandlungsprozesse*, 23.

In the case of using the law to address the Nazi past, taking a historical perspective means above all that we carefully consider the political and social contexts of the investigations into Nazi crimes.[63] This essay attempted to demonstrate that the resumption of prosecutions in West Germany cannot be explained simply by a general rise in moral standards when it came to the subject of National Socialism. To the contrary: the shift in West German priorities and strategies can also be explained by the context of the German-German rivalry of the Cold War era. The East German "blood judges" campaign, conceived as a frontal attack on a central pillar of the democratic state, did not destabilize the Bonn republic as intended. In combination with other events, it did, however, provoke much criticism of West German policy both at home and abroad that made counteraction necessary. Despite the differing interests of West Germany's state and federal governments, the establishment of the Zentrale Stelle in Ludwigsburg was an expression of the political will to deal with some of the Nazis' crimes before the expiration of the statute of limitations even if, at the same time, others would go uninvestigated and unpunished. It was symptomatic of the Federal Republic's adaptability that this defensive strategy was abandoned in the mid-1960s after it was seen to be dysfunctional. A decisive turning point came with the statute of limitations controversy of 1964–65, which led to an active effort to draw on the witnesses and evidence in the Eastern bloc and a substantial expansion of the investigations into Nazi crimes. The most remarkable aspect of this development was that the initiative from that moment shifted clearly to West Germany's advantage. Whereas ten years earlier the GDR might still have acted as the "engine of active confrontation with the past"[64] in West Germany, it came increasingly to act as a brake, adding even more obstacles to that difficult process.

63 For the conceptualization of a German-German history of judicial *Vergangenheitsbewältigung*, see Frei, *Rückkehr des Rechts*, 419.

64 Jochen Staadt, *Die geheime Westpolitik der SED 1960–1970. Von der gesamtdeutschen Orientierung zur sozialistischen Nation* (Berlin, 1993), 156.

10

History in the Courthouse

The Presentation of World War II Crimes in U.S. Courts Sixty Years Later

ELIZABETH B. WHITE

> To see the United States Government uncoil its mighty sinews and reach across time and distance to uncover facts is an amazing and frightening thing to behold. Indeed, seeking to discover the acts of a single individual across the temporal expanse of fifty years and a distance of an ocean and half a continent is a daunting task.
>
> U.S. District Court for the Northern District of Illinois, *United States v. Hajda*[1]

Despite the fact that they deal with the same general subject matter, trials of participants in Nazi crimes in the United States differ significantly from such trials in Europe, particularly Germany. The most obvious difference is that the U.S. government cannot criminally prosecute alleged "Nazi war criminals" who reside in the United States. Crimes committed in Europe by non-Americans against non-Americans were not subject to criminal prosecution in the United States during the Nazi period, and the U.S. Constitution prohibits ex post facto extension of criminal jurisdiction. Prosecutions of alleged participants in Nazi crimes against humanity are therefore civil matters in the United States, and the only judicial remedies that the government can seek are revocation of naturalized U.S. citizenship and removal (deportation) of the perpetrator from the United States. To obtain these remedies, the government must prove that the defendant's involvement in Nazi-sponsored acts of persecution (a crime against humanity under the Nuremberg Charter) rendered him ineligible to remain a U.S. citizen or, if the defendant is not a U.S. citizen, to reside in the United States.

1 *United States v. Hajda*, 963 F. Supp. 1452 (N.D. Ill. April 9, 1997).

There are also significant differences in the types of defendants who are tried in Germany and the United States. Of the 134 persons whom the U.S. Justice Department's Office of Special Investigations (OSI) has sought to denaturalize or remove to date since 1979, only seven were native German or Austrian citizens prior to immigrating to the United States. The other 127 subjects all hail from Eastern Europe or the Balkans and represent 14 different ethnic or national groups, including one Circassian, one Gural, and one Jew (all but one of OSI's defendants have been men). The explanation for this difference in type of defendants lies in postwar U.S. immigration policy. After World War II, U.S. immigration visas were only granted to Germans and Austrians subject to strict quotas, but the United States opened its doors to hundreds of thousands of Eastern Europeans who were displaced from their homes by the war and its aftermath and did not wish or were not able to return. Although the special laws enacted to regulate the immigration of refugees included language prohibiting the issuance of visas to those who had belonged to hostile movements or had assisted the Axis powers in acts of persecution, thousands of Nazi collaborators succeeded in passing themselves off as refugees because the records documenting their deeds were behind the Iron Curtain.

In addition to facilitating the immigration of Nazi collaborators to the United States, Cold War politics also affected the timing and success of subsequent U.S. efforts to take action against such persons. The inaccessibility of witnesses and records in Soviet bloc nations contributed to a general ignorance, even among historians, of the details of how the Holocaust was carried out in Eastern Europe and made it enormously difficult to assemble sufficient evidence to institute proceedings. Even when the Soviet Union proffered documents and witness statements pertaining to the criminal activities of certain emigrés, deep distrust of the Soviets caused American judges and law enforcement authorities to doubt the credibility of the evidence, and the evident propaganda purposes to which the Soviets tried to put such charges did not help matters. Many participants in Nazi crimes who came under suspicion in the United States succeeded in portraying their wartime activities as having targeted only communists and in painting themselves as victims of communist smear tactics. Preoccupation with ensuring national security against a present enemy also left American authorities with little appetite for pursuing the enemies of the past. The obstacles raised by the Cold War, combined with the unresolved status of certain pertinent legal questions in U.S. immigration and citizenship law, had the result that, in the quarter century following World War II, the U.S. government only succeeded in removing one participant in Nazi crimes from the United States.

This introduces another significant difference between prosecutions of Nazi crimes in Germany and in the United States: the passage of time. Whereas all but a few German prosecutions occurred during the thirty years following the end of World War II, the United States did not begin a concerted effort to bring perpetrators of Nazi crimes to justice until 1979. By that point, the passage of time had reduced not only the number of witnesses to the events of World War II but also the ability of some to recall details of those events, as well as the credibility that judges were willing to accord to witnesses' testimony. Moreover, the judges who heard the cases in Germany had for the most part lived through the period when the crimes occurred and had experienced the regime under whose auspices they were committed. They therefore approached these cases with a much better innate understanding of the context in which a defendant acted than is true of American judges, particularly those who, as is now generally the case, have little or no memory of World War II.

Several events in the 1970s led to fundamental changes in the way suspected Nazi persecutors are treated by the U.S. government and under U.S. law. In 1973, the extradition to Germany of Queens, New York housewife Hermine Braunsteiner Ryan, the "stomping mare of Majdanek," awoke the American public to the fact that so-called Nazi war criminals were living freely in the United States. Increased media attention to the situation eventually led to passage of a 1978 amendment to U.S. immigration law, called the Holtzman Amendment after its principal sponsor, Congresswoman Elizabeth Holtzman. This law bars from the United States aliens who, between 1933 and 1945, "ordered, incited, assisted or otherwise participated in the persecution of any person on the basis of race, religion, national origin or political opinion" under the direction of or in association with: (1) the Nazi government of Germany, or (2) one of its allies, or (3) a government established by Nazi Germany or in an area occupied by Nazi Germany.[2] In May 1979, the U.S. Attorney General signaled his commitment to ridding the United States of participants in Nazi persecution by transferring responsibility for pursuing them from the Immigration and Naturalization Service (INS) to a newly created office within the Criminal Division, the Office of Special Investigations (OSI), which was charged with investigating such persons and, if appropriate, with bringing denaturalization or deportation proceedings against them.

The Holtzman Amendment only applies to noncitizens, however, whereas the majority of alleged participants in Nazi persecution who have come to the U.S. government's attention had acquired U.S. citizenship prior

2 Pub. L. No. 95–549, 92 Stat. 2065 (1978).

to passage of the Amendment. The government can only revoke the citizenship of a naturalized U.S. citizen by proving that he or she was ineligible to acquire that citizenship or obtained it by means of fraud or misrepresentation of a material fact. In the years leading up to OSI's creation, the Department of Justice had brought comparatively few denaturalization actions – and only one against an alleged Nazi war criminal – and therefore had not developed extensive in-house expertise for successfully prosecuting them.

A legal blueprint for building denaturalization cases against Nazi persecutors was published in 1981, when the Supreme Court finally handed the government a victory in a Nazi case that had been prosecuted originally by the U.S. Attorney's Office in Miami, with assistance from the INS. This was the denaturalization case against Fedor Fedorenko, an SS auxiliary who had, by his own admission, served as a guard at the Treblinka killing center. The landmark decision in Fedorenko established that the central question to be answered in such cases is whether an individual assisted Nazi Germany in carrying out its policies of persecution and was therefore ineligible for U.S. citizenship. If the government can prove that a defendant's activities constituted assistance in persecution, then the defendant cannot avoid judgment against him by asserting equitable defenses, such as having subsequently been a law-abiding citizen in the United States. In order to demonstrate assistance in persecution, however, the government must prove its case by evidence that is "clear, unequivocal and convincing and that does not leave the issue in doubt," which the Supreme Court has ruled is substantially the same as the criminal standard of "beyond reasonable doubt." The reason the bar is set so high is that "the right to acquire American citizenship is a precious one, and . . . once citizenship has been acquired, its loss can have severe and unsettling consequences."[3]

While the Holtzman Amendment and the Fedorenko decision dismantled many of the legal barriers to prosecuting Nazi persecutors in the United States, few expected OSI to last more than a few years or to have much, if any, success. The challenge of proving what a defendant had done thirty-five years or more after the fact simply appeared to be too great to overcome in all but a few instances, particularly given the assumption that OSI's cases would depend upon eyewitness testimony. Nazi crimes tended to leave few survivors, and those rarely knew the identity of their tormentors or were able to recognize them decades later. The odds that fellow perpetrators

3 *United States v. Fedorenko*, 499 U.S. 490 (1981).

would testify truthfully against their former comrades seemed next to nil. Considering also the advancing age of both suspects and witnesses, it is understandable why OSI for its first twenty-five years informed all new hires that their jobs would last only three to, at most, five years.

The Fedorenko case illustrates the challenges OSI faced. Despite the defendant's admission that he had served as an armed guard at Treblinka and the testimony of survivors that they had seen Fedorenko beat and shoot prisoners there, the government had originally lost the case. Following customary criminal prosecution procedure, the U.S. Attorney's Office had based the case on the admissions and eyewitness testimony. It provided the judge with little evidence about Treblinka's purpose and operation and none about the duties and activities of the guards there. The District Court had rejected all the eyewitnesses' testimony. Moreover, it gave credence to Fedorenko's claims that he had only guarded the perimeter of Treblinka, had not physically mistreated any Jews there, and, during the Treblinka uprising, had fired his gun over the heads of escaping prisoners, not at the prisoners. The District Court found that these activities on Fedorenko's part did not amount to assistance in persecution.

The failure of the Fedorenko case in the District Court made it clear that the government must do a much more thorough job of presenting the historical context of the alleged activities in order for a judge to weigh accurately the credibility of the prosecution's evidence against the credibility of the defendant's claims. Moreover, to meet the terms of the Holtzman Amendment and the standards set by the Fedorenko decision, the government must present evidence showing how the defendant's activities (1) assisted in persecution (2) on the basis of race, religion, national origin or political belief, and (3) were carried out under the direction of or in association with the Nazi government of Germany or one of its allies.

General public knowledge about the Holocaust was much more limited twenty-five years ago in the United States, prior to such events as the opening of the United States Holocaust Memorial Museum, the success of movies like *Schindler's List* and *The Pianist*, and the controversies over the assets of Holocaust victims and the "Goldhagen thesis." Even many of those most interested in the topic did not have the information that could enable them to distinguish between collaboration and persecution or to determine, for example, whether service in the Latvian Legion of the Waffen-SS was more likely to have involved persecutory activities than service in an Order Police battalion in Eastern Poland. For instance, one of OSI's most effective prosecutors was at one point tempted to close an investigation in the early 1980s because he mistakenly assumed that the duties of a guard at Dachau in the mid-1930s and the prisoners he guarded differed little from guard duties and inmates in prisons in the United States at that time.

In order to succeed in its prosecutions, therefore, OSI has to educate U.S. judges in the history of Nazi Germany and its policies and practices of persecution. In addition, because it operates in an adversarial system and must meet such a high burden of proof, OSI has often had to prove facts that are self-evident to most historians, such as that Auschwitz existed and was a place of persecution. As a result of these requirements, U.S. trials of alleged participants in Nazi persecution often seem more like history seminars than judicial proceedings, as OSI presents extensive historical evidence that has no direct connection to the defendant. Unlike German prosecutors of Nazi crimes, who must prove that a defendant committed the elements of a specific crime, U.S. prosecutors of participants in Nazi-sponsored persecution must show the role that a defendant played in the greater criminal conspiracy that was the Holocaust.

The need to present the broad historical context of its cases led OSI to develop a very different personnel structure than that of its counterparts in Germany and than the one it originally started with in 1979. In order to gather the documents that could support and provide context for the evidence in its cases, OSI assembled a staff in 1979 that included two young historians in addition to twelve criminal investigators and a similar number of attorneys. The historians' work not only shed light on the available evidence but also uncovered new evidence in a number of investigations. Documents uncovered by the historians even enabled OSI to identify other members of units that had participated in Nazi crimes and who were residing in the United States. Eventually, thanks in large part to the work of the historians, OSI ceased to depend on outside sources for allegations and evidence and became capable of identifying suspects and obtaining sufficient evidence to prosecute them successfully entirely on the basis of its own investigative initiatives. As the work of the historians enabled OSI to open more investigations and initiate more prosecutions, the office's need for historians increased. In time, they took over many of the tasks originally envisioned for criminal investigators. Whereas the German offices responsible for investigating and prosecuting Nazi crimes have always relied on the usual law enforcement personnel of prosecutors and criminal investigators and have only consulted historians as experts in individual cases, OSI's staff came to consist of ten historians, a similar number of attorneys, and only one criminal investigator.

One key investigative strategy that OSI developed based on the historians' work was its "Research and Development" program. This involves systematically searching for and collecting information that can be used to identify those who assisted or participated in Nazi crimes. The historian in charge of the R&D program is responsible for assembling such information from her own research and the research of the other historians and then for determining whether any of those so identified ever entered the United States. Once the R&D historian has located a potential subject in the United States and developed evidence supporting a reasonable suspicion that the individual assisted in Nazi-sponsored persecution, OSI opens an official investigation, which is then conducted by a team consisting of one or two attorneys, one historian, and one paralegal. Since the mid-1980s, all but a very few of the OSI investigations that have led to prosecutions have been generated by the R&D program.

Thanks largely to this proactive strategy, OSI has far surpassed the original expectations for both its success and its longevity. As of June 2007, it has successfully prosecuted 105 Nazi persecutors, accomplishing 85 denaturalizations and 63 removals.[4]

Although OSI has taken action against a diverse group of perpetrators, including a government minister, two propagandists, a V-2 missile engineer, and even a Jewish kapo, most of its cases have fallen into one of two categories: members of police forces or concentration camp guards. Since it is extremely unusual to find documents showing the specific duties a defendant carried out on a particular day, OSI's prosecutions generally focus on proving that the defendant's unit engaged in persecutory activities as its sole or significant purpose at the time the defendant served in it. As self-evident as this may appear to be with respect to such units as the SS *Totenkopf* (Death's Head) battalions that guarded Nazi concentration camps, OSI must nevertheless not only prove the proposition but also disprove the defendant's claims distancing himself from the activities of his unit. Among the defenses OSI can expect from a concentration camp guard defendant: the camp he guarded held only prisoners convicted of crimes or POWs; as an ethnic German, he was treated as an inferior by the SS and was really little more than a forced laborer himself; he only guarded the perimeter of the camp and was not allowed to enter the camp or speak to the prisoners, so he had nothing to do with their treatment; he never saw that prisoners were killed or mistreated or were even poorly fed; and – if he did not serve at Auschwitz – the camp he guarded was not a death camp like Auschwitz but a labor camp.

4 The office has lost nine cases and dismissed two that it inherited from INS in 1979.

In prosecuting a concentration camp guard case, then, OSI methodically presents evidence that sets the historical context of the case: the escalation of Nazi policies of persecution to ever wider groups of victims; the role of the concentration camps in carrying out this persecution and their development during World War II into institutions of slave labor and mass death; and the organization, purpose, and functions of the SS Death's Head units formed by Theodor Eicke at Dachau and deployed to all the concentration camps. Martin Broszat's expert report in the Frankfurt Auschwitz trial served as a model for OSI when it first sought to establish this broader context for a case against a concentration camp guard.[5] OSI also presents the history of the particular camp or camps where a defendant served, documenting especially the types of prisoners held there, how they were treated, the work that they performed and the conditions in which they lived, in order to establish that those camps were in fact places of persecution. Since most of the concentration camp guard defendants in the United States have been ethnic Germans, OSI often presents evidence on the Waffen-SS's ideological and practical rationale for recruiting ethnic Germans, the formal agreements with other nations permitting it to carry out such recruitment, and the actual conditions of recruitment in a defendant's homeland. For this last point, SD reports on pro- or anti-SS sentiment among the ethnic German population and on the success of the recruitment drives have proven particularly helpful. In addition, OSI introduces wartime German documents demonstrating that the ethnic Germans assigned to serve in the *Totenkopf* battalions were fully incorporated into their units, serving alongside and carrying out the same duties as the Reich Germans, wearing the same uniforms, carrying the same arms, receiving the same pay, benefits, and leave, and swearing the same oath of loyalty to Adolf Hitler. After May 1943, Waffen-SS service even entitled ethnic Germans to apply for Reich German citizenship.

Of particular importance in concentration camp guard cases is establishing what duties the defendant routinely performed. Using various regulations and training materials of the SS Death's Head units – including a picture book produced at Auschwitz to instruct guards with little or no ability to read or speak German[6] – plus postwar statements of fellow guards and their commanders, daily orders assigning companies to a variety of duties, punishment reports on guards who neglected their duties, and many

5 See Martin Broszat, "Nationalsozialistische Konzentrationslager 1933–1945," in *Anatomie des SS-Staates*, Gutakten des Instituts für Zeitgeschichte (Freiburg i.B, 1965), vol. 2.

6 Archives of the Institute of National Remembrance, Warsaw: "Bilderbuch 'Falsch-Richtig' für die Posten im KL-Dienst" (n.d.), Najwyższy Trybunal Narodowy, folder 86.

other types of documents, OSI has succeeded in proving that all the guards in a *Totenkopf* battalion were assigned on a rotating basis to man guard posts in the towers and along the perimeter of the *Schutzhaftlager* (the area of a concentration camp where prisoners were housed), to escort prisoners to and from slave labor sites, and to guard prisoner labor details as they worked. Guards were also routinely assigned to transport prisoners to other camps and to serve on execution squads. In all these duties, the guards' ultimate purpose was to prevent prisoners from escaping the daily infliction of persecution, which was the raison d'être of the camps. U.S. courts have now ruled in dozens of cases that by carrying out their routine duties, SS *Totenkopf* guards assisted in persecuting individuals on the basis of their race, religion, national origin, and political opinion, in that they enforced the confinement of such persons in the places where they were tormented and murdered.

Secondary studies are generally not acceptable as evidence in U.S. courts unless the authors are available for cross-examination. The primary source records OSI presents to support its cases often number in the hundreds. Courts have generally accepted these exhibits under the "ancient documents exception" rule against hearsay, according to which rule records are acceptable as evidence if they are more than twenty years old and appear to be authentic. The process of authenticating a document, or proving it is what it appears on its face to be, can be relatively simple if there are many examples of such documents, such as the applications SS men had to submit to the SS Race and Settlement Main Office before marrying. In other cases, particularly when the document names the defendant, authentication may be complicated, involving, for example, tracing it from its originator to its recipient, proving that those persons existed and held the positions attributed to them, even verifying their signatures through other documents, and then showing how the document came to be housed in its current location. OSI's case against Stefan Leili, for instance, was based on an entry in the "Unnatural Death Book" maintained at Mauthausen Concentration Camp, which showed that Leili had shot a seventeen-year-old French Jew. Although, as Leili later admitted, the youth was simply running away from two SS men who had been beating him, the cause of death was listed as "shot while trying to escape." To authenticate the entry, OSI had to produce evidence showing who kept the book and why and what the entries really meant. OSI was able to authenticate the record in part by presenting correspondence that had survived at Auschwitz and demonstrated that the SS Economic and Administrative Main Office had ordered such books to be maintained and that the entries in the Mauthausen book commenced shortly after this order.[7]

Authentication has proven even more challenging when the key evidence comes from archives that were under Communist control after the war. This was particularly true of cases that were prosecuted prior to the end of the Cold War. Not only did cases involving Baltic, Belarussian, or Ukrainian defendants who had served in indigenous police forces depend upon evidence under Soviet control, but until OSI historians were finally granted access to Soviet archives beginning in 1989, OSI could only obtain such evidence by requesting Soviet authorities to find and provide it. Equally important to such indigenous police cases as Soviet-held documents was the testimony of the defendants' former cohorts and acquaintances who were still living in the USSR. In 1980, which was otherwise an extreme low point in Soviet-American relations, the USSR agreed that Soviet witnesses could give testimony in OSI cases and that they could be cross-examined by defense counsel.

The use of Soviet-supplied evidence and of witness depositions taken in the USSR proved highly controversial, particularly among anti-communist emigrés from areas under Soviet control, some of whom maintained that any evidence that anyone of their nationality assisted the Nazis in persecution was *ipso facto* a Soviet fabrication. Some judges were also reluctant to credit Soviet evidence and testimony – in one case, the judge even accused OSI of "collaborating" with a totalitarian state by taking depositions in the Soviet Union.[8]

To overcome judicial doubts about the authenticity of Soviet-supplied documentary evidence, OSI has submitted the key original records in a number of cases to extensive physical testing and handwriting analysis. In one case, the FBI even found and identified the defendant's latent fingerprint from a document he had signed many decades earlier, during the war.[9] OSI has also sought records in Western and Polish archives[10] that could help authenticate Soviet-supplied evidence, such as by showing that the letterheads, stamps, and signatures were genuine, that the unit named in fact existed and was in the area ascribed, and that other persons named in the document actually served in the unit. In addition, OSI has cited

7 After being denaturalized, Leili voluntarily departed the United States. *United States v. Leili*, No. 86–1370 (D.N.J. December 30, 1986).

8 *United States v. Kungys*, 571 F. Supp. 1104 (D.N.J. 1983).

9 This occurred during the investigation of Valerian Trifa.

10 Poland was the only Communist bloc nation that routinely allowed OSI historians to conduct research in its archives during the Cold War.

the acceptance of Soviet-supplied evidence by German, Dutch, and other courts to support its argument that such evidence could be credited.

Although some judges proved unwilling to accept or fully credit the testimony of witnesses deposed in the USSR, every U.S. court before which OSI has submitted evidence from archives that were then or had previously been under Soviet control has accepted that evidence as authentic. Defendants nevertheless continued to maintain that documents from archives in the former USSR were Soviet forgeries even after the end of the Cold War, but this argument has met with no success. One district court, when presented with this defense, asked, "Why would even the KGB go to the trouble of forging documents implicating [the defendant] in war crimes, and then bar all access to its handiwork for some fifty years, while awaiting the collapse of the government whose evil intentions towards [the defendant] it presumably sought to serve?"[11]

The inaccessibility of Soviet archives to OSI historians considerably hampered OSI's ability to conduct investigations. It could take years for the Soviets to reply to a request for evidence of an individual's activities, and for the most part they answered in the negative if they ever replied at all. Even when they did respond in the positive, the Soviets generally supplied only those documents that named the particular subject of investigation. As OSI later discovered, few Soviet archivists knew German or had more than the most rudimentary knowledge of the captured German records held by their institutions.

The knowledge that an investigative subject served in a particular unit was of little use if OSI could not obtain records establishing what that unit did and where and when it operated. In some cases, OSI historians were able to find sufficient documentation in Western and Polish archives to make successful prosecution possible, but a number of investigations languished for lack of sufficient evidence of assistance in persecution to meet the government's burden. For example, OSI pursued investigations of several members of the Saugumas, or Lithuanian State Security Police, in Vilnius. One of these subjects, Alexandras Lileikis, had been the chief of the Saugumas for the Vilnius region. In the early 1980s, the Soviets supplied OSI with an order in which Lileikis directed that fifty-two Jews in his custody be transferred to the Ypatingas Burys, the Lithuanian squad that carried out the mass shootings of Jews outside Vilnius. The document was a mimeograph copy found in one of the victims' files, however, and did not bear Lileikis's signature, only his typed name. When interviewed

11 *United States v. Lileikis*, 929 F. Supp. 31 (D. Mass. May 24, 1996).

by OSI, Lileikis acknowledged that he had been the chief of the Saugumas but maintained that he had only pursued Communist agents and had held no authority in matters pertaining to Jews. Confronted with the Soviet-supplied evidence, he challenged OSI to prove that he had ever actually signed any such document. OSI could find almost no documentation in the West that pertained to the activities of the Saugumas, nor were there any experts on the subject who could be consulted. Consequently, the Saugumas investigations languished for years for lack of sufficient evidence to support a successful prosecution.

That changed after OSI finally obtained access to the Lithuanian Central State Archive in 1990. In numerous trips to Vilnius adding up to many months of research, OSI historian Michael MacQueen pieced together the history of the Saugumas before and during the German occupation.[12] Within the German Security Police organization in Lithuania, the Saugumas was the Lithuanian counterpart of the Gestapo. As the German Security Police and SD had a staff of only forty to oversee the entire Vilnius area with more than half a million people, it gave far-reaching autonomy to the Saugumas to carry out searches, arrests, and investigations of suspects from beginning to conclusion. Once the Saugumas determined how a suspect should be sentenced, it presented its decision to the German Security Police for confirmation. Communists and suspected communist sympathizers were a chief target of the Saugumas, but they were not its only focus. Like the Gestapo, the Saugumas was divided into a number of sections, each devoted to a certain area of investigation. The section assigned to investigations of communists was actually called the Communists-Jews Section (Komunistu-Žydu Sekcijas). From the very first day of its existence under the German occupation, the Saugumas began arresting Jewish men on pretext charges, such as "as a Jew, suspected of anti-state activities." In July 1941, it began handing over Jews directly to the Ypatingas Burys to be shot.

Once the Jews of Vilnius were enclosed in the ghetto, the Saugumas was responsible for investigating cases involving Jews residing outside the ghetto and the use of false identification papers by Jews. Such cases became

12 For more information on the role of indigenous forces in the Holocaust in Lithuania, see the following studies by Michael MacQueen: "Collaboration as an Element in the Polish-Lithuanian Struggle over Vilnius," in *Kollaboration in Nordosteuropa – Erscheingsformen und Deutungen im 20. Jahrhundert,* ed. Joachim Taubert (Wiesbaden, 2006); "Einheimische Gehilfin der Gestapo: Die litauische Sicherheitspolizei in Vilnius, 1941–1944," in *Holocaust in Litauen: Krieg, Judenmorde und Kollaboration,* ed. Bartusevicius, Tauber, and Wette (Cologne, 2003); "The Context of Mass Destruction: Agents and Prerequisites of the Holocaust in Lithuania," *Holocaust and Genocide Studies* 12:1 (Spring 1998); "Nazi Policy Toward the Jews in the *Reichskommissariat Ostland,* June–December 1941: From White Terror to Holocaust in Lithuania," in *Bitter Legacy: Confronting the Holocaust in the USSR,* ed. Zvi Gitelman (Bloomington, IN, 1997).

particularly numerous during the mass shooting actions in which tens of thousands of Jews in the Vilnius Ghetto were murdered in the autumn of 1941. The Saugumas' role in these investigations was far from passive, for it did not merely wait for instances of escape to come to its attention but actually set up "sting" operations. In four such operations in which OSI subjects participated, the Saugumas arranged for a truck driver to approach Jews and offer to help them escape. A total of thirty-eight Jews agreed to the driver's terms, were picked up by him and a disguised Saugumas officer, and then driven out of the city to a spot where a group of Saugumas men intercepted them, arrested the Jews, seized their belongings, and placed them in the Lukiskis prison. Presumably, they were all shot.

After the mass shootings had ceased, leaving only the Jews who had been spared for work, the Saugumas continued to hunt down suspected Jews residing outside the ghetto. Those arrested were first taken to the Lukiskis prison, which was controlled by the Saugumas and its chief, Alexandras Lileikis. In the prison's records, MacQueen found a number of orders with Lileikis's actual signature directing that Jewish prisoners be transferred to the custody of the German Security Police. The files also contained the subsequent notice dated a few days later recording that the prisoners had been "*befehlsgemäß behandelt*" ("handled according to orders"), in other words, shot. One of the files MacQueen found records the arrest and shooting of a six-year-old girl and her mother.[13]

In 1994, OSI filed a denaturalization suit against Lileikis. In his defense, Lileikis advanced a novel argument that stood the *Befehlsnotstand* defense on its head. Rather than arguing that he was only following orders, Lileikis maintained that he was simply a "disembodied issuer of orders" and therefore should not be held accountable for the logical outcome of his commands. The district court judge was not impressed with this argument and revoked Lileikis's U.S. citizenship in 1996, whereupon Lileikis returned to Lithuania. Under intense pressure from the United States, Lithuania eventually indicted Lileikis but kept postponing the proceedings because of his alleged incompetence to stand trial, an incompetence that did not prevent him from writing his memoirs during this period. Lileikis died in 2000 at the age of ninety-three. Three other Saugumas officials, including Lileikis's deputy, have been denaturalized and have left or been removed from the United States.[14]

13 Lithuanian Central State Archive, Vilnius: Collection R 1673, Series 1, Cards 1426: Kaplan, Fruma and 1425: Kaplan, Gitta (December 23, 1941).

14 They are Algimantas Dailide, Kazys Gimzauskas (deputy chief of the *Saugumas*), and Adolph Milius. After Gimzauskas returned to Lithuania, he was tried and convicted for crimes against humanity in proceedings he was not required to attend, and his sentence was suspended because of ostensible health problems.

The fall of the Iron Curtain led to the discovery of records that not only revived long-standing investigations that had reached dead ends but also opened new areas of research that led to many new investigations and prosecutions. The primary example of this is the complex of prosecutions involving defendants who had been "Trawniki men," that is, members of the Wachmannschaften des SS und Polizeiführers im Distrikt Lublin (Guard Forces of the SS and Police Leader in Lublin District). Based at the Trawniki Training Camp, the Wachmannschaften had provided the manpower for Aktion Reinhard, the operation to murder Jews in Eastern Poland, by carrying out ghetto clearances and mass shootings, escorting transports of Jews to the killing centers and forced labor camps, and guarding those centers and camps. Although Fedorenko had served in the Wachmannschaften and OSI had prosecuted two other Trawniki men in the 1980s, there was a dearth of documentation in the West on the activities and conditions of service of the men who served at Trawniki and very little understanding of how the Trawniki system operated. OSI's intensive effort to correct this situation began in 1990 when, shortly after the Velvet Revolution, the office finally received permission to conduct research in Czech and Slovak archives. A team of four OSI historians immediately traveled to Prague, Terezin, Litomerice, Brno, and Bratislava to survey the archives there. In the archive of the Czechoslovak Federal Ministry of the Interior, Peter Black, then OSI's chief historian (now senior historian at the U.S. Holocaust Memorial Museum's Center for Advanced Holocaust Studies), found a collection of rosters of the SS Bataillon Streibel, a unit formed in the summer of 1944 during the evacuation of the Trawniki Training Camp and commanded by Trawniki's commandant, Karl Streibel. The rosters list hundreds of Trawniki men by name, rank, and *Erkennungsmarke* or identification tag number.[15] With the information in the rosters, OSI was able to track down a number of former Trawniki men who were living in the United States, and thus new investigations were generated.

In addition to leading to new investigations, the Streibel Battalion rosters offered new opportunities to find additional documentation on Trawniki. The names and identifying data made it possible to make specific requests of those governments most likely to control archives with relevant records. Eventually, OSI even obtained access to the largest collection of surviving Trawniki records, consisting inter alia of personnel files, deployment orders, and rosters, in the Central Archive of the Federal Security Service (TsAFSB) in Moscow.

15 The Streibel Battalion rosters are now held by the State Central Archives, Prague: Record Group 114, inventory 242, folders 6 and 7.

From the records it uncovered in Russia, OSI learned that Soviet authorities (specifically, the MGB/KGB) had made a concerted effort after the war to exploit the Trawniki records they had seized in order to identify and prosecute those who had served in the Wachmannschaften. The individuals tracked down as a result of this effort were then investigated and tried, generally in the places where they were residing. The files of these investigations and trials, now located at state or local Security Service archives scattered throughout the former Soviet Union, contain two types of evidence: (1) the original German records pertaining to the subject of investigation or, more commonly, Russian-language translations or extracts of such records; (2) protocols of interrogations of the investigation subject and of witnesses, the latter generally being former Trawniki comrades of the subject.[16] Over the past decade, OSI historians have reviewed trial records scattered throughout Ukraine and Russia, as well as in the Baltic states and Central Asia.

Soviet trials of Trawniki men occurred in two waves, the first during the period from about 1947 to 1952, and the second in the 1960s. During the first wave, Soviet authorities concentrated primarily on proving the fact of the defendant's service in the Wachmannschaften, which was sufficient to obtain a conviction and sentence to a Gulag.[17] In the trials of the 1960s, Soviet prosecutors sought to prove that the defendants personally participated in murder, for which the prosecutors used eyewitnesses, who almost always were fellow Trawniki men. Consequently, the records of the 1960s trials tend to be more voluminous but less likely to contain wartime German documents than the trials of the late 1940s.

In addition to German wartime documentation on Trawniki, then, OSI has collected statements made to Soviet authorities by hundreds of former Trawniki men. Obviously, in assessing the value of such statements as evidence or primary sources, one must keep sight of the interests of both the interrogator and the interrogated and of the system in which these interrogations were conducted. On the other hand, the statements often contain a wealth of information that has little or no bearing upon the ultimate question of guilt or innocence and so raises little suspicion of having been fabricated or coerced, such as how recruitment drives were conducted,

16 The U.S. Holocaust Memorial Museum has copies of at least two such files: proceedings against Alexander Kulinich, RG-06.025–22, and Georgii Andreevich Marusenko, aka Garus, RG-06.025–23.

17 The most common sentence meted out in the first wave of trials appears to have been twenty-five years' hard labor, which was almost always cut short by the amnesty of September 17, 1955. For more detailed information on the Soviet Trawniki trials and the trial records, see the article by OSI Historian David Alan Rich, "Reinhard's Footsoldiers: Soviet Trophy Documents and Investigative Records as Sources," in *Remembering for the Future: The Holocaust in an Age of Genocides*, 3 vols., ed. John K. Roth et al. (New York, 2001), I: 688–701.

or the length and content of training, or when, how, and for what purpose certain forms were completed and passes issued. Among the factors OSI weighs in evaluating Soviet interrogations are whether their details are supported by wartime German documentation, whether they are consistent with interrogations by Soviet authorities of other Trawniki men, and whether they are consistent with statements given by former Trawniki men and their SS and police supervisors to authorities in the German Federal Republic, Poland, Israel, Canada, the United States, and post-Soviet Russia and Ukraine.

One noticeable aspect of the Streibel Battalion rosters that later proved true of other German documentation on Trawniki was the inconsistent spelling of the Trawniki men's names. The first name of a Ukrainian Trawniki man might be given in Ukrainian form in one roster, Russian form in another, and German form in the next – thus Mykola might be identified as Nikolai in some rosters and Nikolaus in others – while last names might be rendered in Polish spelling, in one or more German phonetic versions of the Ukrainian original, or in a German transliteration of the Russian version of the Ukrainian original. Frequent clerical errors add to the variety of spellings of the Trawniki men's names. For example, OSI defendant Fedir Kwoczak shows up in wartime German documents as Fedor Kloczak and Fjodor Klotschak in addition to Fedor and Fedir Kwoczak. (This multiplicity of possible spellings has also complicated OSI's efforts to identify Trawniki men among the population of postwar immigrants to the United States.) The Streibel Battalion rosters are quite consistent, however, in recording the men's *Erkennungsmarken*, and this can also be seen in other German wartime documents pertaining to Trawniki men. Indeed, it is rare to find such a document referring to a Trawniki man that does not include the *Erkennungsmarke*, for it was primarily by this number, rather than by name, that the Germans kept track of the Trawniki men in paperwork.

Starting with the Streibel Battalion rosters, Peter Black collected data on every Trawniki man he could identify from the records OSI amassed on Trawniki. Prior to the large-scale adoption of computer technology by the Justice Department's Criminal Division, this collection of data took the form of an index card system that came to fill multiple wooden card files before it was finally computerized. OSI has been able to identify approximately 75 percent of the somewhat more than 5,000 Trawniki men by name and *Erkennungsmarke*.

By tracking the *Erkennungsmarken* in the German records and tying them to information in other sources, particularly the postwar statements of men whose *Erkennungsmarken* could be identified, OSI has learned a great deal about the recruitment and deployment practices of the SS and Police at Trawniki. Generally (but by no means always), the Germans assigned the *Erkennungsmarken* consecutively to newly arriving Trawniki recruits, and they did not reassign the numbers of Trawniki men who left the system by transfer, dismissal, desertion, or death. Approximately the first 2,500 *Erkennungsmarken* were assigned almost exclusively to former Red Army soldiers recruited from POW camps between summer 1941 and early autumn 1942. Most of the *Erkennungsmarken* higher than 2,500 were assigned to civilians recruited primarily in Galicia, Lublin, and Hrubieszow between late fall 1942 and early summer 1944. Analysis of the records and the *Erkennungsmarken* has shown that the Germans generally inducted recruits in groups and then, after assigning their *Erkennungsmarken* and training them, deployed them in groups of men with consecutive numbers. It was not uncommon for the same group of men with consecutive numbers to deploy together on subsequent assignments. Consequently, it is often possible to determine, just from a Trawniki man's *Erkennungsmarke*, when and where he was recruited, when he arrived at Trawniki, how long he trained, and what he did while in training, and sometimes even to gauge his probable post-training assignments.

OSI has amassed some 7,500 records relating to Trawniki and/or Operation Reinhard. These sources reveal a wealth of detail about the recruitment, training, administration, and deployment of the Wachmannschaften.[18] The Trawniki men were armed, wore uniforms, had their own system of ranks and were eligible for promotion, received local and home leave, and were paid the same *Wehrsold* or service pay as German Army soldiers and Waffen SS men. They were also eligible to obtain family support payments and other benefits, such as medical treatment in German military hospitals. Their training often included practical exercises in the duties they would be expected to perform, such as participating in local shootings and resettlement actions in the summer of 1942 and, later, guarding the Trawniki forced labor camp that was adjacent to the training camp. Trawniki Training Camp served as the base camp for the Wachmannschaften, from which men were assigned to carry out some aspect of Operation Reinhard, whether "resettling" Jews, guarding a forced labor camp, or manning a killing center. All such assignments were temporary, with Trawniki retaining ultimate operational control over the men. Even the commanders of the labor camps and killing centers could not determine which or how many Trawniki men

18 For more information about Trawniki, see Peter Black, "Die Trawniki-Männer und die 'Aktion Reinhard,'" in *"Aktion Reinhardt": Der Völkermord an den Juden im Generalgouvernement, 1941–1944*, ed. Bogdan Musial (Osnabrück, 2004), 309–52.

served under them or for how long. Trawniki Training Camp sent fresh platoons to these facilities to relieve groups of guards periodically – or when desertions and breakdowns in discipline made replacement necessary. Once an assignment had ended, the men generally returned to Trawniki, where they guarded the adjacent labor camp, underwent additional training, or went on leave while awaiting the next assignment.

OSI has used this massive accumulation of evidence to argue that individuals who served in the Wachmannschaften at Trawniki assisted in persecution by making it possible for the SS and Police to murder 1.7 million Jews in Poland in less than two years. U.S. courts have generally found this argument compelling. Since the discovery of the Streibel Battalion rosters, OSI has instituted new proceedings against thirteen U.S. citizens whom it alleges assisted in the execution of Operation Reinhard by serving in the Trawniki-based Guard Forces of the SS and Police Leader Lublin. OSI has won twelve of these cases; the thirteenth defendant died while judgment was pending.[19]

Litigating cases against accused participants in Nazi persecution can pose almost as daunting a challenge as collecting evidence of their activities some fifty or sixty years ago. OSI must present hundreds of documents in a manner that allows the judge to follow the government's theory and persuades him or her to give more weight to the government's interpretation of the evidence than to the defendant's. OSI owes its success in litigation in significant part to the outside historians who have served as expert witnesses in its cases.

While the use of expert witnesses to interpret complex or highly technical evidence is far from unusual in U.S. civil litigation, the employment of historians in such a role certainly is. Nevertheless, OSI's use of historians as expert witnesses in its cases has raised little controversy. On the contrary, a number of judges have cited the usefulness of the historical expert's testimony in their decisions.

OSI's use of historical experts can also be helpful to defense counsel. The number of pages of records that OSI typically provides to the defense during the "discovery" phase of its cases runs to the thousands or even tens of thousands. This mass of material, much of it in foreign languages (although OSI provides the English version of all the records in a case that

19 The defendants who were denaturalized are: Walter Berezowskyj, Bronislaw Hajda, Wasyl Krysa, Andrew Kuras, Fedir Kwoczak, Wasyl Lytwyn, Iwan Mandycz, Jakiw Palij, Jakob Reimer, Dmytro Sawchuk, Mykola Wasylyk, and Vladas Zajanckauskas. Jaroslaw Bilaniuk died before the District Court judge issued an opinion. Prior to 1990, OSI had instituted denaturalization proceedings against the following former Trawniki men: John Demjanjuk, Fedor Fedorenko, and Liudas Kairys. The U.S. citizenship of each of these men has been revoked.

it has translated), can be challenging to assimilate, particularly for attorneys with little or no familiarity with the subject matter of the case. (Indeed, one defense attorney who specializes in criminal cases accused OSI of conducting a "trial by archive" for basing its case against his client on dozens of documents collected in at least five countries.) At or near the end of the discovery period, which is generally several months before trial, OSI provides defense counsel a report that lays out in detail what the historical expert will testify at trial and upon what sources he will base his testimony. This report serves in a sense as a road map through the records produced during discovery as well as providing a preview of how the government will present its case at trial. The defense counsel can question the government's historical expert during a pretrial deposition in addition to cross-examining him at trial.

The role of the historical expert is to explain the factual evidence but not to apply it to the legal issues in the case. Thus, he may testify that a document demonstrates that an individual with a particular name, birthdate, and other identifying data that may match the defendant served in a specific unit, and he may describe the activities of that unit and that person, but it is not his role to interpret whether the defendant's activities constituted persecution. In response to questions from the prosecutor, the historical expert witness explains and analyzes the exhibits, providing their context and their relevance to each other and to the factual questions at hand. The historical expert also plays a role in authenticating the documentary evidence, by testifying whether the records are the type that: (1) historians who study the Nazi era customarily use and rely on; (2) were routinely generated and maintained by German authorities in the course of business; (3) can be expected to be found in the places where the original documents were found.

The historical expert's testimony is much more than a dry recitation of facts, however. Ideally, it is a lively, illuminating, and sometimes graphic depiction of the reality underlying the documents, explaining, for instance, the true meaning of the euphemisms that Nazi officials so often employed and describing what it actually was like for prisoners to work in, for example, a quarry or a peat bog. The historical expert's depiction of the facts in the case often contrasts sharply with the defendant's. Where the latter may describe his concentration camp guard service as occurring only on a perimeter so far removed from the prisoners – and facing outward no less – that he could barely see them and their misery, much less interact with them, the historical expert demonstrates that the guards stood, with weapons pointed, at only six paces' remove from exhausted prisoners struggling to perform heavy labor and just on the other side of barbed wire from where prisoners were starving and dying.

Occasionally, OSI will employ a historical expert to rebut the defense. In 2001, for example, a defense counsel presented OSI a study that purported to prove that the first comprehensive report on the activities of Einsatzgruppe A by Franz Stahlecker, a document that had been seized by the Western Allies at the end of the war and introduced into evidence at Nuremberg by American prosecutors, was in truth a crude Soviet forgery. The principal expertise of the author, who has a Ph.D. in volcanology from the University of Karachi, seemed to rest on the fact that he was a native German speaker. As the defense counsel indicated that he would introduce this "expert" report at trial, OSI asked Christopher Browning to analyze it in a report of his own. After OSI presented Professor Browning's analysis of this report, defense counsel made no further mention of it.

Service as an expert historical witness is not to be undertaken lightly. Thoroughly familiarizing oneself with the documents that pertain to the case and preparing for testimony are time-consuming tasks. Actually giving testimony can be an arduous ordeal, with the prosecution's questioning sometimes lasting several days, followed by withering cross-examination by a defense counsel who may see his client's only chance for vindication as dependent on discrediting the expert.

OSI has been extraordinarily fortunate to have been able to obtain the services of such erudite and articulate historians of Nazi Germany and the Holocaust as Raul Hilberg, Charles Sydnor, Richard Breitman, Dieter Pohl, Henry Friedlander, Ronald Smelser, and Johannes Tuchel, among others. OSI's only consolation for losing Peter Black to the U.S. Holocaust Memorial Museum was that he was then able to serve as the historical expert for Trawniki cases. For the staff historians of OSI, the opportunity to work with leading historical experts is viewed as one of the perks of the job, and we never fail to gain greater insight into our evidence from the knowledge and perspective the experts bring to it. OSI owes a tremendous debt of gratitude to the historians who have served as experts in its cases.

From the perspective of a historian of the Holocaust, the greatest contribution of OSI's prosecutions probably lies in what they have revealed about the role of non-Germans in carrying out the Final Solution. Given the small number of men the SS and police could deploy in the occupied Soviet territories, as well as the linguistic limitations of those men, their success in identifying, isolating, and murdering hundreds of thousands of Jews within a short time span depended upon their ability to recruit indigenous forces who not only were willing to assist the Germans in these tasks but also, in some instances, carried them out with very little supervision. Similarly, in Poland, the success of Operation Reinhard depended in significant part on SS and Police Leader Odilo Globocnik's ability to cobble together a multiethnic force of Eastern Europeans to carry out the day-to-day tasks connected with rounding up, despoiling, transporting, enslaving, and murdering Jews. Likewise, in the concentration camp system, a substantial portion of the SS men who stood guard during the period of highest mortality and who participated in the death marches as the system collapsed were ethnic Germans who were raised in far different surroundings than Reich Germans and had only the most tenuous connection to German culture – indeed, many were practically illiterate and understood little German. A review of the background and activities of the defendants in OSI's successful prosecutions should at least give pause to those who would ascribe the crimes of the Holocaust to the unique values and proclivities of a particular culture.

The greater general historical significance of OSI's prosecutions, however, lies in the body of legal precedent that they have developed. Not only have the general facts of the Holocaust been established and upheld in numerous courts of law in the United States, but the particular details of its mechanism – and of its execution in obscure places where no survivors remained to tell the tale – have been proven in adversarial proceedings by the highest standards known in the world of jurisprudence. In addition, as a result of OSI's prosecutions, U.S. courts have defined assistance in persecution in such a way as to make clear that those who participate in enforcing oppression, whatever their motivation or intent, share moral responsibility for the victimization of the oppressed, even if they did not pull a trigger or crack a whip. A Jehovah's Witness incarcerated in Sachsenhausen was no less persecuted because the SS man who guarded him as he slaved in the brickyard neither beat nor hated him. As one court put it:

> The mere presence of the watchful eye of the conqueror or his deputies, coupled with the often demonstrated presence of both the means and the inclination to persistently inflict various indignities . . . is the personification of mental persecution to anyone, let alone innocent civilian[s] . . . reduced to various degrees of substandard mental and physical well-being.

The court decisions in OSI's cases stand for the propositions that the United States will not willingly serve as a haven for those who played a part in Nazi crimes against humanity and that the passage of time cannot mitigate responsibility for those crimes. Until recently, however, those principles only applied to the crimes of the Nazi era and not to the many similar crimes that have been committed since 1945, for U.S. immigration laws contained no provisions barring the entry of modern "war criminals" and human rights violators. Consequently, participants in state-sponsored torture or mass murder were free to immigrate to the United States and even acquire U.S. citizenship. For too long, it appeared that the lessons of accountability that the United States drew from the Holocaust would expire with the last of OSI's subjects. Fortunately, press reports[20] and activities by nongovernmental organizations[21] drew public attention to the fact that perpetrators of some of the worst human rights violations in the postwar era had found refuge in the United States. On December 17, 2004, President George W. Bush signed into law the Intelligence Reform and Terrorism Prevention Act (IRTPA), which, among its many provisions, charges OSI with responsibility for denaturalizing any naturalized U.S. citizen who committed, ordered, incited, assisted, or otherwise participated abroad in genocide or, under color of foreign law, torture or extrajudicial killing. The IRTPA also makes participation in such crimes grounds for inadmissibility to the United States and a bar to obtaining U.S. citizenship.[22]

Thus, the geographic and temporal scope of OSI's investigations and prosecutions has vastly expanded. The task of assembling sufficient evidence to convict the perpetrators of mass murder in places like Africa and Latin America is different but no less challenging than that of proving participation in Nazi crimes. While the office must develop new areas of expertise in order to carry out its new mission, however, the practices it developed in its World War II–related work of employing historical research and methodology to identify perpetrators and to assemble and present evidence are just as central to its program for pursuing postwar human rights violators. Meanwhile, OSI's pursuit of justice on behalf of victims of the Holocaust continues. On

20 See, for example, Steve Fainaru, "U.S. Is a Haven for Suspected War Criminals," and "Suspect in 'Cleansing' by Serbs Living in Vt.," *Boston Globe*, May 2, 1999, and May 3, 1999; Del Quentin Wilber, "Rights Abusers Can Find Haven: U.S. Immigration Law Enables Torturers to Enter, Stay Safe," *Baltimore Sun*, August 28, 2000; Alfonso Chardy and Elisabeth Donovan, "Scores Accused of Atrocities Committed in Other Countries Are Quietly Living in U.S.," *Miami Herald*, July 22, 2001.

21 Particularly influential were the civil suits brought against defendants in the United States under the Alien Tort Claims Act by the Center for Justice and Accountability on behalf of torture victims. In 2002, Amnesty International called on the U.S. government to draw on OSI's experiences and establish an office within the Department of Justice that would "have primary responsibility for investigating and prosecuting cases of torture and other crimes under international law." See Amnesty International USA, *United States of America: A Safe Haven for Torturers* (New York, 2002), 107.

22 Pub. L. No. 108–458, 118 Stat. 3638 (2004), specifically: Sections 5501, "Inadmissibility and Deportability of Aliens Who Have Committed Acts of Torture or Extrajudicial Killing Abroad"; Section 5504, "Bar to Good Moral Character for Aliens Who Have Committed Acts of Torture, Extrajudicial Killings, or Severe Violations of Religious Freedom"; and Section 5505, "Establishment of the Office of Special Investigations."

March 29, 2007, for example, a U.S. district court found that the defendant in an OSI denaturalization prosecution had shot Jews in the ghetto of L'viv more than sixty-four years earlier, in August 1942, which may constitute the oldest killing ever proved against a defendant in a court of law anywhere in the world.[23] Any pride we at OSI might be tempted to take in this feat must be outweighed by the realization that justice so long delayed is justice diminished. In pursuing the office's new mission, our goal is to build upon the lessons, successes, and disappointments of our World War II work to ensure that the United States does not become a safe haven for the perpetrators of crimes against humanity and that those who do find a way to this country will face swift and meaningful justice.

23 *United States v. Kaymon*, No. 04-60003, 2007 WL 1012983 (E.D. Mich. March 29, 2007). The decision misspells the name of the defendant, John aka Iwan Kalymon.

11

Law, History, and Holocaust Denial in the Courtroom

The Zündel and Irving Cases

CHRISTOPHER R. BROWNING

The issue of "Holocaust Denial" has entered the courtroom in two ways, but only one has also focused on an extensive examination of the historical evidence concerning the Holocaust itself and required historians to play a key role as expert witnesses. When the legal bases of these trials have been "anti-hate" laws (as in the Keegstra case in Canada) or laws explicitly banning such denial (as with the "Auschwitz Lie" law in Germany), testimony by historians was not crucial. The main issues for the court to determine were what the alleged deniers had in fact said or written and what were the effects. But on three occasions – the two trials of Ernst Zündel in Toronto in 1985 and 1988 and the libel suit of David Irving against Deborah Lipstadt and Penguin Books in London in 2000 – the cases revolved very much around the historical validity of particular allegations and the historical integrity of their authors. In these cases, historical expert witnesses played a central role. As I was the historical expert witness for the Crown Prosecution in the second Zündel trial as well as a member of the team of historical experts for the defendants in the Irving-Lipstadt trial, I should make clear that in the following comments I make no pretense of objectivity. They are those of an engaged participant, not a detached observer.

Popular discourse and media headlines about these cases often proclaimed that the "Holocaust was on trial."[1] In the wider sense of what was at stake in the outcome of the trials, this was not incorrect. If the verdict had been in favor of the Holocaust denier in either of these cases, clearly the denier movement would have lost no time in loudly proclaiming that the Holocaust

1 As does the title of D. D. Guttenplan, *The Holocaust on Trial* (New York, 2001), the most prominent journalistic account in English of the trial.

as an historical event had been disproved in a court of law. And certainly a major function of the historical expert witnesses was to provide to the court some of the key evidence that historians have used in writing about the Holocaust, and whose authenticity was challenged, meaning radically disputed, or existence ignored by the deniers. One effect of this exercise, of course, was the presentation of evidence that the Holocaust had indeed happened. But the chief, and in my opinion most complex, task of the expert witnesses in these trials was not just to prove that the Holocaust had happened but more precisely to prove that the deniers had made their claims in bad faith. In this sense, it was not the Holocaust but the practice of History itself that was on trial. Could historians, facing a high evidentiary standard of either "beyond reasonable doubt" (in the criminal case of Ernst Zündel) or "clear, cogent, and convincing" (in the civil case of David Irving), provide the means for a court to make a viable distinction between honest history and dishonest falsification?[2]

Two oddities particular to Canada provided the legal basis for the Zündel trial. The first was an old, seldom-used provision of the Canadian criminal code that made it a felony to "willfully publish a statement, tale, or news that he knows is false and that causes or is likely to cause injury or mischief to a public interest."[3] The second is a provision that a private citizen can lodge a felony complaint, whereupon the Crown Prosecution has the option to take over the case. In this case an Auschwitz survivor invoked the "false news" law to lodge a felony complaint against Ernst Zündel for his publication and dissemination in Canada of the denier pamphlet, "Did Six Million Really Die?" by Richard Harwood alias Richard Verrall, and the Crown Prosecution did take over the case.

In the first Zündel trial in 1985, Judge Hugh Locke declined to take judicial notice that the Holocaust was an indisputable historical event. The issue of judicial notice did indeed present the judge with a quandary. If he took judicial notice, this would remove one of the counts that the prosecution would have to prove "beyond a reasonable doubt" and thus possibly disadvantage the defense, prejudice the case, and expose any guilty verdict to appeal. On the other hand, when he did not, as Lawrence Douglas has observed, "it seemed troubling that a court would refuse to stipulate to the facticity of the Holocaust in a trial meant to demonstrate that certain

2 This point was made by both Guttenplan, who aptly notes that in one respect the trial was the "historian's equivalent of malpractice" (*The Holocaust on Trial*, 14–15), and Richard Evans, *Lying About Hitler: History, Holocaust, and the David Irving Trial* (New York, 2001), 30, 37. But it was made most emphatically in the title of Deborah Lipstadt's own account, *History on Trial* (New York, 2005).

3 Canadian Criminal Code, Section 177, cited in Leonidas Hill, "The Trial of Ernst Zündel," *Simon Wiesenthal Center Annual* 6 (1989): 169.

statements were so beyond the pale of legitimate dispute as to justify the imposition of a criminal sanction."[4]

As a result of Locke's decision, the prosecution did indeed have to prove as part of its charge both that the pamphlet's denial of the Holocaust was false and that Zündel knew it to be false. The prosecution, understaffed and not yet fully aware of the political and publicity dimensions of the trial, did not take full advantage of its expert witness, the preeminent Holocaust scholar Raul Hilberg, to prepare and present its case properly. The prosecuting attorney mistakenly accepted at face value the assurances of Zündel's defense attorney, Douglas Christie, that this would not be a "battle of documents." Thus, Hilberg was not asked to lay out the basic evidence for our knowledge of the Holocaust, nor systematically to dissect and analyze the denial pamphlet Zündel had disseminated. He was basically asked to state his professional opinion about the pamphlet, which he characterized as a mixture of distortions, half-truths, and lies.

Hilberg was then left in the unenviable position of trying to make good these deficiencies in the prosecution case during difficult and aggressive cross-examination by Christie, who fully exploited his advantage of being able to pose the questions and hence control the agenda. While Hilberg's testimony in chief lasted only several hours, his agonizing cross-examination dragged on for days. Several survivor witnesses were brutalized by Christie as well, though at least one, Rudy Vrba, more than held his own in a verbal slugfest with Christie. After Hilberg's unfortunate experience, the prosecution scrambled to improvise a stronger case with some success, including an effective cross-examination of Christie's witnesses and a dramatic and emotionally powerful showing of film footage taken by American military photographers of several of the Nazi camps immediately following liberation in the movie *Nazi Concentration Camps* obtained from the National Archives.

Ever desirous of publicity and perhaps now overconfident, the defense made the mistake of allowing Zündel to take the stand as a witness. Moreover, several of his other publications written under a pseudonym – in particular two gems entitled *The Hitler We Loved and Why* and *UFOs: Nazi Secret Weapons?* – were introduced into evidence by the prosecution. This provided the jury with sufficient insight into Zündel's true nature that he in no small measure convicted himself. However, the conviction was overturned on appeal, in part because the judge had disallowed evidence that

4 Lawrence Douglas, *The Memory of Judgment: Making Law and History in the Trials of the Holocaust* (New Haven, 2001), 224.

the appeals court thought was relevant to Zündel's claims about the honesty of his beliefs and had not instructed the jury with sufficient clarity on the Crown's need to prove Zündel's "actual knowledge of the falsity of the statements" in question.[5] In short, the judge, like the prosecution and press, had been distracted by the issue of proving that the Holocaust had occurred and had not focused with sufficient clarity on the issue of Zündel's state of mind, namely, that his false statements about the Holocaust were made "willfully" as required by the Canadian penal code provision under which he was being prosecuted.

The Crown Prosecution opted to retry the case, and four things in particular changed in the second Zündel trial. First, Zündel did not take the stand. Second, the new judge, Ronald Thomas, did not allow the showing of the film. The judge ruled that its inflammatory impact unfairly outweighed its evidentiary value for the legal issues in question.

Third, the judge took a peculiar and limited judicial notice of the Holocaust. He ruled that "the mass murder and destruction of Jews in Europe by the Nazi regime during the Second World War is a historical fact which is so notorious as not to be the subject of dispute among reasonable persons" and directed the jury to "accept" this as "a fact" not requiring proof by the prosecution.[6] But the individual key claims of the pamphlet, namely that there was no genocidal plan, there were no gas chambers, and millions of Jews did not die, were explicitly not included within the judicial notice. The prosecution case, therefore, was going to focus much more clearly on proving that the denial pamphlet "Did Six Million Really Die?" was demonstrably a fraudulent concoction and that beyond any reasonable doubt Zündel knew it to be such, precisely what the judge identified in his "charge to the jury" as "the most important issue."[7] But the defense was free to advocate the truth of the pamphlet's key allegations, that is, Zündel believed them to be true because they were true, or least that there was no convincing evidence to the contrary, judicial notice of the Holocaust notwithstanding.

And fourth, the prosecution was now fully aware of the political and publicity aspects of the case. The prosecution decided not to use survivor witnesses, both to avoid subjecting them to Christie's sadistic cross-examination and because their testimony would have been irrelevant to the issue of Zündel's state of mind. The crown prosecutor John Pearson also noted privately to me that such cases might have to be proved

5 Hill, "The Trial of Ernst Zündel," 199.
6 *Crown v. Zündel 1988* (hereafter CvZ), 36, 10375.
7 CvZ, 36, 10383.

at some point in time when there would be no survivor witnesses still alive. Thus, the prosecution should learn how to make such a case without them.

Without survivor witnesses or the dramatic film footage of the liberated Nazi camps, the presentation of the prosecution case in the second Zündel trial was necessarily going to depend far more on the historical expert witness than the first. Raul Hilberg declined to appear a second time, but suggested my name. I corresponded and then met with John Pearson for the first time in the autumn of 1987 to discuss and plan for a trial that was scheduled to begin in early 1988.

We knew that we would face a jury composed basically of people who read so little that they had not heard of the first trial. We now had to convince them "beyond reasonable doubt" that the pamphlet in question not only presented historical falsehoods, but also had been purposely and consciously constructed to falsify history. Analyzing the pamphlet paragraph by paragraph, we presented on screen both selected historical documents and the actual texts of secondary sources cited in the pamphlet side by side with the claims that the pamphlet made. When examined one by one, the falsifications of the pamphlet would appear so clumsy and the misuse of sources so blatant, we hoped, that a jury of his peers would reach the obvious conclusion of Zündel's bad faith.

In cross-examination, which lasted three and one-half days against one and one-half days of testimony in chief, Christie followed at least four lines of attack. First, he attacked me as an enemy of free speech. Did it not disturb my conscience to come to Canada to testify against his client in a trial that would not occur in my own country due to the First Amendment? I replied that Canada had an independent judiciary and a democratically elected government to decide how it would interpret freedom of speech, so I had no problem of conscience. If Canada had not been a free country, I would not have come.[8]

Second, Christie pursued a series of ugly personal attacks, many of them shameless in the overt anti-Semitic assumptions that underlay them. "I put it to you that you're not really a historian at all. You're a propagandist for the State of Israel."[9] "I put it to you that you have become part of a scheme to rewrite history. . . ."[10] "You're well aware that the Holocaust and laying it at the feet of the Germans per se is a big business and it's a very lucrative business to the State of Israel."[11] "May I suggest that most, if not all of your

8 CvZ, 14, 3288–9.
9 CvZ, 14, 3290.
10 CvZ, 14, 3294.
11 CvZ, 14, 3248.

writings are published by Jewish sources."[12] On several occasions Christie had me reveal my expert witness fee to the jury and made the accusation that I had come to Canada to enrich myself at the Canadian taxpayers' expense as a "well-paid historian." On the second occasion I noted that historians are in general not particularly well-paid, but conceded that "for this particular episode, I am being paid . . . more like a lawyer than a professor."[13] He did not return to that particular theme again.

Third, he attacked my credibility as an expert. Going rapidly through a long list of questions prepared in advance, he would linger only when he found a book or document that I had not read or a question to which there was no good answer. These matters he would then press at length in a voice oozing with sarcasm and contempt. If I were "really a qualified historian," he repeated ad nauseam, then I "really should have considered" them. Whatever his grasp of the law, Christie was not an ineffective courtroom actor and cross-examiner.

John Pearson had warned me beforehand that for two reasons he would not intrude with objections, even when Christie's questioning was entirely out of bounds, such as in trying to pass off statements of alleged fact in the form of questions. First, it was important that the jury not get the impression that I needed to be protected. Second, by temperament, Christie needed a fight with someone. If I remained calm and if Pearson refused to be provoked into endless objections, Christie would inevitably turn to fighting with the judge. This, Pearson concluded, would damage the defense's case in the eyes of the jury far more than anything he could gain through objecting to Christie's tactics. Pearson's expectation that Christie would clash acrimoniously with the judge proved entirely correct, I might add. And at one point Christie's line of questioning became so outlandish that even the judge in exasperation cut him off, exclaiming "that is preposterous."[14]

The fourth line of Christie's cross-examination was historically and legally more interesting than his various attacks on me as an individual. Initially, he tried to prevent my qualification as an expert witness because "history is not a subject upon which an expert can testify as to the matters of fact."[15] This led to a discussion of the kinds of evidence that both history and the law rely upon, such as eyewitness, documentary, physical, and circumstantial evidence, as well as the uses of such evidence. I attempted

12 CvZ, 17, 3807. The two books I had written by that time had both been published by Holmes & Meier, whose owner, Max Holmes, was indeed Jewish.

13 CvZ, 16, 3800.

14 CvZ, 17, 3857.

15 CvZ, 13, 2935.

to articulate that both history and the law try to establish time- and place-specific events as indisputable facts. Both also try to arrive at persuasive conclusions from the pattern of proven facts, concerning matters like motive, state of mind, intention, or premeditation. The various killings of European Jews, totaling close to six million, as well as the existence of a Nazi intention and plan to that effect, were both historically and legally proven, I argued. Statements about some time- and place-specific events and some historical and legal conclusions might indeed be a matter of speculation or probability because of lack of sufficient evidence, but the Nazi attempt to murder the Jews of Europe was not such a case. Historians did indeed also argue about broad issues of historical interpretation that inherently could not be proven and that were indeed a matter of opinion, such as why did Rome fall or the Nazis come to power, but these were not the kind of issues being contested in the Zündel pamphlet.

Throughout the trial, Christie continued his unrelenting attack on the practice of history and the status of historical knowledge as nothing but opinion and hearsay. Therefore, "a reasonable man might take the position that you so-called historians are a bunch of theologians who may debate and you do not know at all and a reasonable man could disbelieve every one of you."[16] Thus anyone, including his client, could in good faith believe that there had been no Nazi plan to exterminate the Jews and no gas chambers, and that far fewer than six million Jews had perished.

Key individual documents were subjected to the most tortuous analysis to extract alternative meanings and demonstrate their utter indeterminacy as evidence establishing fact. He used the usual denier tactic of treating bureaucratic euphemisms (like *Umsiedlung* or "resettlment") literally and literal language (such as *Vernichtung* or "destruction") figuratively. More sophisticated was his tactic of treating all use of context to establish meaning as simply one man's bias and preconception against another's. We orthodox historians simply assumed the Holocaust had happened and then interpreted ambiguous documents according to that unexamined assumption to reinforce our foregone conclusions. This tactic reached its most absurd when Christie suggested that his valid alternative interpretation of a key section of the Wannsee Protocol ("The inevitable final remainder which doubtless constitutes the toughest element will have to be dealt with appropriately, since it represents a natural selection which upon liberation is to be regarded

16 CvZ, 15, 3559.

as a germ cell of a new Jewish development.")[17] simply reflected the standard Nazi belief "that only the best and the strongest" – including Jews – "should survive, and that was good for society."[18]

In absurd juxtaposition to such crudities, in what Douglas Lawrence described as "a bizarre seminar on historiography" giving an "odd classroom quality" to the trial,[19] Christie read to the jury from E. H. Carr's *What Is History?* "The facts are really not at all like fish on the fishmonger's slab. They are like fish swimming about in a vast and sometimes inaccessible ocean and what the historian captures will depend partly on chance, but mainly on what part of the ocean he chooses to fish in and what tackle he chooses to use.... By and large, the historian will get the kind of facts he wants."[20] Pearson riposted by having me read a different section to the jury: "How then, in the middle of the 20th century, are we to define the obligation of the historian to his facts?... The duty of the historian to respect his facts is not exhausted by the obligation to see that his facts are accurate. He must seek to bring into the picture all the known and knowable facts relevant, in one sense or another, to the theme in which he is engaged and to the interpretation proposed."[21]

In an attempt to give his case a further patina of respectability, Christie went beyond the usual array of pathetic deniers as witnesses. He called to the stand Professor Robert Faurisson, qualified as an expert in text criticism, to repeat the denier mantra but also to argue for the indeterminacy of interpreting documents. He called Fred Leuchter, the now infamous "Mr. Death," to testify on the scientific impossibility of homicidal gas chambers at Birkenau. Science in contrast to history, Christie argued, was not mere opinion. And he called the then best-selling freelance writer and Hitler biographer, David Irving, who for the first time publicly went beyond his carefully crafted Hitler apologetics, proclaimed himself converted by the Leuchter report, and openly embraced the cause of Holocaust denial. He unabashedly stated that the pamphlet in question was at least 90 percent correct.

None of this saved Zündel's case, however, as the jury convicted. In presentencing discussion, Judge Thomas observed to Christie that the key issues, the pamphlet itself and Zündel's beliefs, had been "pushed aside"

17 Christie used the Raul Hilberg translation from *Documents of Destruction* (Chicago, 1971), 94, that translated "bei Freilassung" as "upon liberation" rather than "if released."

18 CvZ, 15, 3466.

19 Douglas, *The Memory of Judgment*, 249.

20 CvZ, 17, 3808.

21 CvZ, 17, 3988.

by the defense to make the trial "a showpiece for the Institute of Historical Review and their right-wing teachings."[22] When preparing to pass sentence, the judge stated bluntly: "The accused man hides behind a veil of honest belief in the truth but the jury has exposed him. It is not the Holocaust that is a fraud, it is Ernst Zündel who is a fraud."[23]

The case was immediately appealed. Christie's more than 100 objections to the conduct of the trial were overruled, but the case eventually reached the Canadian Supreme Court on a constitutional issue. In light of Canada's 1982 Charter of Freedom with its guarantee of freedom of expression, the "false news" law was overturned as unconstitutional, and Zündel's conviction was set aside.

It was precisely David Irving's "coming out" as a Holocaust denier at the Zündel trial, his subsequent publication of the Leuchter report, as well as the numerous, quite unguarded speeches that he gave in the following years, that led to the most recent major Holocaust denial trial. Faced with the devastating consequences of his self-inflicted wounds to reputation and income, Irving tried to recoup by suing Deborah Lipstadt and Penguin Books for libel. The trial was distinct from the Zündel trials in many ways. First, the issue of free speech, with which Christie had cynically tried to muddy the waters at the trial court level and which at the level of Supreme Court review had led to the dubious and vague "false news" law being declared unconstitutional, played little role. Despite his own claims to the contrary,[24] it was Irving who was trying to use English libel law, which clearly privileged perceived injury to personal reputation above the public good of free speech, to silence well-deserved and legitimate criticism of his own self-destructive behavior.

Second, Irving was not attacking History as mere opinion incapable of establishing factual truth. On the contrary, he claimed that he alone discovered new sources and wrote "real history," while we lazy and incompetent professional historians shunned the archives, failed to uncover new sources, and merely sat in our studies plagiarizing one another. In short, while Zündel's defense attorney, Doug Christie, had basically claimed that "history was bunk," David Irving claimed that he was the better historian writing "real" history.

22 CvZ, 36, 10560.

23 CvZ, 36, 10570.

24 Irving argued that a verdict against him would create a "paralysis in the writing of history," forcing every historian to "accept the official version . . . or stop being an historian." *Irving v. Penguin Books and Lipstadt Transcript* (hereafter IvL), March 15, 52.

Third, while Zündel presented a clear and consistent target, Irving switched with bewildering rapidity from one persona to another. At one moment he was the gadfly maverick and super sleuth who claimed to beat the professional historians at their own game and "liked seeing egg on the historians' faces"[25] but who also craved recognition from the historical profession he publicly ridiculed. At the next moment, he was Hitler's self-appointed defense attorney before the bar of history, trying to exonerate his client by demanding that Hitler had to be considered innocent until proven guilty and that all circumstantial evidence and eyewitness testimony be disallowed (unless, of course, it could be construed as exonerating).[26] At other times, he pandered to his only remaining constituency of loyal supporters with blustering Holocaust denial of what he called "purpose-built" death camps, gas chambers, and the Final Solution as a program of planned and systematic extermination. And finally, for the sake of credibility before the judge, he minimized his Hitler apologetics and denied his Holocaust denial.

Fourth, this trial took place before a judge without jury, and Irving served as his own attorney. Given his frequent taunt that the evidence marshaled by historians against Hitler and for the existence of the Holocaust would not suffice to convict a bicycle thief before a humble English magistrate, Irving was now put to his own proclaimed test. He thereby remained the center of attention and earned accolades for his sheer physical stamina but at the cost of a coherent and disciplined strategy of legal defense and experienced and focused cross-examination.

Fifth, the scale of preparation for the Irving trial increased exponentially beyond that of the Zündel trials. In 1985, the prosecution made virtually no effort to prepare Hilberg's testimony or to collect relevant documents for submission in evidence. In 1988, I had roughly two months to prepare, while simultaneously carrying a full teaching load at my university. The documents I selected for submission could fit into one cardboard box the size of a case of wine. For the Irving trial, numerous experts worked for one and one-half years on their reports, several of which exceeded 800 pages in length, and the resulting folders of all the documents cited therein lined the walls of the courtroom. While Christie had spent far more time preparing for the two Zündel trials than the Crown Prosecution, Irving acting as his own attorney was completely outworked and overwhelmed by the Lipstadt-Penguin Books defense team and their battery of experts.

25 IvL, January 15 (day 7), 140.

26 At one point in the trial, Irving turned to the gallery and proclaimed that Hitler was innocent until proven guilty and should not be excluded from the general rule of fair play, which prompted Rampton's riposte that unfortunately Hitler was not there on trial. IvL, January 13 (day 3), 93.

And the final major difference, of course, was that in this case it was not David Irving but Deborah Lipstadt and Penguin Books who were the defendants. Nonetheless, the latter bore the burden under English libel law of proving the truth of her claims, namely that Irving was a Holocaust denier who distorted and falsified historical evidence in the service of his ideology. As in the Zündel case, it would be necessary to prove not only the falsity of the denier's empirical claims but also the mendacious state of mind behind those claims.

To accomplish this task, the defense followed a three-pronged strategy. First, three historians wrote expert witness reports on the state of historical evidence: Robert Jan van Pelt on Auschwitz;[27] Peter Longerich on Hitler's anti-Semitism and the systematic nature of the Final Solution;[28] and myself on the mass shootings on Soviet territory, the gas vans, the death camps of Operation Reinhard, and the Wannsee Conference. Second, Richard Evans and two of his very able graduate students – Nik Wachsman and Thomas Skelton-Robinson – wrote a report documenting the numerous flaws in Irving's own writings[29] – a task considerably more challenging than exposing the fabrications and contrivances of the clumsy denial pamphlet of the Zündel trial. And third, on the basis of the expert witness report of Hajo Funke and the diaries, correspondence, clipping files, and speeches obtained from Irving through discovery, the defense examined Irving's right-wing political ties and racist attitudes.

The press focused primarily on the easily understood evidence of Irving's racist attitudes and more blatant historical falsifications, which I will not rehash. Instead, I would like to concentrate on two key points that received less press coverage but were nonetheless important to the outcome of the case. The first was the understanding and definition of Holocaust denial itself, which the defense maintained was comprised primarily of three points: the denial, first, that there was a planned and systematically implemented murder of the Jews; second, that the Jewish victims numbered in the millions; and third, that most of the victims were killed in gas chambers.

These three criteria, articulated by Richard Evans, were precisely the three points that Christie had identified as crucially distinguishing his client's position in the Zündel trial and which Judge Thomas explicitly did not include when taking judicial notice of the Holocaust. Irving offered two definitions of the Holocaust: that it was either the "tragedy that undoubtedly befell the Jewish people during the Third Reich" or alternatively "the

27 Robert Jan van Pelt, *The Case for Auschwitz: Evidence from the Irving Trial* (Bloomington, 2002).
28 Peter Longerich, *The Unwritten Order: Hitler's Role in the Final Solution* (Charleston, 2001).
29 Evans, *Lying About Hitler.*

whole of World War II" and the suffering and death of any number of innocent people. And he claimed, of course, that he denied neither.[30]

A second issue concerned the definition of and evidence relevant to historical distortion and falsification. Irving made three key claims. First, he should be judged only by the documents that were within the four walls of his study from 1988 to 1992, not what had become available since the opening of the East European archives or was only accessible with the considerable financial resources of the defense experts. He could be held accountable only for what others could prove that he "must" have known at the time, not what others might claim that he "ought" to have known. In effect, without the slightest consciousness of irony, much less hypocrisy, the same David Irving who claimed that he alone found new documents while the professional historians never left the four walls of their studies, now attempted a defense of ignorance, limiting his liability to the documents within the four walls of his study and disallowing the archival discoveries of professional historians! Second, distortion must be proven to be willful and knowing, not negligent and careless. And third, to be deemed a distortion beyond acceptance as a legitimate historical interpretation, his views had to be proven so fraudulent, "so perverse, that no reasonable and unbiased man informed by the same materials and expertise could have arrived at those meanings."[31]

On the first issue, Judge Gray ignored Irving's attempt at semantic evasion. He not only accepted the three criteria of the defense, but also placed special emphasis on additional issues more relevant to Irving's own credibility than to the general phenomenon of Holocaust denial. As the trial progressed, and particularly in his judgment, Gray focused on Irving's denial of Hitler's knowledge of and complicity in the Final Solution. All of Irving's record, especially his portrayal of Hitler, and not just his post-1988 Holocaust denial, was important to the judge.

On the issue of distortion, Judge Gray ruled that accidental error could not be held against Irving. Moreover, he ruled, it was not sufficient for the defense to prove that Irving misrepresented and falsified historical evidence. The defense had the additional burden of proving (as had been the case in the Zündel trial) that such distortions were "deliberate." As Richard Rampton in his opening statement had made precisely that accusation, flatly calling Irving a "liar," this was not a ruling that the defense contested despite its very high burden of proof.

30 IvL, January 12 (day 2), 154–6.

31 IvL, Janaury 25 (day 7), 87–9.

But to the benefit of the defense, Judge Gray crucially ruled that Irving could be held responsible for any "available" documents and evidence that an open-minded historian would have found at that time if he had only looked, not just those documents within the four walls of Irving's study. Ignoring available evidence would constitute an act of "deliberately deceiving himself" and was no different than deciding to distort or suppress evidence. In short, Irving would be held accountable for what he "ought" to have known, not just what he "must" have known. In a memorable phrase, Judge Gray admonished Irving that he "couldn't put the telescope to the blind eye." And to constitute distortion, Irving's conclusions did not have to be "so perverse" that no "reasonable and unbiased man" could have reached the same conclusions. The defense only had to show that he deliberately "misrepresented the facts" because of his ideological agenda.[32]

In effect, Irving was trying to have it both ways. He did not want to be held responsible for or cross-examined about the historical evidence not in his study before 1993, when Lipstadt published her book, on the grounds that he was not yet then an informed Holocaust historian and had not seen it. But he wanted to be able to maintain, again without being examined in court since post-1993 developments were irrelevant, now that he had looked at both the earlier evidence as well as the evidence that had come to light since, that it all supported his earlier instincts, and his claims were justified.[33] If successful, Irving would basically have derailed the expert witness reports of van Pelt, Longerich, and myself (though not those of Evans and Funke) as irrelevant, and the trial would have taken an entirely different course.

With elegant simplicity, Judge Gray made clear that his task in this trial was basically to decide if Irving was an honest historian. "The issue with which I am concerned," he wrote, "is Irving's treatment of the available evidence." And the standard against which Gray constantly measured him was how an "open-minded," "fair-minded," or "objective" historian would have treated the evidence in question. "It is not part of my function," he added, "to attempt to make findings as to what actually happened during the Nazi regime." In the strictly legal sense, David Irving's credibility as an historian, not the Holocaust, was on trial in Judge Gray's courtroom.

I will not go into detail on the issues related to the testimony of Richard Evans, Robert Jan van Pelt, and Peter Longerich, for they have published their own accounts. My own experience, it is important to emphasize, was quite atypical. Clearly, Irving had to vigorously contest the existence of the

32 IvL, January 25 (day 7), 85, 88, 92–4, 105–6. 33 IvL, January 25 (day 7), 96–103.

Birkenau gas chambers with Robert Jan van Pelt and Hitler's role in the Final Solution with Peter Longerich. Likewise, he could not admit to the systematic distortions and falsifications in his own work documented by Richard Evans or to his racism and neo-Nazi connections in Germany documented by Hajo Funke. By process of elimination, therefore, it was in the area of my report that Irving attempted to put on the mask of benign reasonableness and sought to provide a fig leaf of credibility to his belated denial of Holocaust denial.

Following the opening statements, Rampton began cross-examination of Irving on the basis of my report before any of the expert witnesses had appeared. Under this cross-examination Irving admitted that at least one-half and perhaps even one and one-half million Soviet Jews were killed by firing squads, in a planned and systematic manner, known and approved by Hitler.[34] He admitted that the gas van camps at Chelmno and Semlin were "systematic" and not merely "experimental," and his previous statements to the contrary were wrong.[35] He admitted that the Polish Jews had been deported to the Operation Reinhard camps where they "vanished from our general sight," and "obviously something ugly happened to them." On a "balance of probabilities," Irving conceded, hundreds of thousands of Jews sent there had been killed deliberately. But he continued to maintain that, in the absence of definitive documentary evidence ("we are still short of the smoking gun") as opposed to mere eyewitness testimony and circumstantial evidence, it would be "amateurish" to speculate precisely how they met this fate, and as both looting and killing took place in these camps, they could not be viewed "solely" as "purpose-built death camps."[36]

My initial reaction to reading the transcript of Rampton's cross-examination of Irving on my report was that the latter had conceded so much that I might not even be called as a witness. That was not the case, however, and face-to-face in the courtroom, Irving began my cross-examination with exemplary civility and even feigned friendliness. Much of the time he behaved as if we were two colleagues engaged in scholarly discussion at an academic conference, not adversaries in a courtroom. He in fact characterized our courtroom encounter as a "joint journey of discovery and exploration."[37] He was caught up in the role he was playing to the point of snubbing Judge Gray. In this regard, I cannot resist quoting from the transcript. At one point the freewheeling exchange had gotten well ahead of the judge's ability to locate the most recent document under discussion.

34 IvL, January 17 (day 4), 87–116.

35 IvL, January 19 (day 6), 48–74.

36 IvL, January 18 (day 5), 86–94, 125–69.

37 IvL, February 7 (day 16), 31.

After unsuccessfully asking for a citation, Gray broke in once again: "I am sorry to interrupt you, Mr. Irving, but I have to try to digest all this and it is easier . . ." Before he could finish his sentence, Irving replied: "Problem is, my Lord, that both the witness and I have all this in our heads." Gray: "Yes, but it is quite important that you get it into my head too." Irving: "It is not an easy task." Gray: "I am sorry to hear you say that." Irving, backpedaling desperately: "My Lord, the reason I said this is because it has taken me 35 years to get it into my head, the whole history." At which point Rampton opportunistically volunteered: "It has only taken me nine months."[38]

Irving did not frontally attack the major thrust of my report. He did not openly contest the mass killing of Jews in the Holocaust outside of Auschwitz-Birkenau, but raised issues of scale and organization and reliability of evidence, and hinted that if Auschwitz-Birkenau were not a *Todesfabrik* or "death factory" then "on the balance of probabilities" the other camps were not either.[39] And he was still eager to play Hitler's defense attorney, emphasizing that Hans Mommsen and Martin Broszat, both respectable historians, also did not believe in the existence of a Hitler order for the Final Solution, and that I accepted that such an order had never been formal or written. He stated that his own "flagship" biography of Hitler had triggered substantial research on the topic, for which he should be receiving credit rather than blame, while he conveniently avoided any discussion of his more outlandish claims therein, such as that Hitler had had no knowledge of the Final Solution until late 1943, and that it had all been done behind his back by underlings.

Irving then raised the issue that if historians disagreed on many issues, where could one "draw the line" between "permissible debate" on the one hand, and "impermissible debate" on the other. I noted two kinds of issues: the easy case of deliberate invention or distortion of evidence, where the intention to mislead was clear, and the more difficult case of someone who "so identified" with or was predisposed toward an interpretation or position that all evidence was seen through that "default position" and produced a "consistent pattern of distortion" that was not necessarily "calculated and willful."

Irving asked about fallibility or innocent error. I admitted that all historians occasionally made mistakes, noting that he had discovered a mistranslation on my part, but also that that particular mistake had been "against interest" and I was indebted to him because the corrected translation greatly

38 IvL, February 8 (day 17), 52.

39 IvL, January 18 (day 5), 141.

strengthened the point I was trying to make. In contrast, I noted, repeated error from predisposition would not be against interest. "You mean it is like a waiter who always gives the wrong change in his own favour?" This was perhaps the one Irving query in two days of cross-examination that I could answer with a simple and unqualified "yes."[40] As Guttenplan noted, Irving had helped to articulate a standard he would later "have cause to regret."[41]

Throughout the trial, and during my testimony in particular, Irving tried to "plant significant doubts" in the judge's mind about various issues, but especially about the validity of eyewitness testimony as historical evidence. As Irving explained his purpose, if he could "plant significant doubts" in the judge's mind, then he too was "entitled" not to be called a Holocaust denier just because he questioned various aspects of the Holocaust.[42] Gray replied at one point, "I am not finding this very helpful because we all know eyewitness evidence has to be looked at very carefully. Everyone agrees on that." When Irving persisted, Gray noted that "illusive references which are not really followed up do not help me very much."[43]

Only in the last afternoon of my cross-examination did the chameleon Irving adopt yet another persona, this time that of Doug Christie. Irving took a number of Christie's questions directly from the Zündel trial transcript, and we now replayed scenes almost word for word from the courtroom in Toronto. Irving harped endlessly on the Gerstein testimony, one of Christie's favorite topics. Irving continuously brought up Gerstein's exaggerations, which quite intentionally I had already fully documented and conceded in my report. When explicitly questioned by the judge as to whether he was challenging not only Gerstein's exaggerations but also his testimony about gas chambers at Belzec, however, Irving said no, he was only trying to "plant a seed of doubt" in the judge's mind about the general validity of eyewitness testimony, which was "important for the main plank of my case which is Auschwitz." "Rather like Rommel," Irving said, "I am coming around from the rear." The master of sotto voce, Rampton noted in a stage whisper audible to the entire courtroom but not recorded in the transcript, "And we all know what happened to Rommel." When Irving then returned yet again to the issue of Gerstein's exaggerations, Gray finally gave way to a rare display of impatience: "This is all slightly Alice in Wonderland, is it not. . . . you accept there were gas chambers so criticizing Gerstein for saying there were is slightly limited value, I think."[44]

40 IvL, February 8 (day 17), 104–11.

41 Guttenplan, *The Holocaust on Trial*, 216.

42 IvL, February 8 (day 17), 19.

43 IvL, February 8 (day 17), 73.

44 IvL, February 8 (day 17), 154–65.

If my days in the courtroom with Irving were a strange mixture of academic role-playing, Toronto déjà vu, and occasional comic relief, that certainly was not the tone of most of the trial. Ultimately, Irving admitted, however grudgingly, fleetingly, and evasively, to the bulk of the Holocaust. But he stuck most stubbornly and consistently to the denial of gas chambers, particularly at Auschwitz-Birkenau, and to the exoneration of Hitler. Despite Irving's belated and shifting concessions, Gray found that on virtually all contested points he had manipulated and falsified the evidence. The consistent pattern of Irving's falsifications, always minimizing or denying the Holocaust and exonerating Hitler, as well as his tortured maneuverings, clever sophistries, and fleeting concessions in the courtroom itself, ruled out innocent, random error and pointed to the deliberate skewing of evidence on behalf of his political beliefs. Like Zündel before him, Irving's courtroom performance ultimately damaged his own case.

In assessing the relationship in these two denial trials between the law and the courtroom on the one hand and the preservation of the integrity of the historical record of the Holocaust on the other, scholars have come to diametrically opposed conclusions. Richard Evans argued that "in many respects the High Court turned out to be a good place to settle the historical record and methodological points at issue in the Irving case," and "the judgment was above all . . . a victory for history, for historical truth and historical scholarship."[45]

In contrast, concerning the Zündel trials, Lawrence Douglas argued that Christie had "certainly succeeded in hijacking the didactic ends of the trial. Staged to protect and promote the interests of responsible memory, the trial turned into a grotesque spectacle, an offensive and bizarre drama that displayed the perils of relying on legal dramaturgy as a means of buttressing the integrity of history."[46] Or even more strongly, "Christie succeeded in desecrating the courtroom as a space in which to defend the claims of history."[47]

Why such disparate outcomes from the two trials? For Douglas, the problem is systemic, not idiosyncratic, "because the law ultimately will remain less interested in safeguarding history than preserving the conditions of its own complex normativity and discursive neutrality." Inevitably honoring its own neutrality above any didactic affirmation of historical truth, the court became a legitimizing platform for blurring the line between truth

45 Evans, *Lying About Hitler*, 188, 264–5.
46 Lawrence, *The Memory of Judgment*, 225.
47 Ibid., 241.

and falsification when Christie intentionally subordinated the acquittal of his client to the promotion of their mutual political agenda. Christie used the court-validated adversarial process as a platform to parade his array of so-called experts, who ranged from the ludicrous to the repugnant, through the witness box, and he employed all "the structural similarities between the discourses of deniers and of legal advocates" to launch a radical attack on the status of historical knowledge itself.[48]

The dynamics of the Irving trial were fundamentally different, however, because Irving openly embraced and validated a traditional, empirical approach to history. He not only accepted the "rules of the game" but also proclaimed his superiority in finding and analyzing evidence by those rules. Once in the courtroom, Irving did not have to demonstrate that he was a superior historian, the self-proclaimed standard bearer and champion of "real history," but only that he was a "reasonable" and "fair-minded" one. But in the face of the evidence, the more he tried to appear "reasonable," the more he had to concede. And the more he equivocated and distorted to hold his ground, the more clearly his attempt to pose as a "reasonable" historian was endangered.

Another fundamental difference lay in the impression that each trial left in its aftermath. The existence of a lengthy, detailed, and well-reasoned judgment distinguished the Irving trial, while the Zündel trial ended only with a simple guilty verdict subsequently set aside by the Canadian Supreme Court. While the journalists and public could not adequately follow the daily give and take of the Irving trial because they did not have access to the expert reports and the documents under discussion, Gray's written judgment was the final word that clarified the key issues and has become the trial's lasting legacy. In contrast, the courtroom theatrics of Christie, not the guilty verdict, the Supreme Court decision, or even the defendant himself, constituted the most indelible and lasting memory of the Zündel trial.

Whatever the differences in the dynamics of the two trials, the role of the historian as expert witness in both was similar in several regards. In both cases it was our task to uncover and document the bad faith and dishonesty of the Holocaust deniers. Moreover, in both cases we had to lay out evidence concerning the Holocaust, even if proving that that event had actually happened was not part of our legal charge. Finally, and in the long run perhaps most important, we had to model how a "reasonable" or

48 Ibid., 255–6.

"fair-minded" historian deals with such evidence. It was not just the evidence, but as Judge Gray pointed out, the "treatment" of the evidence that was key. We had to set the standard of professional integrity and competence against which the deniers not only of the Holocaust but also of historical knowledge itself could be measured and found wanting.

Index